AN EXTRAORDINARY SCANDAL

An Extraordinary Scandal

The Westminster expenses crisis and why it still matters

EMMA CREWE and ANDREW WALKER

First published in 2019 by
HAUS PUBLISHING LTD
4 Cinnamon Row
London SW11 3TW
www.hauspublishing.com

A CIP catalogue record for this book is available from the British Library

ISBN: 978-1-912208-75-3
eISBN: 978-1-912208-76-0

Typeset in Garamond by MacGuru Ltd

Printed in the UK by TJ International

To our mothers who taught us
to work hard when looking for truth

Contents

Preface and acknowledgements

We met on the 750th anniversary of Simon De Montfort's Parliament in 2015. Andrew, an official in the Commons, was thinking of writing an account of the expenses scandal of 2009 before memories were lost forever. Emma had just published a book about MPs at work in House of Commons during the 2010–2015 coalition.[1] We talked about collaborating to inquire into a range of perspectives on the history of the expenses debacle.

We discovered that we share some perceptions about politicians and their world – a feeling that media attention on MPs and Parliament frequently emphasises extremes, and that the press often seem uninterested in the nature of their work and the complex and challenging working lives of MPs. Politicians perform an endless juggling act to govern, oppose or scrutinise; to pursue issues and campaigns in Westminster at the same time as providing a constantly developing advisory and support service for citizens in their constituencies; to integrate their work with family responsibilities, whether caring for elderly relatives or bringing up young children. We both sympathised with the human cost for MPs and their families that the scandal unleashed.

At the same time we each have our own specific moral sensibility towards money or, more specifically, expenses. Andrew used to work for the Inland Revenue and the Treasury, while Emma has worked for international charities combating poverty in Africa and Asia for years, finding herself annoyed when aid workers stayed in expensive hotels. We came to this research with the view that, collectively, MPs had failed to grasp and respond to public concerns but that this was not the whole story. Since Andrew had been Director General of Resources in the Commons administration at the time of the scandal, Emma did ask: 'Why will anyone believe our version if one of the authors was the official responsible for administering the system?' He convinced her that his wish to honour all sides of the story would win out over a desire to paint himself as the blameless hero of the story.

So we decided to go ahead and embark on an inquiry into the crisis. Andrew had studied history and trained as an accountant; as it progressed our inquiry drew in part on his detective skills, trawling through newspapers, documents and memories of people inside and outside Parliament to reconstruct a persuasive version of the past. This was combined with Emma's anthropological practice as a researcher. Tim Ingold describes anthropology as philosophy with the people still in it: 'Anthropologists follow their noses, sniffing out promising sources and lines of inquiry. They are like hunters on the trail. To hunt, you have to dream the animal; get under its skin to perceive as it does; know it from the inside out.'[2]

Sometimes anthropology involves 'participant-observation', or thorough and long-term immersion into the lives of a group or organisation to find out about their world. Emma had already spent some years in each of the Houses of Parliament (Lords 1998–2001 and Commons 2011–13), and various smaller projects since then, but this time the task was historical. This book is a form of collaborative historical research, strongly influenced by our past experience – by Andrew's 40 years of working in the public service and Emma's participant-observation research with politicians.

To make this inquiry possible, we spoke to MPs, former MPs, parliamentary officials and journalists.[3] We listened to their versions of events, got them talking about what it was like, asked questions about the most puzzling aspects of the crisis and tested out theories. When we talk about the past, we all struggle to remember and to disentangle memory from wishful thinking – most often we want to believe we were better than we were. This was true not just of the people we spoke to but of Andrew himself. With a ferocious persistence, we challenged memories and accounts, discussing at length why someone said what they said, how plausible it was, how it sat alongside other statements or evidence.

As we wrote our account, a similar process ensued, requiring judgement in each specific example to make decisions about what was most plausible or unconvincing and how to deal with contradictions. This book has involved a process of compromise because we have sought to take account of views from many sides of the MPs' expenses story. We have drawn on our own experience and past research, supplemented it with further research, and listened to these multiple perspectives. Since the versions of journalists, officials and MPs are irreconcilably divergent, and even we disagreed in our understanding at times along the way, how did we reach our own shared interpretation? The answer is that we formed a view based on the assumption that it is not about choosing between versions, but about using imagination to create an account that takes into consideration not only the views, but why they might be promoting that version, the context, what other sources indicate, and so on. It is with a sense of detached involvement in the material that an author (or in this case authors) can strive towards the most convincing theory and description of what happened. If you are too involved, you can't see the wood for the trees; if you are too detached, you lose a sense of proportion and fail to see there is a tiny fire burning in the middle of the wood.

Our account has not meant merging or agreeing with all views. Such a task would be impossible. It has meant exercising practical judgement, in the words of the philosopher John Dewey, taking into account generalised values in specific contexts within each decision (sometimes down to the choice of one word above another) in the quest to paint the most accurate moving picture in words that we can.

We are offering a complex answer to the question 'What happened in the expenses scandal?' Of course, we may end up pleasing no one but we hope to give pause for thought, possibly even disrupting well-worn views on what politicians are like and how Parliament works. That task matters in an age where people claim we are post-truth. Working towards truthfulness is far from impossible – and it matters more than anything else – but it does require an extraordinary amount of effort. It is for the reader to judge whether this historical account takes us closer to such truthfulness. We hope it does.

Readers may notice that we have not adopted a monolithic approach to naming individuals. Instead, we have sought to adopt the parliamentary (and anthropological) convention of using the form the individual concerned prefers or is most popularly known by (thus we refer to Betty Boothroyd rather than Lady Boothroyd, or just Boothroyd).

This book has been possible only because so many people from inside and outside Parliament were prepared to give us their views, memories and observations. A contemporary historical ethnography of this kind relies heavily on the candid perspectives – many from opposing points of view – that people have been willing to share with us. We are truly grateful to all those who we interviewed, and who gave us their time freely. Many wish to remain anonymous; but those we can name are quoted in the story and we thank them.

Our advisory panel have given us expert, and sometimes challenging, guidance during the project, which we found invaluable. They are Claire Foster-Gilbert, Caroline Shenton, Aileen Walker and Thomas Yarrow. The book has benefited from thoughtful comments on early drafts from informants and from Michael Carpenter, Tom Goldsmith, Dr Robert Wilkinson, Aileen Walker, Edward Wood and Thomas Yarrow. These comments have been far more than the icing on the cake – they have drawn our attention to flaws, different ideas, and new ways of thinking. Thanks to you all.

Emma would like to acknowledge the support of her colleagues at the Global Research Network on Parliaments and People at SOAS – Richard Axelby, Jas Kar and Bethel Worku, and at the University of Hertfordshire, Chris Mowles, Karen Norman, Nicholas Sarra and Karina Solsø, for their collaboration, ideas and encouragement, as well as the funders for covering her research time (the Arts and Humanities Research Council and Global Challenges Research Fund AH/R005435/1).

The unstinting support we have received from our families, particularly our spouses Nicholas Vester and Alison Walker, has been a real boon. We are particularly grateful to Theo Walker for his cartoons.

Finally, our thanks go to the Haus Publishing team – especially our editors Jo Stimpson and Alice Horne, Asha Astley, Harry Hall, and Barbara Schwepcke – for their professionalism and help during the drafting and production process.

1

A prelude

This is a story about MPs indulging in generous expenses. We are still living with the consequences of the purifying fire of the expenses crisis of 2009, the biggest political scandal for decades or even centuries.[1] It matters that significant historical events are scrutinised. Since Parliament remains our most important UK political institution, and without question the expenses crisis has had a profound impact on the reputations of MPs and Parliament, and probably on the way we do politics, this scandal merits more reflective exposure than it has had so far.

Why good history matters

Why was this scandal important? Since then, the idea of MPs having their snouts in the trough has become a continual refrain, arguably eroding public trust in our politicians. Some claim this increase in cynicism has encouraged people to develop an antipathy to politics more generally.

Ben Worthy suggests,

> As a confirmation of the iniquity of politicians, expenses undoubtedly played into a growing anti-system or anti-politics mood among the public. So, instead of giving us constitutional reform, did MPs' expenses, four years on, actually help give us UKIP?[2]

Could we even speculate that this anti-politics led directly to the disillusionment that influenced the 2016 referendum on whether the

UK should leave the European Union? The evidence is complicated but most scholars seem to agree that the expenses crisis may have contributed to patterns that were already in train: decline in support for the mainstream political parties, increase in support for smaller parties, disengagement from politics and a rise in populist national- ism.[3] It changed Parliament too: in the 2010 election those MPs who received more negative press coverage during the expenses scandal in 2009 were more likely to stand down.[4] But it also galvanised the institution to introduce reforms that have shifted power towards the backbenchers.

So it is worth asking why and how it happened. The blame-filled cartoon-like versions of the expenses crisis, picked up from news- paper reports and undimmed by scholarly articles, don't reveal the real story. The pervasive view among the public is that greedy MPs dipped deep into public funds to pay for a lavish lifestyle and that officials in the House of Commons colluded to assist by maintaining a corrupt system. They bought duck houses to decorate their ponds, cleaned their moats and improved their homes with flat screen TVs because they were greedy; so goes the crude version. While the rest of the population suffered pay freezes, MPs enjoyed increased benefits. Even the most thoughtful accounts blame either the greed of individuals or the flaws of a system. MPs' explanations are often one-track minded in their telling as well. Many of them felt wrongfully accused of embezzlement when the vast majority were following the rules and fraud was only proved in a handful of cases. Few asked why it occurred and how its repetition could be prevented.

This is bad history partly because the cartoon version begins too late and reduces what was a complex scandal into one inaccurate riff. To understand the expenses scandal we have to go way back in time. The story of how campaigners and journalists began to ask questions about MPs' expenses, their persistence and refusal to take no for an answer, is already known. But what was going on inside Parliament is less well understood.

Stories of corruption appeal to our political voyeurism;[5] finding illicit behaviour among our rulers is emotionally satisfying, an outlet for our resentment at being ruled by them (often inadequately) perhaps. It may be disappointing to some, therefore, to read that the illicit corruption found during the expenses scandal was relatively minor. A handful went to jail. The far more significant part of this history is what it reveals about the unseen social, economic, political and cultural changes, both in Parliament and in wider society, that caused the crisis and elevated it to such prominence. The financial crash, the digital revolution, the increase in MPs' constituency work, the Freedom of Information Act, the decline in deference and the rise of audit culture all played a role in this crisis. MPs' feeling of entitlement – derived from their status as elected representatives – clouded their collective judgement so that they failed to adjust to these changes. They could have anticipated the future and adjusted their behaviour, scaling down their claims and making them public. Our account is more about a crisis in the politics of information rather than large-scale corruption, but it lives with us still and its consequences are having a profound effect on representative democracy.

This version of history is told by Andrew Walker, the official in charge of expenses, and Emma Crewe, an anthropologist who has been researching Westminster since 1998. Neither an attack nor a defence, we offer an unvarnished, complex and possibly unpopular version of what happened based on personal experiences, interviews from multiple perspectives and a study of thousands of documents. We will draw on in-depth interviews with MPs, journalists, officials and others who played a part in the MPs' expenses system and the scandal of 2009, as well as on forensic study of parliamentary records and academic studies. As we take the reader in chronological order through the chain of events, from the 1950s in sketchy form and from the late 1990s to the aftermath in 2010 in more detail, some cross-cutting themes will run through the book – secrecy, privacy and entitlement – as well as some recurring characters. These include Speaker Michael Martin (dubbed, much to his irritation, 'Gorbals Mick' by the press); Andrew Walker, the ex-taxman who was responsible for the Fees Office throughout the period; and Heather Brooke, the transparency campaigner and investigative journalist, determined to challenge male entitlement. They operated within the culture of the Westminster village, which was beginning to change and become more responsive to societal developments, but not quickly enough; and the changing relationships between the media, government, Parliament and constituents.

This story emerges in part out of our experience. When Andrew ran the Fees Office as Director General of Resources, he tried to improve the regime internally and struggled with the onslaught of exposure caused by MPs blocking attempts to be more transparent. He regrets underestimating the potential for public fury: for example, after he referred to the 'John Lewis list' during a court case, it became the focus of endless attack. Emma undertook the first ethnographies of the UK Parliament (1998–2002 and 2011–13) and is sometimes accused of being too sympathetic towards MPs. Compiling this piece of history centred on discussions between the two of us during 2017–19, interspersed with searches into our memories; interviews with MPs, clerks, officials, peers, journalists and academics; and (re) readings of public and private documents from Parliament and the media.

As two people who have been involved in Parliament in different ways, we had the benefit of access to people and knowledge, but needed to take the task of achieving detachment more seriously than outsiders would have done. All along the way our constant refrains to each other have been, 'Is this credible?' and 'How can we substantiate this from another source or two?' Our approach was to write an account that aims to be scrupulously accurate about past events, weaves in a multitude of different perspectives, and points to critical moments rather than offering a comprehensive survey of facts, as though history unfolds in an even way. We hope this history is persuasive, but also offers a provocation about what we might learn from the past of a scandal that still lives with us.

The distance from strangers

Strangers, meaning visitors, were once forbidden from Parliament. In 1584 a stranger who had sat in the House of Commons for two hours was apprehended, strip-searched and sworn to secrecy. It was thought that strangers would diminish the dignity of the House and distort debate. Also, and perhaps more importantly, the proceedings of the House were private for fear of the King. Gradually the Members[6] and the Speaker would indulge the presence of strangers unless they were voting or a Member objected, in which case the stranger would be thrown out. To understand expenses, a starting point is MPs' long habit of keeping strangers at a distance when dealing with matters they deem private. Perhaps the secrecy disposed observers to be suspicious and to sometimes misread what they saw. Some strangers were rather shocked by parliamentary informality in the eighteenth century: 'It is not unusual to see a Member stretched out on one of the benches while the rest are in debate. One Member may be cracking nuts, another eating an orange or whatever fruit may be in season, they are constantly going in and out.'[7] This visitor from Prussia was also horrified by the way MPs abused each other and concluded, 'Anyone who wishes to observe mankind... and study human nature in the raw, should go to the House of Commons.'

Until one hundred years ago Members of Parliament were over-whelmingly male, pale and rich. They wore silk top hats, top boots and greatcoats in the House of Commons and received no salary because they had an income already. Some bought their seats. Until the 1832 Reform Act over 50 seats were 'rotten boroughs', with so few voters that they could easily be acquired through patronage. However, bribery and intimidation of voters continued until secret ballots and the 1883 Corrupt and Illegal Practices Prevention Act finally put a stop to it. Other forms of corruption did not cease, of course. Most notori-ously, Lloyd George sold honours in exchange for campaign contribu-tions and various Conservative MPs were alleged to have accepted cash in return for asking questions and lobbying within Parliament in the 1990s. But the examples of corruption in the last one hundred years are relatively rare. It was probably more the perception of politicians' secrecy, distance and greed that may have predisposed journalists and the public to expect the moral worst of their elected representatives.[8]

Deference in decline

The expenses scandal of 2009 was not so much a manifestation of past practice but a signifier of change. It was in all their relationships with those both inside and outside Parliament that MPs were facing huge shifts. Deference has been in decline since the 1960s: one former Labour MP told Emma that when he visited the BBC in the past, someone would have met him at reception, taken him for a drink and then escorted him to the interview.[9] These days, he reported, you make your own way and get something in a plastic cup if you are lucky.

The relationship between Parliament and the media dramatically changed after the televising of Commons debates from 1989. Lobby journalists had camped out in Parliament for years: it was a briefing to a Lobby correspondent before his 1947 Budget that led Hugh Dalton to tender his resignation to Clement Attlee, when the journalist inad-vertently published the information before Dalton had reached the relevant section of his speech.[10] Since then the relationship between lobby journalists, Parliament and the government of the day has changed, with trusted correspondents being invited to 10 Downing

Street for briefings, and with the increasing appetite for No 10 press secretaries such as Bernard Ingham and Alastair Campbell to give an off-the-record spin on the day's main political events.

The relationship between MPs and their constituents also changed beyond recognition during a similar time period. Until the 1950s, many MPs worked out of the gaze of their constituents, hardly visiting their constituencies or consulting with members of the public. John Biffen (MP from 1961–97) used to spend only one hour a week answering constituents' mail in the earlier years, while larger and more urban constituencies produced a larger volume.[11] Nowadays two hundred or more emails a day are reported by MPs as normal, alongside Facebook posts, tweets and mail. The stories about the rarity of visits to constituencies are the stuff of legend. Visits to constituencies used to be so rare that MPs were met at the railway station by a brass band. In the 1959–64 Parliament less than one third of MPs listed addresses that were in their constituencies, whereas in 1987 for the first time the majority of MPs had a constituency address.[12] Edmund Burke's attitude to representation is regularly quoted, especially by Conservative MPs:

> Parliament is not a *congress* of ambassadors from different and hostile interests; which interests each must maintain, as an agent and advocate, against other agents and advocates; but parliament is a *deliberative* assembly of *one* nation, with *one* interest, that of the whole; where, not local purposes, not local prejudices, ought to guide, but the general good, resulting from the general reason of the whole.[13]

In this outmoded view, if the MP is the only one to judge the singular interest of the constituency, or even the nation, then visiting regularly is not only unnecessary, it would have been politically counterproductive. These days, the attitude of most MPs to representation has lost this aloof simplicity. It is assumed that constituents can only be represented, or at least satisfied, if their elected representative is seen to be fighting for their plural and diverse interests locally as well as nationally. And local MPs are frequently consulted as trusted advisers and a sympathetic ear to help resolve local problems. Nowadays it is difficult to find an MP who fails to visit at least fortnightly; most spend their weekends in their constituency. Andrew recalls sitting with a London MP in his constituency surgery where citizens brought all kinds of issues to him, ranging from problems with the NHS or housing needs to family disputes. He dispensed common-sense advice as well as offering to take up cases of injustice of failing public services with the relevant authorities.

Emma found during a study of seven constituencies in England, Scotland and Wales (and another two subsequently) that MPs and their staff compile an ethnographic knowledge of their area.[14] This has become necessary because the 'claim' to represent tens of thousands of diverse constituents, as Saward puts it,[15] creates endlessly different expectations and meanings in the relationships between parliaments, parliamentarians and groups within any society. Any constituency will contain within it a multitude of interests and perspectives. The Burkean idea of trustee representation – where an MP represents their constituents by weighing up the evidence and using their judgement to decide the constituents' collective interests – is straining in many countries under people's plural demands to be heard. Constituents write to their MPs in ever increasing numbers demanding that they act as their mouthpieces to advocate causes, fulfilling a form of delegated representation, or to solve their problems and grievances, frequently arising out of failures of the welfare state. MPs derive huge satisfaction from interacting within their constituency, where they tend to be respected as individuals in contrast to the remote loathing they receive via social media as one of the collective of elected politicians. As the demands of constituency work translated into more regular visits, and MPs' lives got busier and busier, the second home allowances blossomed.

In the thirteenth century boroughs and shires paid wages to their representatives in the Commons; knights received four shillings a day, citizens and burgesses two shillings.[16] But payment had ceased by the end of the seventeenth century, so for a time only wealthy men could afford to be MPs. The Chartists advocated payment of MPs but it wasn't until 1911 that Members were entitled to draw £400 per annum from public funds. £400 was six times the median wage – proportionately much more than MPs' current pay. But during the Depression it was cut to £360, and did not rise significantly until 1937, when it was increased to £600. Thereafter it grew more in fits and starts than as a smooth progression.[17]

MPs' pay 1911–2009 (£)

1911	400	1987	18,500
1931	360	1988	22,548
1934	380	1989	24,107
1935	400	1990	26,701
1937	600	1991	28,970
1946	1,000	1992	30,854
1954	1,250	1994	31,687
1957	1,750	1995	33,189
1964	3,250	1996	43,000
1972	4,500	1997	43,860
1975	5,750	1998	45,066
1976	6,062	1999	47,008
1977	6,270	2000	48,371
1978	6,897	2001	51,822
1979	9,450	2002	55,118
1980	11,750	2003	56,358
1981	13,950	2004	57,458
1982	14,510	2005	59,095
1983	15,308	2006	60,277
1984	16,106	2007	61,820
1985	16,904	2008	63,291
1986	17,702	2009	64,766

Current and former MPs recall that when party leaders urged MPs to reject pay increases recommended by independent bodies, they promised their members that they would be compensated by better allowances and pensions. Tam Dalyell MP, who retired in 2005 after 43 years in Parliament, was reported as saying that the abuse of expenses goes back to 1963. Apparently the then Conservative chief

"It's an unofficial strike for more pay by MPs. Wouldn't try to cross the picket line, Sir, they're in an ugly mood!"
Cartoon by Joseph Lee,
Evening News, 16 June 1952

whip Brigadier Martin Redmayne said, 'We know there are a number of MPs in poverty, and it's impossible to put up MPs' salaries, so in the circumstances we will introduce some allowances.' He claimed that various chief whips acknowledged that MPs' pay was falling behind civil service pay levels but 'We will see you all right.' The Fees Office were instructed to be generous:

> A very nice man in the Fees Office said, 'Look, Mr Dalyell, you really would be much better off if you designated your London home as your first home and your home in Scotland as your second.' Now my home in London was two rooms above a public lavatory, and my home in Scotland was the first house asked for by the Scottish National Trust. The point is that the Fees Office was trying to be helpful to me, and why was this? Because they had been instructed by the government.[18]

Receipts were not usually required and honour was assumed: the MP's signature on expenses claims was sacrosanct. MPs felt entitled to respect, trust and deference; on the whole, most officials obliged. This changed when the scope and value of expenses increased. But as the regime for accounting for them tightened up after 1997, the relationship between MPs and officials running the system became more fraught.[19]

Helping MPs with their finances, or being relaxed about expenses, was one strategy for the party whips when trying to secure the co-operation of backbench MPs. One former Government Chief Whip (GCW) merits quoting at length. He explained to Emma how in the old days the whips oiled the wheels of the political machine to secure the support of backbench MPs for the decisions of their party leaders. It is well known that their 'whipping' used to involve the promise of rewards or punishments ('Vote with the party or you won't get promotion'). Stories about financial assistance, or turning a blind eye to misbehaviour of various kinds, used to circulate as gossip in Westminster. This Chief Whip was not typical – his approach was unusually emollient (to put it politely) according to other MPs – but his claims conjure something of the spirit of the whipping culture in the 1970s and 80s:

> GCW: People would come to see me who were in desperate financial difficulties... You could find them a job or a part-time... I mean, the last one I had was when a couple of East End demolition contractors said they wanted a parliamentary adviser and they said they'd pay £10,000 a year or something for advice...
> Emma Crewe: But why were you helping them?
> GCW: Because, the Chief Whip... Chief Whips have always done that, all that sort of thing, to keep the show going.
> EC: Just so that they can keep functioning as MPs?
> GCW: Sure, sure. Sure. Just to keep the show on the road. And, you know, and when you say to... one of the things... if a chap gets really in debt, you come to the conclusion that the only way out of it... we can bail this chap out, is to sell his flat, which is his only asset, to somebody with some money and then he can rent it back from them. And now, in my day, in the House of Commons, the people who had money to buy flats were [MPs like] Alan Clarke, who could afford it... But I mean, you know, you try and find solutions

for these people. What I'm really saying is that you will not find many Members of Parliament who tell you of the extreme pressures that they are under, because they've got to keep their peckers up.

[...]

One of the things that I would do as Chief Whip is, and nobody's supposed to know that we do this, but I would always, [in] the House of Commons, in particular, where they allow credit in the restaurant, you'd look at the overdue accounts. And you would find it's the same people living beyond their means who didn't know how to cope and that was a signal of something. Occasionally you would look at the claims for mileage allowances on their cars and you'd sometimes see that it was miles above what was reasonable. But there was no point in humiliating the guy, what you've got to do is get it right. So one of the whips would say to him casually, 'There's a bit of a blitz on mileage allowances old chap. Just check you've got yours right. I mean, some damn fool's charged his wife's mileage in as well as his own', you see. Which gives him the excuse as to why he can then go back and get it down, you see. And you know perfectly well this guy's going to go and have a look and he realises that he's been fiddling, because he's got a guilty conscience. He then goes from the Whip's office to the Fees Office, where these things are dealt with, and says, 'Look, I think I've made a mistake. I want to submit new claims because I've included my wife's mileage in as well as my own. Can I put it right?' And they say, 'Oh, quite understand. These things happen, you can put it right.' He doesn't know I knew that that's what he was doing, so you do it. So you manage these things in a way, not to catch people out but to try and get the show back on the road. Now, that's all part of the pressures that these people are under. That's really the message.

[...]

I used to keep in the bottom left hand drawer of my desk any cases that were reported to me of infringement of the postal regulations. You know, the free post that Members of Parliament get. And every now and again you get a case brought to you where a chap has sent a circular out using the free post, or his office has or something. Well, I suppose strictly the right thing to do is for me to go to the Opposition Chief Whip and say, 'Your chap has been abusing the system, what are you going to do about it?' you see. Well, my attitude to it was to, if I could, put it in my drawer, so when he came in to see me and say, 'Well, I've got an infringement and your fellow's been using these...' I'd say, 'Oh yes, I was going to have a word with you about it.' And I'd bring one out of about equal severity and slap it on the table and say, 'I think what we should both do is have a word with our respective Members and see if we can get this to stop because it's an abuse.' And you found ways of resolving these things which weren't great rows because it made the show work. You couldn't do it with an absolutely blatant, dishonest... anything really serious, you'd do something straight away. But if you could smooth it through you did, because that made the show work.[20]

His view was that these tactics enabled politicians to focus on the big issues – the 'show' was making laws and running the country. Whether the detail is true or not, and it is difficult to imagine that there were many MPs rich enough to assist by buying flats (especially outside the Conservative Party), it is clear that whips saw themselves as there to help MPs in difficulties where possible. This was only possible because solutions to keep the show on the road could be concealed. Everything changed with the Freedom of Information Act, which came into force in 2005. But we are getting ahead of ourselves: we need to set the scene, before we explain how and why the curtains were drawn, exposing the inside workings of the Commons for the first time.

The Fees Office

We need to go back further to look at the way the House of Commons organised its administration to fathom how the system of expenses developed.

The Fees Office has existed since at least the eighteenth century – long before MPs' pay began in the twentieth century. Like many parliamentary functions, the role of the Fees Office changed over time. Since at least 1485, the key parliamentary officials – the Speaker, the Clerk of the House and the Serjeant-at-Arms – were each paid an allowance by the Crown, but the amounts were insufficient for high officers of state, and the Monarch is thought to have supplemented their allowances from time to time, on the basis that the amounts they had been paid were inadequate. But, for all three officials, the salaries and gifts from the Crown were a minor part of the rewards of office.[21] They needed additional sources of income, and one of the most important was 'fees'. Normal public bills going through Parliament attracted no additional rewards for these officers, but private bills did.[22] Thus in 1607, the Speaker ruled (and the House of Commons agreed) that a bill for amending highways in Surrey, Sussex and Kent was a private not a public bill, because it affected only three counties. Its sponsors had to therefore pay private bill fees of £5 to the Speaker for each sponsor of each bill. The Clerk of the House also received a fee. As private bills grew in number (many sponsored by the City of London as its prosperity increased), so did the fees.

The Clerk's fee for private bills was initially only £2, but the Clerk had more opportunity to extend these, for example by charging an extra 10 shillings for a proviso benefiting a private person in a bill, and further fees for additional work such as preparing a revised copy of a bill following amendments by a committee. Promoters would also tip the Clerk as a way of securing his favour for a private bill. The City of London records for 1548 mention 'such accustomed fee as the Clerks of the Parliament House have heretofore commonly used to have at every session of the parliament, of the free gift of the said city.'[23] Such practices would not be acceptable by today's standards of propriety, but they were common – and open as the City's records show – in Tudor England. In 1549 the amount paid was five marks (£3 6s 8d).

The Serjeant-at-Arms was not significantly involved in private bills, but he could still generate fees through his security duties. In 1585 the Serjeant could charge 20 shillings for arresting a culprit in Parliament and 10 shillings a day while in his custody. From 1649, a scale of fees was established, and by the eighteenth century an office had been set up in the Clerk's department to collect the fees. The officials in the office would have been paid by their masters (the Speaker, Clerk and

Serjeant) out of their own fees. This was the beginning of the Fees
Office. But the Fees Office's role was not to benefit or reward MPs
(other than, of course, the Speaker).

Limited free stationery was given from 1911. This was supplemented
by limited free travel in 1924. Some time later in the twentieth century
the Fees Office took on the role of administering MPs' pay and allowances, and in due course was moved to the new Administration
Department, while private bill fees continued to be collected by the
Clerk's Department. At that point, the connection of the Fees Office
with private bill fees came to an end. Like so much historic termin-
ology in Parliament, its name had become a complete misnomer, but
it was a name that MPs had become familiar with so it stuck. When
the Fees Office's name became widely known in public during the
scandal, many people – including journalists and some MPs – wrongly
assumed that 'fees' meant MPs' expenses.

In 1997, the House of Commons appointed Andrew Walker as the
new Director of Finance and Administration, to manage and reform
both finance and human resources. He would also run the Fees Office.
Following a senior management review, it had been decided that
major efforts would need to be put into improving finance, business
planning and HR. In contrast, it was assumed that the Fees Office did
not need to be changed. When he arrived at the House of Commons
in January 1997 to start his new job, Andrew went to see his boss, Sir
Donald Limon, the Clerk of the House. He was urbane and affable.
He said he would see Andrew for a chat once a month, but otherwise
he was on his own. By the way, he said, when you get to your office
you'll find a critical report on your desk. It points out what needs
putting right in your department. Your predecessor kept coming up
with new ideas, which is not what was wanted. And he spent too
much of his time at meetings. 'Oh, and by the way, you'll be responsible for the Fees Office. Don't get too involved in that – it will look
after itself.'

When he arrived in Dean's Yard, the quiet cathedral close hidden
away behind Westminster Abbey, he was introduced to his secretary,
shown his vast office, and for the first time met the three heads of
office who would work for him, leading Finance, Personnel and the
Fees Office respectively. It was by then midday. 'Come with us and

we'll brief you,' they said, and led the way to the Palace of West-minster and the sumptuous Strangers' Dining Room. The briefing took place over a full lunch and a couple of bottles of Barón de Ley Rioja. Clearly working at the House of Commons was going to be very different from the austere and punctilious atmosphere of the Inland Revenue.

When Andrew proposed in the late 1990s that the title 'Fees Office' should be changed given that it was a misnomer, Betty Boothroyd, who was then Speaker, called him in and told him politely but firmly, 'Don't touch my Fees Office, Mr Walker.' So the name was kept.

The (dis)organisation of the House of Commons

It will help to illuminate later events if we paint a picture of the unique and often Byzantine internal 'management' of the House of Commons. When our story began, there was little by way of management that would be recognised by those trained in conventional management approaches. The advantage was flexibility, but mostly for those at the top of the hierarchy; the disadvantage was it relied on trust. MPs are elected representatives; they have no boss, aside from constituents, they are not employees and they decide for themselves how best to do their job. Equally, although MPs are collectively responsible for how the House is run, most have minimal understanding of and no prac-tical say in its administration. MPs have political party bosses, but the parties' interests are mainly to get MPs to develop or back their leader-ship, policies and electoral campaigns. The parties have no direct say (and little interest) in the House's administration, which is rigorously non-party political. The Fees Office was part of that administration: its inner workings were a mystery to most MPs.

Back in the late 1990s, the House of Commons administration was fragmented. It had grown up piecemeal, and had escaped the Thatch-erite financial and management reforms of the 1980s and 90s. While the Civil Service was being cut back, the House of Commons staff-ing had continued to grow; but the staff organisation had no single or clear line of responsibility, no straightforward way to take decisions and no clarity about where the buck stopped.[24]

The House administration was overseen by the House of Commons Commission, a committee of senior MPs chaired by the then Speaker, Betty Boothroyd. Often described by journalists as shadowy, it had been set up under the House of Commons Administration Act 1978. Its focus was predominantly on internal matters such as staffing, internal budgets, IT, buildings and a variety of other administrative issues. Later, the Commission was to become the natural focus in the House for Freedom of Information issues, though many MPs were unaware even of its existence, let alone of its activities. Quite often MPs asked Andrew, 'What is the Commission – I've never heard of it?' It met once a month for a couple of hours on a Monday evening. That allowed insufficient time to run the House of Commons administration effectively – that task was delegated to a Board of Management chaired by the Clerk of the House.

The Board had been set up following a critical report in 1990 by Sir Robin Ibbs, once a director of ICI.[25] It comprised the heads of the six departments of the House, which had been viewed as six different employers. The Clerk of the House was its chair, but he was not Chief Executive. He was described as *primus inter pares* – the first among equals. It was a strange body. The internal workings or challenges of the six departments were not discussed. Meetings were often tetchy and inchoate. On one occasion the then Clerk of the House went round each individual member of the Board of Management giving his opinion of each – in the most unfavourable terms. Fragmentation, rivalry and mutual suspicion were rife.

Part of the governance of the administration was three 'domestic committees'. These were select committees of MPs whose role was to set out Members' requirements for services. MPs did not get much kudos or recognition from being appointed to these committees, so attendance was often poor, and committee membership changed frequently as MPs got themselves appointed to more interesting committees. The relationship between these committees and House staff was often strained: the committees frequently asserted that they were in charge in each of their areas of interest (accommodation, information and administration), and grumbled if officials did not do what they wanted. But when the Accommodation and Works Committee was accused in 2000 of operating a 'buy British' policy in commissioning the building of Portcullis House, which would have been against EU law, the Committee distanced itself from any hands-on responsibility. It was a parliamentary official who took the rap. (A subsequent review exonerated him.)

Above the three domestic committees was the Finance and Services Committee. They decided on the annual budget for the administration and acted as audit committee. Some committee members resented officials' attempts to improve financial management and accountability. During a particularly difficult meeting in the late 1990s about financial reforms, one committee member threatened the Finance Director – 'I'm going to stop your budget' – a clear sign that interference by officials was not welcome.

Curiously, the Fees Office was not overseen by any of these committees because of the arcane way in which the House of Commons budgets were organised. In those days the House was financed from two entirely separate budgets with distinct funding.[26] The Administration Estimate was the House's budget for paying House staff, running the buildings, catering, security, printing and so on. It was overseen by the Commission and the Finance and Services Committee. It was the House's own money, and not subject to government control. In contrast, the Members Estimate was technically money provided by the government to pay MPs and their staff, and to fund their pensions. The accountability arrangements were messy and incomplete; years later, this was to become a factor in the crisis. And, of course, the members of the Commission and the Finance and Services Committee were bemused (and sometimes irritated) that they were responsible for only part of the overall budget. MPs usually felt they should be in charge; though in Andrew's experience, most were unaware of the requirements of modern financial accounting or governance. This was particularly evident when the House of Commons switched from cash accounting to accruals accounting in the early 2000s.

To explain these administrative complexities is not to excuse, but the combination of a fragmented and sometimes chaotic management set-up, a variety of MP committees and a lack of clarity about where the buck stopped does at least go some way to illustrate why there was not a single, straightforward institutional approach to the disclosure of information about MPs' expenses.

A cloud no bigger than a man's hand

In the late 1990s the cloud of the expenses crisis was no bigger than a human hand, far away on the horizon. As Dick Allen puts it:

> It approaches from the sea, too small
> For thunder and lightning
> But ominous as a closed fist
> And what it will bring
> Nearing us, growing larger,
> Is completely unknown.[27]

Nevertheless, there were voices in Westminster proposing that the rules applied to the MPs' expenses system should meet a higher standard of probity. 'It was a different regime in the old days,' said one Fees Office member of staff, 'all done by a nudge and a wink.' The Fees Office had a reputation among MPs for being there to maximise the amounts MPs could claim through the allowances system. But even then, they did not automatically pay up just because a Member told them to. In his early days Andrew was told by a colleague of an occasion when a well-known MP had some years earlier claimed for black satin sheets in his second home; Andrew was reassured to be told that the Fees Office had turned down the claim.

Black Dog column, Mail on Sunday, *21 April 2019*[28]
Ten years on from the MPs' expenses brouhaha, Andrew Walker, the ex-Commons official who oversaw their claims, reveals one scandal that never saw the light of day – the MP who asked: 'I've got black satin sheets in my main home – why can't you pay for black satin sheets in my second home?' Teasingly, Walker – who said the claim was rejected – won't name the 'very well-known' culprit. Spoilsport.

Changes began to take place in 1997. The 'old school' Head of the Fees Office soon left. Improvements in the expenses rule book (nicknamed the Green Book) and the tightening-up of the system and its governance began.

THE IRRESISTIBLE FORCE OF BETTY BOOTHROYD
MEETING THE IMMOVABLE FORCE OF THE WHIPS

May 1997 saw a new Green Book to replace the previous rambling, cyclostyled version that had been issued in 1987. In the foreword, Betty Boothroyd said, 'It is important that Members observe both the spirit and letter of the arrangements described.'[29] The new Green Book emphasised that payments of the allowances were for reimbursement of costs incurred to enable them to perform their parliamentary duties. One clause caused a furore among returning MPs when they took their seats after the May 1997 General Election: it was a requirement that for car travel in their constituencies, MPs should identify journeys 'in sufficient detail to show for each journey the places visited, the mileage involved and the vehicle used'. The Fees Office, backed by Betty Boothroyd, felt that this new requirement was reasonable. After all, anyone else using their car for work and claiming mileage expenses would be required to keep a record of the journeys.

The irresistible force of Betty Boothroyd and the immovable object of the Whips' Offices met head-on. The Fees Office was squeezed in the middle.

The National Audit Office was asked to help. Several weeks, and many difficult meetings later, a deal was brokered. MPs would still be required to give details of the car journeys they made in their constituencies, but only if they wanted to claim for more than 350 miles a month. So the large majority of MPs claimed for exactly 350 miles. Some complained bitterly that they had been denied claiming the full, larger amount because the requirement to keep records was unreasonable. The episode highlighted a serious weakness in governance. Strong and popular though Betty Boothroyd was, her decision to require properly documented mileage claims from MPs and the furore that followed illustrated that the force of the Speaker's personality alone was insufficient to modernise the expenses system.

While no significant public concerns had been raised by then, there were signs that trouble would brew if nothing was done. Andrew and a Fees Office colleague went to see a key cabinet minister in 2001 to express concerns about risks inherent in the expenses system. For example, if the public knew the kinds of things MPs could spend taxpayers' money on, and the fact that there was no external validation, there was a risk that it would damage the reputation of the House of Commons. They said that, under the current system, the Fees Office was not allowed to question beyond the MP's signature. They could give advice to MPs, check arithmetic and ensure that the items claimed were within the rules agreed by the Speaker. But beyond that, they were required to treat Honourable Members' expenses claims as being above suspicion. The Green Book stated that MPs were responsible for ensuring the validity of their own claims, and ensuring that the expenses were used wholly, necessarily and exclusively for parliamentary purposes. If an MP signed to say that they had used the items purchased for parliamentary purposes, then they had. Andrew and his colleague told the minister that there was a likelihood of skeletons in cupboards that would be revealed if full scrutiny was applied to the system. The minister listened carefully, and reflected on what had been said; in the end the response was, 'Mr Walker, thank you for bringing your concerns to me. But I really don't think the public will be interested – they have never shown any interest in the past.'

But however right the minister was in that assessment based on past experience, subsequent events would prove that judgement painfully wrong for the future. And therein lies a typical predicament for parliamentary officials when anticipating trouble ahead: if they do too little, they may worry that they are not protecting Parliament vigorously enough; if they do too much, they may find themselves threatening democracy. We will return to this dilemma in Chapter 7.

By the late 2000s, the main allowances were:

Allowance	Purpose	Max value (2008) (£)
Additional Costs Allowance (ACA)	To allow MPs to live in two places, often called the 'second home allowance'.	24,006
London Supplement	Extra amount to help meet living costs in London. Available to London MPs *instead of* ACA.	2,916
Incidental Expenses Provision (IEP)	Mainly for the cost of running a constituency office.	22,193
Staffing Allowance (SA)	Costs of employing staff in the constituency and at Westminster.	100,205
Travel	Travel costs to and from the constituency and within the constituency, and up to three visits a year to official European institutions. Also limited family and employee travel to and from London.	Variable
Communications Allowance (CA)	For non-party political communications with constituents (e.g. newsletters).	10,400
IT equipment	Provided free (on loan to MP).	Approx. 3,000

A watershed

History is never even and small events can have seismic consequences. 5 July 2001 would turn out to be a watershed, a pivotal moment, with both an attempt to improve governance and a massive increase in the second home allowance. The occasion was the parliamentary debate on the motions put forward by the new Leader of the House, Robin Cook MP. The Leader of the House is the Cabinet Minister responsible for the House of Commons and, working with the Chief Whip, they plan and manage the government's business in the House. Until 2010, the Leader was also responsible for government aspects of the MPs' expenses system, for example laying the annual Estimate (budget) for MPs' pay and expenses, and tabling any necessary motions on the floor of the House. Cook proposed to accept the Senior Salaries Review Body's (SSRB) recommendations on MPs' pay (an increase of £2,000, which would take their salary to over £50,000) and on the Office Costs Allowance, which was to be reformed.

But backbenchers complained about what they regarded as inadequacies in the support for their expenses. When the SSRB recommended a 42 per cent increase in the House of Lords overnight subsistence allowance from £84 to £120 a night, backbenchers led by the Member for Sheffield Attercliffe (Clive Betts) proposed the same proportionate increase in MPs' second home allowance – the Additional Costs Allowance (ACA) – from £13,628 to £19,469.[30] And the allowance was tax-free. Robin Cook acknowledged a former MP's suggestion that the 'post of MP attracts the average pay of a saxophonist with the job security of a football manager',[31] but asked MPs to hold fire on the increase. His appeal to them failed – the increase was voted through (ayes 229, noes 117).

'The problems started from then,' said a perceptive senior MP, referring to the 2001 increase in the second home allowance. And they started in more than one way. First, although many backbenchers felt that the ACA had until then been insufficient to meet their extra accommodation costs in London, for the most part their commitments were nowhere near the additional £5,841 they would now receive each year. What could they spend it on? The published records show[32] that many MPs spent close to the maximum of their allowance year by year: they now had enough funding to carry out repairs and renovations, to pay for decorations and cleaning, to buy furniture, kitchen equipment, entertainment systems, toilet rolls and bath plugs.

The second problem was the timing of the Freedom of Information Act. The first year of the increased ACA was 2001/02. Coincidentally, that was also the earliest year of MPs' expenses records that would still be available when FOI requests became possible on 1 January 2005. And, of course, it was the ACA that was to be of greatest interest to the media and public, because it opened a window on the home lives of MPs, and was the allowance that seemed least justifiable to many citizens.

Getting a grip on governance

Following the constituency mileage debacle in 1997, it was clear that some form of improved governance was needed. The SSRB report published in March 2001[33] reported on a comprehensive review of the system of allowances for running MPs' offices. Instead of an Office Costs Allowance, which covered the rental of a constituency office, staffing and a whole variety of other costs, two new allowances were introduced: a Staffing Allowance and an Incidental Expenses Provision. And MPs would be loaned computers that were compatible with the parliamentary IT system, rather than having to buy their own. The Staffing Allowance was increased and ring-fenced to ensure that staff would be properly paid and that MPs could increase their staff support to meet the rapidly increasing demand for help from constituents. MPs who had been elected before the 2000s report a massive increase in constituency work during the decade. The increase in staffing reflected that growing demand, giving MPs greater capacity to deal with local issues in addition to their participation in Westminster politics. It is possible that the more they met demand, the more constituents made claims on their time.

It was felt that it should not just be left to the new Speaker (Michael Martin, elected in 2000) and the Fees Office to develop the system to underpin these more complex allowances. A committee to advise the Speaker was proposed. This committee, the Speaker's Advisory Panel, was an innovative creation, as it comprised both MPs and senior officials. The committee's membership was announced in a written parliamentary answer:

Ms Drown:
To ask the President of the Council what progress has been made in setting up the Speaker's Advisory Panel.
Mr. Robin Cook:
Following the debate in the House on 5 July 2001, I am pleased to announce that the Speaker has appointed to the Advisory Panel the hon. Member for Sheffield, Hallam (Mr. Allan), my hon. Friends the Members for Cambridge (Mrs. Campbell) and for Streatham (Keith Hill), the hon. Members for Beckenham (Mrs. Lait) and for West Derbyshire (Mr. McLoughlin), my hon. Friends the Members for Dundee, West (Mr. Ross) and for Enfield, Southgate (Mr. Twigg), as well as the Director of Finance and Administration, the Head of the Fees Office and the Director of Communications. It is hoped that the first meeting of the panel will be held soon.[34]

The panel was chaired by the thoughtful and independent-minded Anne Campbell MP. At early meetings of the panel, the issue of control of expenditure, including the vexed question of when receipts would be required, was discussed on several occasions. Some MPs resisted the idea of having to justify themselves to Fees Office officials. It was not so much that most of the Fees Office staff were junior, but that *Honourable* Members had the legitimacy of having been elected, whereas officials, whether junior or senior, were no more than employees – serving Parliament. Ernie Ross MP referred to Andrew as a 'mole from the Inland Revenue', presumably because of his aim to introduce arrangements that Mr Ross felt put bureaucratic controls above democracy. An advantage of the Panel, said one of its members, was that it provided an opportunity for a more systematic and consistent approach. [35] Ross, with a trade union background, wanted to promote fairness of pay and conditions for the MPs' staff who were paid from the public purse. This led to the creation of standardised job descriptions and pay bands for MPs' staff whose salaries were paid by the House, which have subsequently proved to be of enduring benefit. Other improvements were made, too, like getting rid of the antiquated travel warrants system and replacing it with a payment card, so it was both easier for MPs to buy air and rail tickets and easier for the Fees Office to spot misuse (though the MPs whose cards were later stopped when they failed to account for proper usage were of course not pleased).

The ACA allowed MPs to claim the additional costs of food while they were away from home. How much should have been allowed for this, bearing in mind that the Members' Dining Room served high-quality food to MPs at a hugely subsidised price? An MP could eat like a prince for a few pounds a day. The panel decided that MPs should be allowed to spend up to £400 a month on food without needing to provide documentary evidence. This looked generous to people outside Parliament, and would later attract critical comment. The £400 figure was intended to place a cap on claims; but in light of events it was a misjudgement.

Sir Roger Sands became Clerk of the House in 2003. As Accounting Officer for the Members Estimate, he was keen to improve the governance and accountability of the allowances system further. His brainchild, the Members Estimate Committee, was set up in 2004. It had the same membership as the House of Commons Commission and the two committees were often thought of as the same body.[36] It would later become the forum for endless agonising over fighting FOI battles through the courts, but in 2004 it carried out a number of reforms, such as reducing the length of time MPs had to finalise their expenses claims after the year-end, so that the financial accounts could be audited and published in good time. It also acted as a brake on the Speaker's personal decision-making on MPs' expenses arrangements. It was set up under the House's Standing Orders in a form analogous to a select committee – so its deliberations were covered by parliamentary privilege, and disclosure of its proceedings could not (and still cannot) be forced under FOI. There was much internal debate about whether it was *actually* a select committee or just analogous to one. Successive Clerks of the House took differing views.

Considered from the inside, it looked as though the House of Commons was beginning to get a grip on the expenses system: the governance was better, though still secretive, the Fees Office was challenging MPs to provide receipts and other information to support their claims. But did the House have the collective will to continue the process of improving regulation and accountability? And, even if it did, would that be enough to avert a crisis later on?

Ingredients of a perfect storm

A further SSRB report on MPs' pay and allowances was published in October 2004. The Clerk and the Finance Director had written to the SSRB to draw attention to the fact that the way the expenses system operated – in conjunction with the provision of free office accommodation in Westminster – was having the perverse effect of incentivising Members to accommodate their staff on the already overcrowded Parliamentary Estate in Westminster rather than in the constituency.[37] The SSRB accordingly recommended: 'The amount of IEP that may be claimed by MPs should be abated by £7,500 for each permanent workstation occupied by their staff on the Parliamentary Estate. The maximum amount should be available only to those MPs who have no permanent workstation for their staff on the Parliamentary Estate.'[38] In addition, the SSRB recommended cutting the rate of MPs' Motor Mileage Allowance to the Inland Revenue maximum tax-free rates.

Some MPs were incensed by these recommendations and when Peter Hain, the then Leader of the House, introduced the motions to give effect to the changes, there was an ill-tempered debate before the House voted on them.[39] Following a strong speech by Anne Campbell in favour of the reduced mileage allowance, the change in mileage rates was accepted, but the IEP restriction was rejected. Campbell, the Clerk and the Finance Director would all suffer for their impetuosity: the whips were on the warpath. Anne Campbell and Andrew were both sacked from the Speaker's Advisory Panel. Andrew was given a dressing-down by the Speaker in the presence of whips from the two main parties. The House's domestic committees would also be reformed. 'It was intended to punish us,' said Roger Sands: the prevailing view was 'these officials need more controlling by Members'.[40] MPs regarded the structure of the allowances as their preserve.

The House's split personality was on view. On the one hand, some MPs were keen on stronger accountability and much better provision of information to the media and the public. On the other hand, it seemed that many MPs were against change, against interfering officials and against openness. And there were many who were still blissfully unaware of what was round the corner. When John Biffen wrote in 1989 about MPs' pay, he did so with prescience: 'Settling MPs' pay has been a miserable parliamentary experience. The Commons is rarely at its best when dealing with so self-conscious a matter.'[41]

The stage was set: reform was under way and accountability was growing. MPs' jobs were getting more challenging: they needed more staff and financial support and, being self-governing, they voted for the increases in expenses that they believed they needed. Meanwhile, preparations were in hand to implement the Freedom of Information Act. Taken together, these would prove to be a heady mix, with FOI as the key catalyst in the scandal. One MP close to Michael Martin, Sir Archy (now Lord) Kirkwood, was pressing for MPs to back up their expenses claims with receipts.[42] He had fought hard for this, but he had not foreseen that it would give the *Telegraph* more to disclose when they started to publish details of MPs' claims in 2009. 'I was conscience-stricken', he told us – not because it wasn't the right thing to do, but 'because it gave the media more to disclose: the story could be painted in detail. It was the detail – an MP spending money on talcum powder – that caught people's imagination and their prurient interest... It created a perfect storm.'[43] As Robert Winnett of the *Telegraph* observed, part of the problem for the House of Commons was being caught in the attempt to clean up. A move to supplying more detailed claims supported by receipts was needed, but it was those details that gave the story. In his view, the need for accountability was what led to the transparency problem.[44]

2

Secrecy cracks open

Elegantly bound in leather, and filling metre upon metre of shelf space, the hundreds of volumes of historic Hansard bear record to the openness of Parliament in making full and accurate records of its debates available to everyone – lawyers, academics and ordinary citizens alike. Today, over two hundred years of debates have been digitised and are available free online, alongside thousands of other parliamentary documents and records.[1] But it was not always so.

A parliamentary shift to openness

In the early eighteenth century, Parliament was a highly secretive body, publishing only a brief record of its decisions, not of its deliberations. Those who published Parliament's proceedings were deemed to have breached the privileges of Parliament. That began to change in 1771, when the Lord Mayor of London was imprisoned in the Tower of London for failing to punish a printer named John Miller who had published parliamentary debates. Following legal manoeuvres and public protests, the Lord Mayor was released, and it gradually became acceptable to publish a record of the debates. In 1812 Thomas Hansard began to issue his daily record, having taken over the job from William Cobbett, who had been jailed as a result of his campaign for free speech. Hansard has been a feature of Parliament ever since. In 1909, Parliament itself took over publication of the daily record of debate, though the title Hansard has stuck, not only in the UK but also in some overseas countries. Thus, in the space of little over one hundred years, Parliament moved from being virulently opposed to making its full proceedings public to being vigorously and fully in favour of the openness of its deliberations. In 1979 it even set up a dedicated phone line for enquiries from the public, ready to explain about the business, membership or history of the House and its committees. In recent years there has been much pride within Parliament about just how open the legislative process has become: 'It would be hard to find an organisation who provides more information than us,' notes one official.[2] Readers can see today's debates online within minutes, or elect to watch or listen to them live or after the event on Parliament's website.

There are still some exceptions to openness. The reasons for this are often obscured from the view of outsiders. For example, MPs sitting on select committees assume that their inquiry reports will have more clout if their conclusions appear as if they were unanimously supported by all committee members. The political impact of their reports would be undermined, they assume, if these differences were exposed. In private this often means reconciling differences of opinion through gentle persuasion, and debate, even trading points. But secrets have become rare.

Politics used to rely on secrets far more than it does now with the parties in Parliament. Whipping once depended upon the 'usual channels' – that is, the business managers including the Leader of the House, shadow leaders and whips – keeping a tight control on information. Only they knew the diverse views of its Members on particular issues at any one time. They used bribery, persuasion and even threats to prevent potential rebels from defying the party line. But this has broken down in modern times, in part with the fragmentation of political parties but also with the explosive transparency provided by 24/7 media – securing the obedience of party members through secrecy has collapsed.

Parliament's culture of openness is reinforced by the presence of journalists. Quite a number of Lobby correspondents – the parliamentary reporters of all the major news organisations – prowl the corridors cheek-by-jowl with politicians, political staff, parliamentary officials, police and other contractors. The reporters mostly occupy the 'Burma Road', a long upper corridor overlooking Speaker's Court. Before smoking was banned in 2007 and new fire safety standards were adopted, walking down the Burma Road involved choking in a fog of smoke and tripping over higgledy-piggledy piles of old papers – a continual risk that the events of 1834, when Parliament was burned down, might be repeated.[3]

Parliamentary life and proceedings were regularly reported and, when first microphones and then TV cameras were allowed into the chambers, openness triumphed. In recent years instant commentaries have become available, with MPs tweeting their opinions about the issues and those championing them from the Chamber, committee rooms and even party meetings.

In other ways Parliament remained secretive and unaccountable. A senior House of Commons clerk recalled how in the early 1990s concern had been growing in the Members' Interests Committee about MPs' jobs on the side as lobbyists.[4] A register of MPs' outside interests was introduced to discourage such behaviour by making its existence public. Ironically, this greater transparency had the effect of making the practice more respectable, and the Speaker would call on MPs whose names were on the list when a relevant topic was being debated in the House. The system was severely tested in late 1994 when Mohamed Al-Fayed accused MPs Neil Hamilton and Tim Smith of accepting cash to ask questions in Parliament.[5] But at least Parliament was seeking to bring such practices to light, albeit on its own terms.

2019 saw another important milestone in parliamentary openness. Erskine May, the authoritative guide to Parliament's procedures and practice, had first been published in 1844 and had been updated regularly, but the cost of a printed copy is over £300. On 2 July 2019 a new edition finally became available online, free to all users. For the first time this has made the inner workings of the House of Commons procedures easily accessible to the general public.[6]

It is ironic, then, that the story of this book has parallels with that eighteenth-century reluctance to open Parliament up to greater public scrutiny, though the timescale has accelerated from the hundred-or-so years it took to get Hansard established: it took less than a decade to reveal expenses in full after the FOI Act was passed. This resistance and then shift to openness is more central to our story than greed; the significance of the scandal is about the dangers of secrecy more than corruption.

The FOI saga begins

'You idiot. You naive foolish, irresponsible nincompoop. There is really no description of stupidity, no matter how vivid, that is adequate. I quake at the imbecility of it.'[7] So wrote Tony Blair about his decision to introduce a Freedom of Information Act in his memoir after Labour lost the 2010 election.

The secrecy that had once applied to parliamentary proceedings had been abolished for more than two hundred years, but secrecy in executive government was rife (or protected, depending on your viewpoint) in the post-war years. All new civil servants were covered by the Official Secrets Act from the time they took up duty. In government departments, managers and trainers emphasised the awful consequences of being careless with or misusing 'official information'. (Even the canteen menu counted as official information in those days.) Public servants in the UK were drilled in the need for confidentiality. How else could government operate effectively? Of course government did publish some information: departments started issuing more informative annual reports and accounts, gradually opening the window on internal administration, and academics were beginning to look behind the curtain,[8] but the normal workings of the Civil Service remained a closed book to most citizens.

Before Labour won the 1997 election, Tony Blair had said,

> [It] is not some isolated constitutional reform that we are proposing with a Freedom of Information Act. It is a change that is absolutely fundamental to how we see politics developing… information is power and any government's attitude about sharing information with the people actually says a great deal about how it views power itself and how it views the relationship between itself and the people who elected it.[9]

But, as Blair discovered, the Freedom of Information Act came to be used not by ordinary citizens but by the media, campaigners and even by politician against politician. It begged the question of how much of government's internal deliberations should be opened up to scrutiny before the archive files were eventually opened up 30 or 40 years later.

Preparing the FOI legislation

Civil servants who join the House of Commons Service find the culture different from what they have been used to in government departments. When Andrew joined the parliamentary staff in the late 1990s, he found a real contrast with the everyday confidentiality that he'd experienced in the Treasury and Inland Revenue. The culture in Parliament was more open, perhaps because parliamentary staff had daily dealings with politicians and the many public visitors to the Palace of Westminster.

Parliament's openness is tangible. It is not just that debates in the chambers of the Commons and Lords are open, but so are meetings of parliamentary committees, with most hearings held in public, and regular publication of research papers and other documents. In the pre-digital age, each day when Parliament was sitting a small folded sheet of pink paper would appear (known as 'the pink'), setting out every document that was issued on that day – often dozens of items, ranging from brief statutory instruments to weighty reports. And although parliamentary staff have a general duty of confidentiality like employees in many other organisations, they are not subject to the Official Secrets Act in the same way as government employees.[10]

The Government's white paper on FOI was published in December 1997. It recognised that much government activity was carried out in ministries behind closed doors. So the white paper pledged to deal with unnecessary secrecy in government and to encourage more openness and accountability. It proposed to exempt Parliament from the FOI legislation, stating, 'Parliament, whose deliberations are already open and on the public record, will be excluded.'[11] So it was already recognised that Parliament was different from government in its requirement to be open, but no details were given.

It was the House of Commons itself that proposed that the new legislation should be applied to Parliament. The Public Administration Select Committee (PASC) took no evidence on the proposed exclusion of Parliament from the forthcoming legislation; but in May 1998 it said in its commentary on the white paper:

> Proceedings of many Committees take place in private, and the privacy of these would need to be respected. However, the proposed exemption for the integrity of decision-making is likely to protect these discussions. The papers held by individual Members, parties and their Committees, do not relate to Parliament's public functions, and would therefore not, presumably, be covered by the Act... But there are many administrative functions carried out within Parliament which, it seems to us, do not need to be protected, any more than do those of the police. The justification for the exclusion of Parliament has not been made out. The exclusion may well convey the wrong impression to the general public, given the purpose of this legislation.[12]

There is no hint that the committee understood the impact this would have on the information about MPs' expenses, their home lives, their travel patterns, and a host of other details that were held by Parliament as part of the administrative arrangements. This included members of the committee itself, some of whom later had to make repayments for their over-claims.[13] As Michael Carpenter, a later Speaker's Counsel, remarked: 'It is perhaps regrettable that evidence was not taken as to the "administrative functions" of the House so that these were more fully understood.'[14]

When the draft FOI Bill appeared in May 1999, both its drafting and the subsequent scrutiny left much to be desired. As suggested by the PASC, it now included the House of Commons and the House of Lords as public bodies that were to be covered by the Act. But the PASC did not focus on the issue any further, even though they published another extensive set of recommendations on other aspects of the FOI Bill in July 1999.[15] Nor did the House of Commons or the House of Lords consider the inclusion of Parliament when the FOI Bill passed through its various parliamentary stages.

Safeguards were put in place to prevent the disclosure of information if it would curtail parliamentary privilege, or if it would prejudice the effective conduct of public affairs, but neither of these exemptions would prevent disclosure of MPs' claims. There was a technical flaw in the drafting of this part of the Act. It applied the legislation to the 'House of Commons'. To a lay observer, that might seem perfectly sensible; but not to a parliamentary lawyer. The House of Commons is not a legal entity in the normal sense, so the term 'House of Commons' was not sufficiently precise. It conducts its administrative business through the House of Commons Commission, which employs the staff of the House, and through the Corporate Officer, the Clerk of the House, who is responsible for contracts and most other legal matters.[16] One or both of these entities should have been specified. A consequence of the sloppy drafting of the legislation is that when the House of Commons ceases to exist a month before a general election, the FOI Act does not apply to it for that period.[17] There is nothing for it to apply to.

A hidden benefit of the FOI Act was that its introduction applied the 1998 Data Protection Act (DPA) to Parliament. Through an oversight, the original DPA had never been applied to Parliament. This would apply protection of personal privacy to MPs, parliamentary staff and others, though it would not prove to be a strong enough protection to prevent the later disclosure of personal information about MPs in the context of their expenses.[18]

FOI and parliamentary privilege

The Freedom of Information Act received Royal Assent in November 2000; but it did not come into force until January 2005, to the irritation of some campaigners.[19] The delay in implementation would allow Parliament time to prepare.

A senior House of Commons clerk was put in charge of implementation for the House, and within months he recruited Judy Wilson as a specialist adviser to lead the work on preparing an FOI policy for the House, and to begin drawing up a wide-ranging publication scheme. At this point some clerks worried about how greater openness would impact on their work, according to a pro-FOI official, typically asking questions of one another like: 'Surely we don't have to give members of the public what they ask for?' and 'How are we going to do our work at all?' Even if this was a caricature, it reveals a sense of the tensions around transparency.

There were anxieties on constitutional grounds. Article IX of the Bill of Rights of 1689 provides that 'freedom of speech and debates of proceedings in Parliament ought not to be impeached or questioned in any court or place outside Parliament'. Would this important constitutional principle be weakened if the courts demanded to apply FOI principles to the proceedings of select committees? Would the House's decisions based on Section 34 of the Act, which allows the Speaker to certify that information is exempt from disclosure on grounds of parliamentary privilege, be overturned by the Information Commissioner or the courts? In fact, this has not turned out to be a significant problem in practice in the 14 years of the Act's operation, but it was uncharted territory back in 2001.

When Ben Worthy and Gabrielle Bourke interviewed key politicians and staff five years after the FOI Act came into force, few were concerned with the impact of FOI on parliamentary privilege, and they could not cite any examples of impact.[20] Guidance was written for MPs involved in committee work.[21] A system was developed for deciding on a case-by-case basis what privileged information could be released. In practice, plenty of background information had been given out by now, particularly by select committees as they became more attuned to the developing culture of openness.

On the face of it, parliamentary privilege might seem to have little to do with the expenses scandal. The Fees Office had never regarded information about MPs' expenses as protected by privilege. But it later became clear that some MPs thought it should be. We return to this, and other inventive ideas for keeping MPs' claims private, in a later chapter.

Expenses as an FOI crunch point

While much of the attention of the Commons clerks in the Palace of Westminster was taken up by the possible effect of FOI on the parliamentary business of legislation and scrutiny, staff in the Department of Finance and Administration started to address the likely impact of greater disclosure of information about administration. An early task was to prepare for the application of data protection legislation to all the House administration's holdings of personal data – staff and members of the public as well as MPs.

But they also quickly recognised that expenses would be an area of public interest. In parallel with Judy Wilson's appointment as an adviser, an experienced member of staff, Bob Castle, was transferred to work on data protection and the MPs' expenses aspects of FOI. Many senior staff involved in the early days were unfamiliar with the inner workings of the expenses system, which was operated largely by junior staff away from their normal sphere of operation. So even though Judy Wilson, Bob Castle and their colleagues had become aware that MPs' expenses could become a crunch-point issue, it took them a long time to convince others of its importance.

Wilson and Castle worked closely together for the next four years, carrying out research and preparing advice for both politicians and officials with a view to ensuring that Parliament's implementation of the Freedom of Information and Data Protection legislation was timely, lawful and professional. It was a major challenge and a steep learning curve for everyone. No one knew for certain what would have to be disclosed. They started talking to the Information Commissioner's Office (ICO), who would play a major part in developments on MPs' expenses disclosure in subsequent years. The ICO advised them on compiling a publication scheme that would list documents covering a wide range of parliamentary activities such as planning, administration and finance, as well as political and legislative activity. These documents would be released proactively, pre-empting the need for members of the public to make FOI requests to see them. The House of Commons was the first to publish its publication scheme, before local authorities and others. Two particular questions had to be resolved: did the FOI Act apply to MPs at all? And, if it did, how much privacy would MPs be entitled to? With hindsight, the answer to the first question now seems obvious, but it did not back in 2000, at least to many MPs. MPs have told us that the potential impact of FOI on disclosure of their expenses only began to occur to them after the FOI Act had been passed. 'MPs are not public bodies so they did not think initially it would apply to them,' said ex-MP Sir Nick Harvey.[22] Even so, not all MPs took this view. Norman Baker, the Liberal Democrat Member for Lewes, did believe FOI would and should apply to MPs' expenses.[23] He submitted an FOI request as soon as the legislation took effect, asking for details of MPs' travel expenses.

But it was the question of how much privacy MPs should be entitled to that would prove the more difficult one. It was an issue on which there were widely differing views, which would only ultimately be resolved through the courts. We return to this in Chapter 4.

In those early days some MPs suspected that the ICO's caseworkers were FOI fanatics, with a brief to ensure that as much information as possible was made public. The experience of Andrew and his staff was more nuanced: ICO caseworkers were committed to achieving greater openness, sometimes to the point of making mistakes in the law, but most were also determined to help. For example, they advised on compiling the House of Commons' publication scheme.

Top-level legal advice was sought about whether MPs' expense claims would have to be released if someone made a request and, if so, what level of detail should be provided. Could requesters be limited to receiving annual totals of claims under major headings such as office costs, staff costs, travel costs, accommodation costs, and so on? Or would they be entitled to see information about each individual claim, or maybe see the claim forms themselves? The legal advice was guarded: there would certainly have to be disclosure of expenses, but it was difficult to predict what the courts might decide on how much detail would have to be revealed if the issue was put to them.

Andrew and a colleague raised the issue with the late Robin Cook, who was Leader of the House of Commons between 2001 and 2003. They visited him in his palatial office in Carlton Gardens. Although it was still early days, he immediately saw the practical and political challenges that FOI would bring. He appeared to be no fan of the FOI Act: 'I was on a plane at the time the House voted on it', he quipped, but then went on to add, 'We should publish and be damned.'[24] But that view wasn't shared by others. Many MPs were slow to focus on the risks. One senior government minister thought that the public would never be very interested in something so mundane, while others assumed that the information would be protected by their right to privacy because it contained information about their houses, children and household spending. Another MP – a lawyer – later argued that the House of Commons did not 'hold' MPs' claims at all: they remained the property of each MP making a claim, and the House therefore had no right to disclose the information to a third party. His argument did not succeed.

The habitual trust between the Fees Office and MPs was beginning to break down as staff challenged claims more often. Some MPs complained that senior Fees Office staff were no longer 'on their side'. As the rules for expenses were tightened, for example to require receipts, Fees Office staff were challenging claims more than they used to and some MPs felt that the Fees Office was too keen to publish information about their claims as the FOI deadline loomed. The perception that the Fees Office was there to meet MPs' wishes unquestioningly was fading fast.

One aspect of the new legislation that required attention was how long to keep information, especially of a personal nature. The Data Protection Act made it clear that personal data should be used only for the purpose for which it had been collected, and should be retained only for so long as it was needed to fulfil that function. The Parliamentary Archives led the work to draw up a draft data retention policy and a schedule of disposal arrangements, for agreement by the authorities of both Houses. The aim was to ensure that documents of historical and archival importance did not get destroyed, but that administrative information was disposed of securely once it was no longer needed. One of the categories to be looked at was MPs' expenses records, where the Fees Office and the Archives co-operated closely. This threw up difficult choices, including whether claims should be destroyed once the annual accounts had been audited; whether they should be kept for longer in case the tax authorities wanted to refer to them; or whether they should be kept in perpetuity as part of a national archive. There were arguments in favour of all these options.

The National Audit Office was consulted: for its purposes, it did not see a need to keep MPs' individual claims once it had completed its annual audit work on the House of Commons accounts (usually in the year following the year of claim). Consultants had suggested that the Inland Revenue would require claims records to be retained for six years, but the Revenue explained that, as the claims related to PAYE rather than to Corporation Tax,[25] a retention period of a couple of years after the year of claim should be sufficient. In the light of advice, the House of Commons Commission decided that the House Administration should err on the side of caution and retain MPs' claims for three years after the year of claim (i.e. for a maximum of four years).

This meant that by the time members of the public could request disclosure of MPs' past claims (when FOI came into force on 1 January 2005), claims made before 2001 would no longer be held by the House.

Later, the House would be criticised for operating this policy when there was the possibility of litigation. The Information Tribunal in 2008 described the destruction of some such data as 'regrettable', though they saw it as incompetence rather than intent.[26]

Denial and panic

Alan Keen MP: This Freedom of information stuff – it actually applies to us as well?

Speaker Martin: Look – calm down. After some thought on the matter, I've decided that the best course of action is to certify categorically under section 34 of the Act. This means no disclosure.

[Pause – colleagues speechless]

Martin: What? You don't think I could have thought of that on my own? Is that it? [...] I've got this Freedom of Information thing under control. This is the House of Commons, with centuries of authority behind it. Nothing's going to change. Nothing.[27]

On Expenses, the TV fictional drama on the scandal, is inaccurate in detail but captures the mood of denial among many MPs in the early days of FOI. In the TV film, the Speaker is portrayed as weak and petulant but, as one senior MP put it, he was canny – 'nobody's fool... nor was he malicious.'[28] He was proud of having been a sheet metal worker in Glasgow and of having climbed the greasy pole of politics by his own merit and efforts. Not an intellectual, he resented what he saw as the scholarly arrogance of the Commons clerks who surrounded him, anger that would bubble over from time to time when he felt manipulated by them. But he resented equally media references to his humble origins. He loathed being dubbed 'Gorbals Mick' by Quentin Letts,[29] both because he was not from the Gorbals and because he saw the term 'Mick' as anti-Catholic abuse. The late Tam Dalyell said, 'The epithet "Gorbals Mick" was an ill-judged, unjustified, nasty invention of certain metropolitan sketch-writers.'[30]

"I'VE GOT THIS FREEDOM OF INFORMATION THING UNDER CONTROL!"

As a former shop steward with the Amalgamated Union of Engin-
eering Workers, he had a natural affinity with many of his Labour
former colleagues. It had been normal for a Speaker, once elected, to
distance himself from his former party group in order to emphasise
the impartiality of the speakership. Not so Speaker Martin. His continuing loyalty to his former Labour colleagues was widely noticed:
'His colleagues in the Tea Room had voted him in, so he felt he owed
them,' observed one MP.[31] But that is the view of a non-Labour MP,
so has to be treated with caution: Speaker Martin's loyalties were
broader, according to other MPs, as he was also close to some MPs in
other parties who he had known for decades. He 'appeared to see his
role as that of a shop steward for MPs', said Norman Baker MP.[32] In
the words of a senior official: 'Michael Martin felt he'd been elected
by grassroots MPs, so he wanted to help backbenchers... his instinct
would be hostile to FOI: he set the tone. It is conceivable that a

different Speaker might have set a different tone.'[33] One non-Labour senior politician expressed sympathy: neither Michael Martin nor his wife Mary had been properly briefed by their officials, so they were unprepared for many of the issues and pressures that faced the Speaker when he came into office in October 2000, just a month before the FOI Act received Royal Assent. 'His staff should have supported him better,' he added.[34]

Freedom of Information was to be one of the defining themes of his speakership. But from the outset, he started to show unease when his officials explained the implications to him. In 2002, Andrew had visited his opposite number in the Irish Parliament, the Houses of the Oireachtas, to see how they were dealing with similar issues. 'Mr Walker, who authorised you to go to Dublin?' asked Michael Martin when Andrew briefed the House of Commons Commission on preparations for the release of information about MPs' expenses the following year. Andrew was nonplussed at what was clearly intended as a rebuff. The Irish experience was cautionary: the Oireachtas administration had run into problems with both MPs and with the media, so Andrew's report back to MPs in London was not encouraging.

While many MPs' heads were in the sand, the Commons Commission spent more and more time discussing how to apply FOI to expenses. Should MPs' permission be sought if someone asked for information about them? Could MPs be told who had asked for the information? They considered whether they should publish expenses information automatically, without waiting for it to be requested, and debated several times what information could be refused. A former Clerk of the House, Sir Roger Sands, who attended the meetings, said they spent as much time on FOI – mostly in relation to MPs' expenses – during these years of preparation as on all of their other business put together. With the benefit of hindsight, it might have been helpful for MPs to alert their colleagues informally that they should think ahead. They could have encouraged them to be sure that there was nothing in their claims that they might be uncomfortable about if it was made public. But the Commission dug their toes in, determined to keep what they saw as private information out of the public domain. 'They were constantly looking for a way out,' Sir Roger told us.[35]

A member of the Commission confirmed that they would have preferred to keep FOI at arm's length: 'they would try to hold the line'.[36] He described how the 2002 dispute with the Standards Commissioner Elizabeth Filkin, when the Commission had refused to renew her contract, had left a sour taste. The Commission had taken this line because many MPs were unhappy with Filkin for what they regarded as an anti-MP attitude, and because she revealed the names of those she was investigating, thus effectively blackening their reputations. 'This bad relationship infected subsequent discussions: there was a psychological effect that carried over... so the Commission started in the wrong place,' he added.

In the early days, the Commission was conservative in its outlook; it was in favour of preserving the status quo. Among its members were Sir Patrick Cormack (Conservative) and Sir Stuart Bell (Labour), described by Nick Harvey, a Commission colleague, as 'the two most conservative MPs in England, and of course Speaker Martin, the most conservative man I have ever met. As far as those three were concerned, there was nothing to change.'[37] Some were shocked at the idea that FOI might relate to them. Parliament, after all, was sovereign: they assumed that if they were fleet-footed, they could keep the wolf from the door. A siege mentality was beginning to develop: another official who attended the meetings said, 'Michael Martin was in denial... he would stamp his foot quite regularly.'[38]

One commissioner, Sir Archy Kirkwood, did sound a note of warning to a colleague: 'The expenses regime and the FOI Act are on a collision course. It will end in tears.'[39] So at least one MP said out loud that it might be impossible to maintain the secrecy.

Un pour tous, tous pour un

If no one asked for anything to be disclosed, there was nothing to worry about. But as the FOI implementation date of 1 January 2005 crept closer, public interest was beginning to grow. Some MPs, especially those who championed the cause of FOI, decided that it would be best to make their own expenses claims public anyway. Norman Baker published his. With a reputation as a campaigning MP since he was elected in 1997, he would quickly emerge as a strong advocate of publishing details of all MPs' expenses, and take a case against the House to Tribunal.

The Commission and its parallel body the Members Estimate Committee (MEC) met several times to discuss what to do. They took on an experienced media adviser, John Stonborough, to help. His advice was to take the bull by the horns and publish annual summaries of the expenditure of all MPs, rather than wait to be asked. Otherwise, there was a danger that, as details of individual MPs' expenses were requested, there would be a damaging drip, drip, drip that would never stop.

They also decided on a policy of 'one for all and all for one': MPs should stick together through thick and thin. So if the House was asked to disclose information about one MP – for example their office expenses or travel costs – the same information would be provided for all other MPs. This meant that in due course the Publication Scheme could be extended to cover hitherto unpublished details as new requests were received. There was much agonising about how much to publish. The consensus view was to publish the minimum amount of information that would stand a chance of satisfying the likely interest of the media and the public. Despite its cross-party political make-up and differing views on secrecy, the Commission and, from 2004, the Members Estimate Committee tried to present a united front.[40]

The Commission had to decide what to publish and when. They had taken legal advice and received guidance from the ICO about what level of publication would satisfy the requirements of the FOI Act. Michael Martin wrote to MPs in December 2002 and again in 2003 telling them that the Commission had decided to publish annual totals for each Member's allowances, adding that he believed that this would meet the House's obligations under the Freedom of Information Act.[41] The figures would be released under nine headings: Additional Costs Allowance (ACA), London Supplement, Incidental Expenses Provision, Staffing Allowance, Members' Travel, Members' Staff Travel, Centrally Purchased Stationery, Centrally Provided Computer Equipment and Other Costs. No individual items would be disclosed, nor would expenses claim forms be released. So the Fees Office was instructed to begin preparations to publish three years of information about MPs' claims: 2001/02, 2002/03 and 2003/04. Publication would take place some time in 2004, in the hope that early publication would satisfy public interest before the right to submit FOI requests became available the following January.

Public interest intensifies

Meanwhile, public interest in MPs' expenses had been growing. It was not just FOI that fuelled interest. A growing demand for greater accountability, increased scrutiny and more openness was having an impact. The cash-for-questions affair in 1994 had led the then Prime Minister John Major to set up the Committee on Standards in Public Life (CSPL), chaired by Lord Nolan, to establish a high-level code of ethics for MPs, ministers, civil servants, executive agencies, the NHS and so on. The seven principles established by Nolan – including the principle of openness – had become widely accepted and used. Parliament itself developed the habit of subjecting government organisations to vigorous scrutiny on the basis of these principles, and in recent years had extended the scope of such scrutiny to private sector organisations, too.

It was the principles developed in light of Parliament's own cash-for-questions scandal that helped to develop the environment within which Parliament itself could scrutinise others and hold them to account. And it was ironic that the same principles and expectations started to be applied to MPs' expenses. Public interest in MPs' expenses was awakening well before it became possible in January 2005 to make FOI requests, and would contribute to the mood of expectation. Three cases illustrate this: Henry McLeish, Michael Trend and David Blunkett.

Henry McLeish had become Scottish First Minister in 2000; but early in 2001 he was accused of failing to notify the Fees Office of income he was receiving from subletting his Edinburgh offices (before becoming Scottish First Minister he had been a Westminster MP). He rushed to register the income, but the damage was done. In November 2001 he resigned as First Minister, just a year and thirteen days after he had taken up office.

"Regular or not, sir, you can't claim this as your second home."

The Hon Michael Trend, CBE MP, the Member for Windsor, had claimed expenses for an overnight stay in London when in fact he'd spent the night at his family home in Windsor. When the matter was investigated in 2002, the truth turned out to be more serious. Trend had told the Fees Office that his main home was in London, so he was claiming expenses on his Windsor home. But his Windsor home was his family home, and had been for years. It was his main home. In fact he didn't have a proper home in London at all, but stayed overnight with a friend when he needed to – stays which he admitted were infrequent.[42] He should not have been claiming expenses for a second home at all. Trend paid back £90,000 immediately.

This was the starting pistol for an increasing number of allegations against MPs. Not all of them were found to be true, but the snowball had begun to roll down the hill and was – slowly at first – gathering pace.

'Blunkett fights for his political life' was the headline in the *Telegraph* on 29 November 2004.[43] The allegations were that he had abused his position as Home Secretary to help his former lover, Kimberly Quinn,

Allowances or expenses?

A common conversation in the House of Commons in the run-up to the crisis was whether the payments that MPs could claim for their offices, second homes and travel were allowances or expenses. To most this will seem an abstruse point, but it was meaningful for MPs and reflected the culture at the time. The point was this: an *allowance* was seen as something an MP was entitled to in full.[44] They were not obliged to have it all. Indeed some decided to have none at all. But it was theirs if they wanted it. In contrast, an *expense* was a cost you incurred in doing your job, and could claim back from your employer. MPs normally talked of allowances rather than expenses, and would sometimes correct people who called them expenses. Unsurprisingly, the 2003 Green Book, the internal guide to the arrangements, uses the term 'allowances' 136 times and 'expenses' only 50 times.[45]

The pay, pensions and allowances for MPs were founded on resolutions of the House. Such resolutions are broadly equivalent to internal legislation for Parliament.[46] In this case they often referred to allowances. But they also spoke of expenses, suggesting that the terms were interchangeable. For example, the second home allowance is described as follows: 'Provision should be made for Members who are Members for constituencies other than those specified in the Schedule set out below at paragraph 3.2 below to receive an allowance in respect of the additional expenses necessarily incurred by any such Member in staying overnight away from his only or main UK residence for the purpose of performing his parliamentary duties.'[47]

So why did MPs insist on using the term allowances? A brief history will help. Back in 1911, the Liberal government introduced an annual salary for MPs, following a legal judgement that prevented trade unions from providing financial support to MPs from a political levy. The Chancellor of the Exchequer Lloyd George answered the accusation that this would lead to a professional class of MPs by saying, 'It is not a remuneration, it is not a recompense, it is not even a salary. It is just an allowance, and I think the minimum allowance.' The following year, the Inland Revenue decided that it combined salary and allowance, and taxed only three-quarters of it: the remainder was regarded as covering out-of-pocket expenditure and was therefore free of tax.[48]

> So, for MPs there had long been a broad equivalence between pay
> and allowances, despite the fact that the resolutions of the House
> and the Green Book made it clear that the allowances were for strict
> reimbursement of expenses incurred in parliamentary work.[49] Many
> MPs had a deep-rooted perception that the allowances were in some
> way an addition to salary. This went alongside the common view, as a
> number of MPs and ex-MPs told us, that if pay was restrained, it was not
> unreasonable to seek a commensurate increase in allowances. By 2008
> it had begun to dawn on many MPs that this approach did not meet
> public approval, and the names of the allowances began to be changed to
> 'expenditures'.

by helping her to get a visa for her Filipina nanny, having her chauf-
feured to his weekend home in Derbyshire in his government car, and
giving her one of his first-class rail warrants issued by the Fees Office.
Soon afterwards, Blunkett resigned as Home Secretary. The most
damaging issue had been the visa, but the rail warrant played its part.
Blunkett admitted giving Quinn the rail warrant, and the Standards
Commissioner's investigation[50] published on 21 December criticised
him – mildly – for the error.[51]

The idea that MPs were routinely 'sleazy' was now taking root more
widely. Parliament and politicians had of course never been held in very
high regard, but that was not especially linked to corruption: between
the 1920s and 1990s it was scarcely discussed in British politics.[52] There
had been political scandals of various kinds decade after decade, but
there had been little by way of scandal about MPs' expenses,[53] though
it was no doubt suspected that there was the occasional rotten apple
in the barrel. So maybe the cabinet minister who thought in 2001 that
the public would not be interested in MPs' expenses was right histori-
cally. But societal developments were changing expectations: factors
including the internet and the information revolution, a more aggressive and investigatory approach by the media, and the decline of deference may all have played a part.

Unhappiness as publication day gets closer

In early 2004, each MP was sent their expenses figures that were to be published on the parliamentary website in the autumn, and given time to check them. Many MPs were nervous. Some released the figures on their own websites to get ahead of the game. The *Times* phoned MPs to ask for their data before it was published by the Commons. Publication was set for 21 October. The Commission's spokesman, Sir Archy Kirkwood, announced: 'This is a significant step towards openness and accountability and I welcome it. It's the first time that we have ever published so much information. The tax payer can really see how their money is being spent.'[54]

Publication day was a Thursday. The newspapers ran the story the following morning when MPs were back in their constituencies. Gisela Stuart, the MP for Edgbaston, was astonished when she arrived to take her constituency surgery that she was pilloried as one of the high spenders. She'd had no idea about how her spending compared with other MPs, because each MP had only previously seen their own figures; they didn't know what others had spent. The Commission had been told that they couldn't warn the high spenders in advance – the Commission hadn't in any event seen any of the figures beforehand.[55]

The Fees Office released the data in alphabetical order, in locked PDF format, to try and prevent publication of league tables, but that was a naive and forlorn hope. The press were determined to create league tables, regardless of the format the data reached them in. The locked files simply served to irritate them, which was counterproductive, because it reinforced their feeling that the House was resisting the public interest, and was trying to hide something. Many MPs thought the newspaper presentation was unfair. One MP told us that newspapers tended to miss out any context and did not, for example, take into account that an MP with a huge constituency in the north of Scotland was bound to have higher travel costs than an MP with a small constituency close to Westminster.[56]

Implementation day for the FOI Act was now close. The atmosphere on MPs' expenses had become febrile following the October release. Some MPs started to pay back money, and asked for the records to be adjusted to reflect the repayments they had made. The Commission's media adviser at the time, John Stonborough, said, 'We all knew it was going to be a nightmare, but no one ever realised quite the degree to which it would explode.'[57] One commissioner felt they were unprepared for the media reaction: in retrospect he thought the PR had not been handled well. Thus the hope of drawing the sting and letting things settle before the FOI Act took effect was not realised. Instead, the media and public appetite had been whetted. Significantly, it was in 2004 that Heather Brooke, the anti-secrecy campaigner, first telephoned the House of Commons to ask about MPs' expenses. She would later become a key player in the story as it unfolded.[58] The black clouds had not blown away as MPs went home to spend Christmas with their families.

As 2005 dawned, no one was happy. MPs were dispirited. Their sense of being 'got at' was increasing. Some MPs had made a point of publishing more information about their expenses on their websites; others resisted pressure to disclose information they regarded as private. They felt that the Commission and the Fees Office had let them down and, although the Speaker had assured them he would hold the line, the omens did not look good. A general election was imminent, when they would be held to account and could lose their seats. The House of Commons Commission, aka the MEC, were disgruntled: the PR advice they had been given had not proved effective and the problem would not go away. They asked for regular updates on FOI requests and responses, but were uneasy about what they heard.

Heather Brooke and other journalists were dissatisfied. Why was the House of Commons refusing to give more information when they requested it? The natural conclusion was that they had something to hide. They suspected the House of trying to conceal wrongdoing. The Fees Office and the FOI team were caught in the middle. MPs, the Commission and journalists were all at odds with them: they felt like meat in the sandwich.

3

Closing ranks on privacy

Heather Brooke telephoned the House of Commons in January 2004 to track down information about preparations for FOI.[1] She spoke to Judy Wilson, who later sent her an email stating that MPs' expenses would be published in October 2004.[2] Disappointed – though evidently not surprised – that the aggregated expenses figures released in October did not satisfy her interest, she started making requests the following January, as soon as the FOI legislation took effect. Over time she made requests for the names and salaries of MPs' staff, MPs' travel claims and, in March 2006, details of MPs' claims for Additional Costs Allowance. When the requests were refused, she became 'determined to highlight MPs' blazing hypocrisy'.[3] Without her dogged campaign, the expenses scandal would never have happened.

Emma asked Heather what propelled her persistence. Her history of investigating financial accountability in the US started her off. The contrast between transparency at every level of politics in the US and secrecy in both local government and the Westminster Parliament was a shock. She wondered what they were trying to hide. Her feminist convictions gave her critique a specific twist: this collusion between entitled men at the centre of government is bad for democracy, she thought, but also downright aggravating. She did not have contacts within Parliament and did not know how it worked or related to government, which may have helped her maintain her determination.

An earlier exchange with an MP reveals the danger of closeness in Parliament:

MP: They hug you to them close, they want you to feel part of the institution. The result is that you are less likely to speak out critically.

EC: Is this a conscious tactic?

MP: No, it is just the way it works. They know that if you love the institution, you are less likely to be critical but it is not an intentional strategy.[4]

Norman Baker MP describes how he felt he 'should not hold back from making waves where there was an important issue at stake'.[5] So in January 2005 he, too, asked for details of MPs' travel costs. Like Heather Brooke, he would pursue his campaign through the various appeal stages all the way to the Information Tribunal.

Campaigns begin

January 2005 saw a torrent of FOI requests. Out of 196 requests the House received in 2005, one third related to expenses – by far the largest category – and most of these were received in the first couple of months. Many requested details for multiple MPs. A number of requesters were given some additional information, but those who were asking for breakdowns of the expenses figures contained in the October 2004 release were told that 'disclosure of information additional to that in the publication scheme would not be consistent with the data protection principles and is therefore exempt from disclosure'.[6] Each time a request was received, the Fees Office wrote to the MPs concerned to tell them about the request and how it had been answered. MPs often asked for the name of the requester, but the Fees Office would not tell them – they did not want to encourage disgruntled MPs to take up the cudgels against requesters.

While the number of requests began to decline after the initial flurry, three requests were made on 4 and 5 January that set the course for the crisis four years later. They were summarised in the 2008 Tribunal judgement:

(1) On 4 January 2005 Mr Thomas, a journalist who writes under the bye-line 'Jon Ungoed-Thomas', made a request for details on the ACA claimed by Tony Blair in 2001/2, 2002/3 and 2003/4, 'specifically, a list of the items totalling £43,029' under the ACA.

(2) On the same day Mr Thomas also made a request with regard to the ACA claimed by Margaret Beckett over the same period, asking 'exactly what items the allowances were spent on and the amounts spent on each of the items over each of the three years' and 'if refurbishments or works were paid for out of the public purse', 'what these refurbishments or works were.'

(3) On 5 January 2005 Mr Leapman, who is also a journalist, requested copies of the original submissions, with copies of receipts, rental agreements or mortgage interest statements, from named MPs in support of their claims for ACA in each of the same three financial years as Mr Thomas's request. The named MPs were Tony Blair, Barbara Follett, Alan Keen, Ann Keen, Peter Mandelson and John Wilkinson.[7]

Both Jon Ungoed-Thomas of the *Sunday Times* and Ben Leapman of the *Evening Standard* were experienced investigative journalists. The House of Commons Commission and MEC soon realised that their hopes, and those of most MPs, that the issue would subside were misplaced. The die had been cast. The October 2004 publication, which fell short of journalists' and campaigners' hopes, and was presented in a form that irritated them, may have had the opposite effect to the one the House authorities had hoped for. They had misjudged the media reaction: instead of earning them 'brownie points' or drawing the sting of criticism, the October publication had, with hindsight, acted as an incendiary bomb.

Fourteen months later, another important FOI request was submitted, this time by Heather Brooke. It was summarised by the Tribunal:

On 20 March 2006 Ms Brooke, who is a freedom of information campaigner and freelance journalist, requested a detailed breakdown of MPs' ACA. At a later stage, after reference to the cost limit set under [FOI Act] section 12, her request was recast as being for a detailed breakdown of ACA claims for 2005/6 and all information held by the House, in relation to the claims made by Tony Blair, David Cameron, Menzies Campbell, Gordon Brown, George Osborne, John Prescott, George Galloway, Margaret Beckett, William Hague and Mark Oaten.[8]

The need to communicate?

As we saw in Chapter 2, over the centuries the House of Commons had had mixed feelings about communicating with citizens. With our twenty-first century perspective, it seems odd to us that a Parliament elected by citizens would not want to communicate extensively with those people. But Parliament believed it *was* communicating – through Hansard, through *Today in Parliament* on the radio, through the television, and through MPs. MPs saw themselves as communicators for the House of Commons, so much so that staff who urged a more professional and coherent communications effort in the early 2000s were often told that they were treading on MPs' toes: individual MPs were the voice of Parliament to the public. The corollary of this was that many insiders had a view that the House of Commons had no persona of its own, other than through MPs collectively, and proceedings of the House in formal session.

In parallel, a number of journalists began asking for information too. That created a quandary. The FOI team, once set up, realised that few requesters would be asking for information with a view to painting the House of Commons in a good light: the House's responses to FOI requests would inevitably lead to criticism by individuals or the media. Such criticism might well be justified, but sometimes it might be seriously ill informed if the information supplied was misunderstood or was used out of context. The FOI team therefore tried to encourage internal providers of information to supply more information than had been requested, so that it could be seen in context.[9]

Senior officials urged the House of Commons Commission and the Members Estimate Committee to hire professional advice on public communications. The Commission's spokesman, Sir Archy Kirkwood MP, supported this and the media adviser, John Stonborough, had been engaged in December 2001 (see Chapter 2). He advised the Commission on a number of occasions on the presentation of MPs' expenses, but he resigned in December 2004 – just before FOI requests began to pour in. A series of other advisers followed. But the House remained reactive, with the result that it was always on the back foot. This had not mattered as much before the publication of expenses information began. There had, of course, been occasions when the House authorities attracted bad publicity, such as over the building of Portcullis House,[10] but the advent of FOI meant that unwelcome stories based on FOI disclosures were to become weekly, and sometimes daily, occurrences and the House was not ready to respond.

What communication strategy might have helped the House on MPs' expenses? As we have seen, one of the problems was the near-secrecy of the rules and the system. Sir Christopher Kelly, who was to head up the Committee on Standards in Public Life (CSPL) in 2008, told us that he had no understanding of the system of MPs' expenses before he joined CSPL, even though he had spent much of his career as a top civil servant in regular contact with Parliament. A diligent Parliament-watcher could no doubt have examined SSRB reports, which made recommendations on MPs' allowances every three years or so, or they could have read Parliament's detailed resolutions carefully. Indeed, from May 2005, they could have read the House's own 'Concordance of Resolutions'[11] relating to MPs' expenses. But it was not an easy read and it would be time consuming for most to find this information. So the general perception given by news stories was frequently one-sided: the House of Commons had presented little, if any, contextual material that journalists could draw on.

The House's complex governance and incomprehensible internal organisation got in the way. What was needed was a concerted, co-ordinated, holistic approach to communications. This would involve listening to and monitoring the public mood, engaging with citizens both directly and through the media, and openly explaining how the House of Commons worked, why its apparently crazy way of doing things was important, and how it sought to reflect the interests and concerns of people throughout the UK. The House set up a Modernisation Committee and in 2004 it produced a report about communicating better with the public.[12] The following year, a committee chaired by the British film producer and peer David Puttnam proposed a more strategic approach to public communications by the House of Commons: '[Parliament's] communication strategy... should be based on the optimum principles of accessibility and transparency; participation and responsiveness; accountability; inclusiveness; and best practice in management and communication.'[13] The report was wide ranging, including recommendations about the House's administration. But progress was slow.

When John Pullinger was recruited to run the library, outreach and communications in 2005, he saw that a more vigorous approach was needed, and set about persuading staff colleagues and politicians to move in that direction.[14] But this took years to germinate, and only took root when the expenses crisis was in full swing. John Pullinger and Aileen Walker (then Director of Public Engagement) expanded Parliament's education services, established a regional parliamentary outreach service, introduced awareness-raising activities and vastly improved information services for visitors. During this time MPs were polarised on communications: many on the then government's side, already in the mood for modernisation, were eager for the House to look outwards. Many Conservatives felt that the House itself shouldn't claim an identity. Their line was typically that

> there is no such thing as the House of Commons. MPs are the public face of the House of Commons. In a parliamentary democracy the relationship with the public is through MPs. There are 650 of them and they are the ones who relate to the public, so there is nothing for the House of Commons to do.[15]

One initiative entailed the Speaker writing to all new voters when they reached their 18th birthday, explaining their responsibility as citizens in a democracy, but MPs objected. One asked how the Speaker could write to *his* constituents. (It was stopped as part of the House's savings programme, hastened when they discovered that a few of the young people receiving the letter had died.) Many MPs were even more resistant to the idea of the Commons expanding its media capacity, horrified at the idea that Parliament itself might embark on New Labour-like spin. Speaker Martin was among the sceptics. The result was that, when the expenses scandal unravelled, the institution was paralysed without the media skills to know how to reply to the stories. Rather than trying to respond by explaining, the institution tried to stop the exposure in its tracks.

For the media and public to understand MPs' expenses in context, they needed not only to know what expenses MPs were given, but also to understand more of the context about their work and lives: the need for non-London MPs to live in two places at once, the unpredictable and often long hours, the challenges they had with caring for their families (or even staying in touch with them), dealing with the mounting and conflicting pressures, and so on. There appeared to be little awareness, for example, of the fact that by the mid-2000s the majority of MPs worked very long hours for six days a week either in constituencies or Westminster, even when Parliament was not sitting. This was in stark contrast to the period up to the 1970s, when MPs were routinely advised by colleagues to spend as little time as possible in the constituency (see Chapter 1). But John Pullinger's initiative came too late to ameliorate the expenses crisis: the idea that Parliament as an institution should explain itself to the general public in interesting, clear and accessible terms was simply not accepted within Parliament in the early 2000s.

Uneven press attention

Andrew's collection of press cuttings from May 2003 onwards represents only a partial sample of what the media were saying about the House of Commons, specifically the areas of his responsibility, but it reveals the ups and downs of the scandal. Unsurprisingly, there was a big increase in press coverage in 2008 as court cases were lost and public interest grew, and then an explosion in 2009 following the leak to the *Telegraph*.[16]

Before the publication of expenses information about all MPs in October 2004, most media attention was aimed at government ministers' grace-and-favour homes, highlighting the fact that they were also able to claim their parliamentary second home allowance on top. The press returned to this theme several times over the succeeding months.[17] While Tony Blair, Margaret Beckett and John Prescott were targeted, so was Michael Martin. Speaker Martin appears in several headlines, again as 'Gorbals Mick', as part of a wider campaign against him by the *Mail on Sunday*. But expenses as a regime hardly attracted attention at that stage. Even after figures were published on 21 October, the media flurry soon died away. On 28 October the *Guardian* reported, 'Many

[MPs] relieved at voters' mild reaction to publication of claims.'[18] It was a similar story for 2006, with the main concern being 'this ministerial free house scam'.[19] Speaker Martin also attracted media attention over the failure to curb thefts from parliamentary buildings and for allegedly trying to shoehorn his son into office in Scotland. Media interest in expenses as a broader issue began to grow in 2007, with both claims and legal cases popping up for scrutiny.

So, despite the FOI Act coming into force in January 2005, that year was to be quiet on MPs' expenses. The most important debating issues in the run-up to the general election that year were health, taxation, crime, immigration, education and the economy; expenses did not feature. In parallel the FOI requests received by the House of Commons began with an initial flurry at the beginning of 2005. But after that, requests about MPs' pay and expenses dipped in 2006, started to grow in 2007, then tripled in 2008.[20] On the surface, it might look as though MPs breathed a collective sigh of relief in 2005 – the media coverage had mostly been mild and MPs' expenses were not an issue in the General Election.

But Nick Harvey MP, who was appointed to the Members Estimate Committee after the 2005 election, told us that he, at least, saw problems ahead, and was 'absolutely shocked' that some colleagues from other parties were so resistant to reporting MPs' expenditure in more detail.[21] Some felt that it would be a breach of Parliament's sovereignty if further disclosure were to be required: to put it in a more personal way, they were also anxious about loss of privacy.

Privacy at what price?

To MPs, information about what went on 'behind the front door' (a phrase they used in the years running up to the crisis[22]) was private and should remain so. Media attacks on their children were even more painful for MPs than those on themselves; journalists could be merciless about politicians' children when they misbehaved. But there were differing views within the House of Commons about privacy as well, in keeping with its nature as a body where issues are hammered out by adversarial debate in the face of ideological differences. These reflect perspectives on privacy and power in wider society; after all, the issue of whether public representatives should be allowed any privacy is not a new one.

In the eighteenth century, Henry St John, 1st Viscount Boling-broke wrote that rulers should live as though their private lives were public, for if they try to conceal vice, they will get found out anyway: 'for want of a sufficient regard to appearances, even their virtues may betray them into failings, their failings into vices, and their vices into habits unworthy of princes and of men'.[23] He thought the position of those in authority was different from others, so our expectations of them should be higher:

Let not princes flatter themselves. They will be examined closely, in private as well as in public life: and those, who cannot pierce further, will judge of them by the appearances they give in both. To obtain true popularity, that which is founded in esteem and affection, they must, therefore, maintain their characters in both; and to that end neglect appearances in neither, but observe the decorum necessary to preserve the esteem, whilst they win the affections of mankind.[24]

On the other side of the argument, those who believe in the need for more bottom-up accountability would view political traditions in the UK more critically. Public office has been an opportunity to increase one's wealth, prestige or influence for centuries, or to further one's relatives' careers, so misconduct by MPs has a long history.[25] It used to be an offence to speak ill of the government, so exposing the corruption of our leaders was extremely difficult. In bottom-up forms of accountability the public interest in exposing corruption in public office might trump the rights of our elected politicians to protect their privacy. When they are using public funds – tax donated by citizens – as if it is their private money, then we want reassurance that it has been spent with probity, even if this means that the public/private boundary collapses for MPs. We return to what this reveals about MPs in Chapter 7.

There was wide agreement in the House about one thing: MPs should be allowed at least *some* privacy. As they saw it, their jobs were stressful enough already, without having the added complication of opening up personal aspects of their lives, and that of their families, to the public gaze. But Heather Brooke took the opposite view: 'There's nothing private about an MP's expenses' was the headline of her article campaigning for full openness in April 2006. She went on to say, 'As I so often hear from the state when it invades my privacy – what's the problem if you have nothing to hide?'[26] The suspicion that politicians were hiding something that ought to be public fuelled ordinary citizens' interest. She pointed out when we met that we need to know where MPs live in order to check their use of their second home allowance and to make sure they are not neglecting their constituencies – as public servants they should be accessible.

The question of whether it was in the public interest to see into MPs' home lives, or whether what the media called the 'public interest' was mere prurience, was to become an important theme in the Information Tribunal hearings in 2007 and 2008. As the crisis of 2009 revealed, MPs did have something to hide. But, leaving aside those who were making fraudulent claims, the over-generosity of the system and the lack of rigorous audit, there were also genuine anxieties among the many MPs who were neither personally greedy nor negligent. Even something apparently innocuous, like MPs' mundane weekly travel arrangements to and from their constituencies, led to concerns. If it became widely known that an MP usually travelled on a particular train each Thursday evening, and then returned to Westminster at the same time each Sunday evening, there was a worry that it could lead to unwelcome intrusion, or even physical attack. Some MPs felt especially vulnerable: long before Stephen Timms was stabbed in 2010 and Jo Cox's murder in June 2016, stalking had become a fact of life for a number of MPs, and especially women. A survey of MPs in early 2010 reported that over 80 per cent of those who responded had experienced intrusive or aggressive behaviours in the previous 12 months: 15.5 per cent had been followed, 18 per cent had been attacked physically, and 42.3 per cent had been threatened.[27] A parallel study showed that women MPs were significantly more likely to have been stalked than men.[28] MPs' concerns were well founded.

One of the most worrying aspects for MPs was their home addresses. While MPs' constituency homes were generally well known locally, they were usually part of the local community and felt safe there. But it was a different matter in London. Many MPs lived on their own in Central London in small flats (some rented, some owned), to which they would return from Westminster in the evening, sometimes very late. Some MPs felt vulnerable, and there were cases of mugging and assault, so their privacy concern was that, if their London address was disclosed publicly, they would become even more of a target. The police team at the Palace of Westminster and the Serjeant-at-Arms often gave advice about safety – ensuring their doors were properly secure, for example. Their anxiety about the public knowing where they lived had a solid foundation: MPs were in danger, especially women.

A third anxiety was stirred up by the spotlight being turned onto their lives at home, and especially what their family members were up to, for the public to gawp and gasp at. Why should the media and public have the chance to pore over the details of their living arrangements (including what equipment and supplies they were buying), which were allowed under the second home allowance? It was exactly these details that would be the most compelling aspects of the *Daily Telegraph*'s reporting from the leaked data three years later, and raised the question of whether MPs should have been allowed to claim for such household items and supplies in the first place.

Small steps to tighten up

The media and public reaction in late 2004 and early 2005 to limited revelations about MPs prompted at least some MPs to start putting their house in order. It was too late to do anything about the past, but more effort was put into trying to prevent disclosure than into reforming the system. With hindsight, it seems that most MPs simply did not read the warning signs.

One MP told us he had counselled party colleagues to get prepared for public scrutiny, but his warnings appeared to have gone unheeded when in 2005 six MPs accepted cash payments from the landlord of their mansion block in London to buy out their long leases and replace them with shorthold tenancies, even though their rent had been paid wholly from the Additional Costs Allowance.[29] The revised arrangement could have led to higher rental costs, payable by the Fees Office, in future years. Surely they should have turned down their land-lord's offer or, if they had accepted it, passed back to the Fees Office the buyout payment they received from the landlord? They later reported themselves to the Parliamentary Standards Commissioner, who decided that they had been in the wrong. Four of them had to repay substantial sums in 2010 and lost their seats at the 2010 election. (Others got away with keeping property that had been partly or even wholly bought by mortgage interest paid out of allowances.)

But, in parallel, the Members Estimate Committee took steps to introduce more rigour. Some measures had been introduced in the 2003 Green Book to require receipts for items over £250, and to require copies of second home mortgage and rental agreements to be lodged with the Fees Office. It also prohibited MPs from 'renting' a second home from themselves and paying themselves rent from the ACA. The 2006 Green Book went further by prohibiting MPs from claiming expenses for a property rented directly or indirectly from a family member.[30] In 2006 they also tightened the rules about increasing mortgages on second homes. Until then, MPs had been allowed to increase their second home mortgage if there was sufficient headroom in the annual ACA ceiling. The Fees Office noticed that some MPs were increasing their mortgage on the same property, while the House of Commons paid their higher interest bill. In other words, they were able to get a secured loan with the arrangement fees and the interest paid by the public purse. The MEC were informed, and seeing that this could justifiably attract criticism, closed the loophole. This may, however, have had the perverse unintended consequence of increasing the likelihood of 'flipping' – switching the designation of the main and second home to gain a financial advantage – which the media would criticise MPs for in 2009. There were three main advantages: first, the opportunity to use up more of their ACA if they had a bigger mortgage on their other home; second, the possibility of juggling their 'only or main residence' designation for capital gains tax purposes; and third, the possibility of using their ACA to pay for renovations on both properties in succession.

A case of misuse of expenses was found almost by accident in 2005. Jonathan Sayeed, MP for mid-Bedfordshire, was accused by a party col-league in his constituency of wrongly using parliamentary stationery.

But, when the Fees Office investigated further, they found that Mr Sayeed had been claiming expenses on both his main home and his second home, which was not allowed under the rules. After criticism by the House's Standards and Privileges Committee, the Conservative Party whip was withdrawn from him and he stood down at the May 2005 General Election. He was suspended from the House for two weeks and he repaid expenses of more than £16,000. It looked like a single rotten apple at the time, with the House of Commons policing itself effectively and rooting out misconduct. But it was worrying that the Fees Office's scrutiny of his claims had not been careful enough to spot the erroneous items much sooner; and it would later turn out that Mr Sayeed was not the only MP to be claiming for an ineligible property.[31]

'Sleepers awake!'[32]

While the original FOI requests, appeals and counter-appeals were slowly trudging through the legal system, there was an opportunity to do more to reform the system, despite there being little new media pressure for change on the expenses in 2005 and 2006. An important development in 2006 was the Communications Allowance. A consensus was emerging in the House that MPs needed resources to communicate more systematically with their constituents. A number of MPs already did this, but there were complicated rules about mailshots. First, it was (and still is) important for parliamentary resources not to be made available to sitting MPs for party political campaigning or electioneering, as this could disadvantage competitors and help an incumbent MP to remain in office. Secondly, the internal rules themselves were complicated and disparate: the Serjeant-at-Arms was in charge of providing franked envelopes and headed stationery (a legacy of a much older system), while the Fees Office provided funds for purchase of postage stamps and other stationery. The Serjeant's rules and the Fees Office rules did not fit together well.

The House passed a motion in principle on 1 November 2006 that a Communications Allowance should be introduced and the rules clarified, despite a warning from various then opposition MPs, including

Lib Dem MP Jo Swinson: 'I agree that communication is important, but the proposed allowance could be an additional £6 million of tax-payers' money, and it is being driven not by the inability of current Members to communicate but by failure to enforce the existing postage rules to combat some of the extravagant claims made by a small minority of Members.'[33] Arguing for the allowance, Sir Stuart Bell (Labour, also a member of the MEC), argued that the allowance was needed to make up for perceived lack of media interest in Parliament:

> ... the bridge between civil society and political society is the media. We are generally able to communicate with our constituents only through the media. The media have changed, however, and they now have a different analysis of the situation. I do not wish to comment on particular instances, but there are newspapers around the country that have cancelled the contracts of their parliamentary reporters. They no longer have a parliamentary reporter here. How are the Members of Parliament in such constituencies to communicate with the electorate? Regardless of what people may think about the various allowances and expenses – I should say 'allowances', rather than 'expenses' – every allowance is fully approved by the House authorities. However, there are distortions within those allowances that we need to take into account. The communications allowance will provide a way of doing that, which is why I give it my full support.[34]

The MEC would be asked to work out the details and submit them to the House for a further vote in 2007. During the debate, the Conservatives and Lib Dems expressed reservations and in March 2007, when the House debated the MEC's proposal for a £10,000 annual ring-fenced allowance for MPs' communications, Theresa May (Conservative and then the Shadow Leader of the House) again expressed concerns, particularly about advantages to incumbent MPs and how it might look to the public:

> It is fair to say that people's scepticism about politicians led them to think that we all had our noses in the trough. Of course, that is not true. There is a need to ensure that the budget and expenses

available to MPs enable us to do our jobs effectively, and there is a responsibility on the media to be careful in their reporting of such matters, but we must be mindful of the views of those who bestow on us the privilege of sitting in Parliament.[35]

She voted against the measure, even though she was herself a member of the MEC, but the House voted for it (Ayes 283, Noes 188), and the Communications Allowance was introduced the following week.

So a need to improve communication had been perceived and acted on. But the Communications Allowance concentrated on MPs as individuals rather than on the House of Commons as an institution. The scheme itself was flawed: it was easy and tempting to abuse, and in the months that followed there were many complaints (usually by political opponents) that an MP was flouting the rules by including party political material in newsletters paid for by the taxpayer. This forced the Fees Office into a policing role for the first time – a new responsibility for which they were not well suited.

But perhaps the most significant development was growing disagreement between the political parties about the allowances. Although a couple of Conservatives had voted in favour of the Communications Allowance, and some Tory MPs made use of it, the Conservative leadership remained sceptical. In January 2008 the Conservatives came out positively against it,[36] and in September 2009, the then Leader of the Opposition David Cameron said:

> We've already said we'll get rid of the £10,000 yearly 'Communications Allowance' that every MP gets. It may sound new-fangled, but let me tell you: it's nothing less than old-fashioned, state-sanctioned propaganda. It's there for every MP to pay for sending newspapers and leaflets to their constituents to tell them how great they are, what a brilliant job they're doing and why they're the best thing since sliced bread. It's anti-democratic, it's a waste of money, so it's gone.[37]

Further party differences about MPs' expenses would emerge over time.

Defending the front door

Anxiety was growing in Westminster. Some politicians felt that parliamentary officials – especially Andrew Walker and Bob Castle – were not batting hard enough or effectively enough with the Information Commissioner's Office. In late 2006 there was a political initiative to try and reach a deal with the Commissioner himself. Four senior MPs – Jack Straw (Leader of the House), Theresa May (Shadow Leader), and two Liberal Democrats, Nick Harvey and David Heath – went to see him. Straw, May and Harvey were all on the Members Estimate Committee. One of their concerns was that MPs' correspondence with local authorities and other public bodies might be disclosed as a result of FOI requests to those bodies. Many MPs were bothered about this, feeling that it could undermine the trust and confidentiality they had with constituents.[38] The *Telegraph* reported this as Jack Straw trying to conceal expenses.[39]

But the main issue was MPs' second home allowance, the ACA. Notes of the meeting reveal that there was already by this stage an acceptance – at least among senior politicians in the main parties – that there was no objection to releasing further details of MPs' office expenses. The problem lay with the ACA, and the feeling that it would be intrusive on MPs' privacy if the public were able to look behind the front door of the second home. Two of the MPs at the meeting said that releasing details of expenditure on, for example, essential renovations and repairs would be the cause of 'unwarranted focus'. The Commissioner suggested to the MPs that if they could go further and disclose more information about the ACA – for example by breaking down the overall annual figures into categories of spend such as rent/rates, utilities, telephone, cleaning and repairs – he might be able to support the House of Commons position. The candid report of the meeting by a Fees Office official went on to say:

> My reading of this discussion is that it was a clear, and well-prepared, offer of a compromise by the Commissioner – provide more information about the generality of claims, and he would be in a better position to rule that the details fell on the private side of the balance.[40]

But even these relatively open-minded MPs baulked at compromise:

> The Members did not accept that this approach was a possibility and when pressed by the Commissioner confirmed that in their view the figure reported in the autumn for overall ACA expenditure was the extent of information that should be provided – all the rest, including a categorised breakdown, would be 'behind the front door' personal and private information. My impression was that the Commissioner was disappointed with this outcome.

Nick Harvey[41] told us that he had supported the Information Commissioner's proposed compromise, but Michael Martin had rejected it outright, with Sir Stuart Bell's backing. Bell saw it as an epic battle: 'We shall fight on the beaches', he said, quoting Churchill's speech to Parliament in 1940.

December 2006: Mr Maclean's daring failure

While three MEC members were trying, and failing, to get a behind-the-scenes deal with the Information Commissioner, another MEC member, David Maclean MP, tried something bolder. He would seek to get a bill through Parliament to exempt MPs' expenses from the FOI Act altogether. Maclean was well connected and influential – he had been a minister in the Major government in the 1990s and Opposition Chief Whip between 2001 and 2005.

The bill – described as 'breathtaking in its audacity' by another MP – would have removed references to the House of Commons and the House of Lords as public authorities, and would also have secured the confidentiality of MPs' correspondence on behalf of constituents with local authorities, health trusts etc.[42] If passed, the legal requirement for the House of Commons to disclose MPs' expenses details would have been removed. Hardly anyone noticed when the bill was introduced on 18 December 2006. The bill had support from both Labour and Conservative MPs, including government ministers. When the bill came up for debate in April and May 2007, Maclean emphasised the importance of protecting the confidentiality of MPs' correspondence with public authorities. Private Members' bills rarely make much progress, and never without the support of the 'usual channels',[43] but through clever management (and suspected help from the whips) the bill got to its Third Reading in the Commons on 18 May.

The debates were held on Fridays when most MPs were back in their constituencies. But Maclean had persuaded more than usual – particularly London MPs – to stay in the House and vote. Norman Baker MP and Simon Hughes MP, both Liberal Democrats, tried to talk it out but failed. The House of Commons passed the Bill by a comfortable majority of 96 to 25. Although no Liberal Democrats voted for the bill, and a number of both Conservative and Labour MPs did vote against it, the overwhelming sentiment was that FOI should *not* apply to MPs. One senior MP told us that, having seen the way FOI had been used to 'do down' Scottish MPs and their legitimate travel claims, he supported the idea of not applying the FOI Act to Westminster MPs.

But Maclean's victory was short lived. A media storm followed, with the *Telegraph*'s political correspondent claiming the bill would place MPs above the law.[44] The bill still had to go through the House of Lords, and the following month the House of Lords Public Bill Office confirmed that no Member of the Lords had come forward to sponsor the bill by the deadline of 13 June.[45] Maclean's bold dash had failed.

Maclean's bill illustrates the unpredictable, even sometimes chaotic, way the internal affairs of the House of Commons worked. When making law, or administering the departments of state, the government has an iron grip on Parliament as long as it has a majority. But Parliament itself is not run by the government even when it has a majority; it is run by a mix of committees and individuals, principally the Speaker but also the Leader of the House (who represents Parliament in government and government in Parliament). Maclean was a member of one of the committees, the MEC, but it did not formally support his attempt. He was a Conservative, but many Labour MPs including ministers supported him. He was aware of the inevitable negative media reaction, yet he and many others thought it worth the risk. In the end, it added to the impression that MPs were self-interested and secretive and could not be trusted to run their own expenses system.[46]

It was ironic that almost exactly two hundred years earlier, William Wilberforce had succeeded in his campaign to abolish the slave trade. The Slave Trade Act was passed in 1807,[47] arguably showing Parliament at its reforming best. Thus, while Parliament was celebrating the bicentenary of this initiative to improve human rights and liberties, it was also seeking to protect its own practices from public scrutiny.

Freedom of Information progresses

Jon Ungoed-Thomas's and Ben Leapman's FOI requests were grinding through the appeal system. First, they had to ask the House of Commons for an internal review. When that confirmed the House's refusal to disclose the requested information, they appealed to the Information Commissioner. Only after that, when they were dissatisfied with the Commissioner's decision, could they appeal to the Information Tribunal. Each stage of the process took weeks or months. Meanwhile, Jonathon Carr-Brown of the *Sunday Times* and Norman Baker MP had both asked in January 2005 for a breakdown of MPs' travel expenses. After the House of Commons' refusal, they each appealed to the Information Commissioner in April 2005, and he gave his adjudication in early 2006. In both cases, the Commissioner upheld the requesters' complaints. Officials advised the MEC that, while there was a case to appeal, the probability of success was not great, and would bring the possibility of adverse publicity. The House of Commons ignored the advice and appealed. The House engaged a talented barrister, Eleanor Grey, and the two cases were heard together by the Information Tribunal in January 2007. Despite Ms Grey's advocacy, the House lost the case: it was ordered to supply the information within 30 days, and did so.

Another case followed hard on its heels: a number of requests were made for details of travel undertaken by Anne Moffat, the controversial Labour MP for East Lothian. A Green Party activist, Michael Collie, had challenged her high spending on travel. Again, in August 2007, the Information Tribunal found against the House of Commons, and the additional information was published.[48] Moffat lost the support of her local party and was deselected as an MP.

While neither of these cases caused a huge stir, they added to the gradual increase in pressure on the House of Commons authorities, and the step-by-step increase in what was published. So, for example, after the Baker case, the House had stuck to its policy of treating all MPs equally and publishing equivalent information about all MPs, not just specific MPs whose details had been requested.[49]

2007 – Opportunities missed

The Committee on Standards in Public Life's (CSPL) role was to promote better public life ethics, including in Parliament. Their chairman from 2008, Sir Christopher Kelly, told us that the CSPL had had a number of discussions about the need for reform of MPs' expenses.[50] They thought that it was an open secret that Mrs Thatcher had said that MPs could increase expenses to compensate for pay restraint, and had identified what they saw as the 'feebleness of the Fees Office' as encouraging MPs to claim. They also saw a discrepancy between the things most people experienced in their ordinary lives and the different standards MPs applied to themselves. But their first public formal expression of concern was not until March 2007, when they said:

> The publication of Members of Parliament's use of the allowance and expenses system of the House of Commons has attracted significant press and public interest. The Committee has discussed this issue on a number of occasions during the last year because any allegations made that members claim excessive levels of allowance can damage the trust in which the public holds Parliament, politicians and public office-holders in general.
>
> This concern is separate from issues that relate to the misuse of the allowance and expenses system in respect of the rules that govern the system. Such misuse is an explicit breach of the MPs' Code of Conduct, and the system for dealing with such breaches has worked well and continues to do so. The Committee's concern – and one that we believe concerns others – relates to the system itself, particularly the potential difficulties in publicly distinguishing between salary and allowances and the perception that the rules

that apply to MPs for seeking reimbursement for justified expenditure are less rigorous that those for all other public office-holders, and indeed private sector employees.[51]

The CSPL comment did not lead to any specific action. Why? Although it was before his time, Sir Christopher Kelly explained to us that while remaining independent, by convention the Committee always consulted the Prime Minister on its reviews, and tended to have most effect when 'working with the grain', making recommendations they knew would be accepted. But allegations of misconduct by MPs about their use of expenses became increasingly frequent. The main one to hit the headlines was Derek Conway MP's inappropriate employment of his son Freddie, exposed by the *Sunday Times* in May 2007. The newspaper report was picked up by the Parliamentary Standards Commissioner. It would have a devastating effect when his report on Conway was published the following year.[52]

Inside the House of Commons, more voices were being raised. In 2004, the MEC had set up an audit committee, the Members Estimate Audit Committee (MEAC), to monitor the Members Estimate accounts. It comprised two politicians plus two independent external members: Sir Thomas Legg KCB QC, a former Permanent Secretary to the Lord Chancellor, and David Taylor FCA. Early on, the two external members had begun to express concerns about the expenses scheme. In December 2004 they had submitted a paper 'drawing attention to the reputational risks to the House of not having a clear and defensible system for ensuring proper accountability'.[53] The paper was sent to Speaker Martin, who replied the following February that 'the MEC was not minded to pursue the issue of external verification any further'.[54] Legg and Taylor continued to express their concerns, but progress was glacial.[55] They returned to the issue in 2007, when the House's Internal Auditor and PricewaterhouseCoopers reviewed the administration of the expenses regime.[56] The report argued for stronger audit of MPs' claims. This was to be influential the following year, but the House rejected the proposals.

The Blair government had commissioned the Senior Salaries Review Body (SSRB) to carry out its triennial review of MPs' pay and allowances in 2007. The report was ready in July: it recommended an additional pay increase for MPs, plus extra money to allow MPs to hire an additional staff member.[57] The pay increase was proposed because the previous methodology for the annual uprating had been flawed: it was supposed to keep MPs' pay in line with Civil Service pay, but the formula had allowed MPs' pay to slip back in relative terms. This exacerbated the problem that had contributed to the growth of MPs' expenses.[58] The government (now headed by Gordon Brown) became jittery and held back publication until the following January. Had the issue been settled before the 2007 summer break, it might have passed without incident. As things turned out, it was to fan the flames already beginning to burn more brightly in January and February 2008.

4

Ebbing privilege

The tinder was smouldering. 2007 had seemed relatively calm on MPs' expenses, so the sudden build-up of events in early 2008 came as a surprise. The dripping tap of cases of alleged misconduct being considered by the Parliamentary Commissioner for Standards (PCS) continued. In the final quarter of 2007, eight MPs[1] were found to have misused the Communications Allowance. By the beginning of 2008, several investigations were in progress, which would have an explosive impact when their results were published. In parallel, the hot potato of the Senior Salaries Review Body's report into MPs' pay and expenses entitlements, which had been delayed by the government since mid-2007, could not be held back any longer. And in January 2008 the dates were announced for the long-awaited Information Tribunal hearing of the most important legal challenge to the secrecy about MPs' expenses claims: the hearing would take place over two days on 7 and 8 February. One Commission Member, Nick Harvey, told us that while he himself was not optimistic about the outcome, Speaker Michael Martin was convinced the House of Commons would win the case.[2]

Parliament and MPs had graver worries in early 2008. In July and August 2007 the London financial markets had become volatile, with credit much harder to get and bank lending plummeting. In September 2007 there was a run on the Northern Rock Bank; investors queued in the street to get their money out. The government quickly provided emergency funding, and the Banking (Special Provisions) Bill was rushed through all its House of Commons stages in a single day, 19 February 2008. The House sat until midnight to achieve this. Northern Rock was nationalised three days later. 'Austerity' was born, and would continue for many years. Both government ministers and Parliament had matters of state on their minds, against which the expenses issues no doubt seemed relatively minor. David Amess MP said in 2009 that 'there are much, much more serious issues at stake other than the claims MPs make in terms of allowances.'[3] While the government and Parliament's prioritisation of action on the financial front may have distracted their attention from addressing the MPs' expenses system, the credit squeeze and accompanying austerity only emphasised that MPs were protected from the financial problems being faced by others. Many employees – including House of Commons staff – had their pay frozen for three years or more, while MPs' pay and expenses continued to grow.

Internally, the House of Commons Administration was undergoing a major restructuring following a report by Sir Kevin Tebbit on their management functions. A new Management Board was created, and the six previous departments merged into four larger units.[4] The effective date for the management reforms was 1 January 2008. This engaged the House of Commons Commission, managers, staff and the trade unions: there was some turmoil internally just at the time things were beginning to hot up on expenses.

Preparing for the tribunal

Preparation for the forthcoming tribunal had been going on for months in the House of Commons. The tribunal would look at the requests made three years before, in January 2005, for details of the second home expenses claimed by seven MPs: Tony Blair, Margaret Beckett, Barbara Follett, Alan Keen, Ann Keen, Peter Mandelson and John Wilkinson. Seven more names had been added to these in 2006: David Cameron, Menzies Campbell, Gordon Brown, George Osborne, John Prescott, William Hague and Mark Oaten. The Members Estimate Committee believed that none of these MPs would want details of their claims disclosed. As the tribunal remarked in its judgement, however, 'there was no evidence that any of the 14 MPs whose expenses details were sought had made any communication to Mr Walker's office requesting that the details should be withheld.'[5]

While some members of the MEC still thought the case was win-nable, Nick Harvey told us that before the tribunal, some MPs began to panic: they were horrified at the prospect of the exposing of their domestic lives – such as travel habits, home address, and family arrangements – if details of their claims were published.[6] Whatever the thinking of individual MEC members, much detailed work had to be done to prepare the case, involving MPs, several lawyers and House officials.

The MEC had considered who should be called as witnesses. Should some MPs take the stand? One possibility was that one or two of the 14 MPs whose expenses claims were the subject of the case would come forward and say why disclosure would be damaging for them. But that would be a political risk for any of them, and none of them volunteered. Andrew spoke to one MP, who said he'd consider being a witness, but then he decided against it. Even if an MP recognised that this was a deeply political situation, requiring a political defence of how and why MPs protected their privacy, none could face the inevitable backlash that would be entailed in arguing for the unpalatable. An alternative would have been for a member of the MEC – effectively the owners of the expenses system – to represent the Commons. That, too, was turned down. In the end, they decided that Andrew, now the Director General of Resources, should be the House's only witness. On the one hand, it was logical as he was the official responsible for the administration of finance including expenses. On the other hand, it may have been a misjudgement as it gave the appearance of MPs shirking responsibility. He spent the lion's share of the two-day hearing on the witness stand.

Two significant events were to take place in January that would influence the tribunal decision. The first was a damning report on the behaviour of Derek Conway MP, to which we will return. The second was the long-delayed SSRB report and recommendations on MPs' pay and allowances, which was published on 16 January.[7] It recommended a backdated pay increase for MPs, followed by an annual uprating in line with Civil Service pay for the following three years *plus* an additional £650 for each of the next three years. More money would be made available for MPs to employ staff. The second home allowance, the ACA, was to be kept at the same level – £23,083 per year. 'We are concerned that it is in the area of ACA that the greatest scope for abuse is thought to exist', said the report, but added, 'We are satisfied that ACA is necessary and set at an appropriate level.' On account-ability, MPs should provide receipts for all items over £50, and the National Audit Office should carry out an audit of a representative sample of MPs each year. The SSRB appeared to be unaware that the NAO already did this, as was to emerge in the tribunal hearing three weeks later.

On the same day the government announced its own counter-recommendations: MPs' pay for 2007 should be allowed to increase, but more slowly than the SSRB proposed; no pay increases were agreed for future years, but there should be an independent review of the mechanism for setting MPs' pay; the SSRB's proposed increase in the allowance for MPs' staff should go ahead, but the SSRB's other rec-ommendations on MPs' expenses 'should be referred to the Members Estimate Committee to examine.'[8] The government's recommenda-tions were debated – and accepted without a vote – in the House of Commons on 24 January. The debate focused mainly on pay; but over the following weeks, MPs would become more alert to the growing concern about their expenses. In the months ahead it would be expenses rather than pay that caught the public's attention.

'I am not a crook'

Four days later, a grenade exploded. It was bound to happen, as the story had already been trailed in the *Sunday Times* the previous May.[9] But the Committee on Standards and Privileges' report,[10] published on 28 January, was damning, causing a furore in the media and urgent activity in the House of Commons.

Derek Conway was MP for Old Bexley and Sidcup. He had employed his son Freddie in a part-time role for a number of years while he was a full-time student in Newcastle. Neither Derek Conway nor Freddie could provide evidence of the work he had done to justify a salary of £11,773 (equivalent to a full-time rate of £25,970), nor to justify annual bonuses ranging from £1,766 to £6,300. Noting that Freddie 'seems to have been all but invisible during the period of his employment', the Committee recommended that Mr Conway should

repay both Freddie's excessive bonuses and excessive pay, and that he should be suspended from the House of Commons for ten sitting days.

Conway protested that he had stuck to the spirit, if not the letter, of the rules. He apologised to the House and was duly suspended. But he defended himself to the media. 'I am not a crook', he told the *Mail* the following Sunday,[11] opining that he was just the unlucky one who failed to get away with it. As the sketch writer Quentin Letts put it: 'Mr Conway simply had the misfortune to be caught. Maybe he is not the only one.'[12] Letts perhaps voiced what others were thinking: Derek Conway's protestations may have served to reinforce a view that MPs were somehow separated from ordinary people's worlds. Many MPs at the time employed family members, though there was then no complete register of them, so precise figures are not available.[13]

The question of MPs employing members of their families had come up a few years earlier, when one of Iain Duncan Smith's staff had alleged that Mrs Duncan Smith had been employed by her husband under a contract with a job title of Diary Secretary, but had not obviously performed any duties. A journalist, Michael Crick (then of the BBC), took up the case in 2003 and complained to the Parliamentary Standards Commissioner. The Commissioner's inquiry was wide ranging. In his report to the Standards and Privileges Committee in February 2004, the Commissioner did not uphold Mr Crick's complaint that Mrs Duncan Smith was improperly employed by her husband.[14]

After this, MPs faced a dilemma. In the competitive world of the Commons, MPs trust few people with information about themselves, often require their staff to work long and unsocial hours, and have scarcely any time with their families. The parliamentary rules allowed them to employ family members. Husbands, wives and other family members were usually trusted by the MP, and they would frequently go above and beyond the call of duty, working long days alongside the Member, writing last-minute speeches, arranging constituency functions, and so on. Collette Conway, Derek Conway's wife and PA, is reported as saying: 'Quite often if he's working late, I will carry on working in the office and we'll catch a half-hour supper, then he'll go back and vote, then we'll walk down the road together. I'll do business lunches for him in his office.'[15] But to people looking in from the outside, it could have appeared that MPs were feathering their own nests. It was another nail in the coffin of public trust.[16] The lack of openness and transparency was at the root of this; and the concern applied to other aspects of MPs' expenses, too, not just to their staffing arrangements. The same concern was at the heart of the Information Tribunal hearing a few days later. The Conway story was kept alive on the first day of the Information Tribunal hearing by Nick Cohen announcing in the *Evening Standard* 'I know the mole who dug out how Derek Conway MP diverted hundreds of pounds of taxpayers' money to his wife and sons.'[17] The article was wrong in detail, but the suspicion remained that a temporary worker had indeed been put into the Fees Office to leak information. The events of January helped to convince the MEC that radical reform of the expenses system was needed. On 31 January, the Speaker announced that the MEC would meet urgently, and later the same day the House resolved to suspend Derek Conway. The following Monday the committee met, and the Speaker wrote to MPs that same evening promising a 'root and branch' examination of the system.[18]

The scene was set for the tribunal hearing. Throughout January MPs' practices – and the lack of openness about them – had been brought to public and media attention on an almost daily basis, and had highlighted the very concerns that would be aired in the tribunal hearing. The privacy and private lives that MPs wanted so much to protect was under threat from the increasing public demand for transparency, openness and accountability.

Facing the tribunal

The tribunal took place in a Georgian building in Bedford Square.[19] It was a lot grander on the outside than inside, where the tribunal room was kitted out with 1960s vintage civil service metal desks. Heather Brooke relates how she 'forcefully' took Andrew Walker's seat at the tribunal.[20] It didn't matter too much to him, as he then spent most of the two days' hearing in the witness box at the front of the room. Both felt far more ill at ease than they appeared. When Heather walked into the small court there were no free chairs near her lawyer. She nearly went to the back, struggling with a feeling that she did not belong – even that she had no right to be there. Then she remembered it was her case, it was her lawyer: she forced herself to move towards the front. She noticed a chair with a hat on it and moved the hat so she could sit down just behind her lawyer.

When Andrew approached, saying that she had taken his seat, she stuck to her guns: here was the embodiment of entitled male culture, in her eyes, free from doubt or uncertainty. Why should she give up her chair for him? Andrew, meanwhile, was not in the least relaxed. But adversaries often misread each other's vulnerability for certainty.

There was no official record of the hearing, and detailed accounts differ. Experienced lawyers were representing the various parties. The House of Commons was the appellant, and the Information Commissioner was the respondent. Heather Brooke, Jon Ungoed-Thomas and Ben Leapman were additional parties. With so many players, cross-examination stretched across two days. Eleanor Grey was Counsel for the House of Commons; her style was gentle. Hugh Tomlinson QC, acting *pro bono* for Heather Brooke, was a contrast – relentless and skilled at funnelling Andrew Walker, the only witness representing the Commons, into places he did not want to go.

"YOU'RE IN MY SEAT."

How was the experience from his perspective?

> *Andrew Walker's experience of the tribunal*
>
> I had mixed feelings as I took the stand. As the boss of the Fees Office, I rightly had to be seen to take responsibility for the operation of the system. But I had little experience of either legal process or political communication and knew that I had to operate within constraints. Thinking about it in advance, I knew that I would have to try to duck political questions. What was I to say, for example, if asked whether there was sufficient checking of claims, or if I would like to see more rigorous audit, or how strongly my staff could question whether an MP really needed a new TV, or what they had done with the one they bought the previous year? And what if I was asked why the allowances

were generous? I had spent years trying to tighten up the rules. But equally my job in general, and my task in the tribunal, was to serve Parliament and respect that the ultimate decision-making power rested with MPs in relation to everything within the House of Commons, not with me as an official.

As the only witness I would have to answer not only for myself and my team as public service administrators, but also on behalf of MPs and the political authorities – the committees of MPs who decided on the scope of the system and the rules governing it. I was not normally given to sleepless nights, and had practice at appearing calmer than I felt, but I mulled over and over whether I would be asked questions that I would find it impossible to answer, either because to do so would be disloyal to the House or MPs, or because I was not always aware why a committee had taken a certain decision. For example, the Fees Office was forbidden to include in the Green Book the rule that MPs could spend £400 a month on food without producing receipts. Many commentators felt the allowance was too generous, but it was the fact that the rule was not included in the Green Book that was more damaging at tribunal, as it appeared to reinforce the notion that the rules were an inadequate basis on which to run a robust and fair system of administration.

Giving evidence was gruelling. My anticipation that there would be difficult questions proved true; and when they came thick and fast and seemed brilliantly designed to trip me up, I found it increasingly difficult to maintain my composure. 'It was a bear pit,' said another House of Commons official who was present.[21] The questions that threw me off-kilter required either economy with the truth[22] or imagining the reaction of the public, a task that I was entirely unused to. As one commentator put it, 'He was asked a number of questions that any public servant (as opposed to an elected politician) would find difficult,'[23] for example whether the allowances system commanded public confidence, and whether the House's decision not to disclose full details of MPs' claims had lowered the public's opinion of MPs.

When I tried to explain the strange nature of MPs' work – how they have no boss and are really only accountable to their constituents or how vulnerable they were in security terms – I met scepticism. The work of MPs is often misunderstood and in those days we lacked the rigorous evidence of security threats to MPs that has since come to light, even if it was clear to parliamentary officials from reports by the MPs themselves.

Under cross-examination, certain facts and details came to light for the first time. Assiduous Parliament-watchers would have been aware of many of them, but the details that emerged enabled commentators to paint a picture that the general public now saw for the first time. I revealed that MPs could claim up to £400 a month without receipts as a food allowance. Both the generosity of the allowance and the lack of scrutiny were challenged. The availability of the second home allowance for MPs with constituencies in outer London – well within the commuter belt – was also met with critique. I was criticised sharply for failing to produce a single comprehensive manual covering all the rules for expenses. And the generosity of the regime was questioned again and again. At one point I explained that MPs could not claim for an iPod, because it was not an additional cost of staying away from the MP's main home, but one of the lawyers later pointed out that if an MP bought an iPod at Tesco's with their weekly food shop, the Fees Office would never know as they didn't ask to see grocery receipts.[24]

In representing Parliament I was constrained by politics without the expertise or liberties of politicians. Hugh Tomlinson QC, acting for Heather Brooke, led me into various traps. When I explained that the Fees Office precedent list was known in the Fees Office as the 'John Lewis list', Sam Coates of the *Times* gasped. I gave it as an example of how my staff checked and controlled Members' claims. I should have anticipated the media and public reaction. But I had misjudged it, and the example backfired. If only I had used a different example, or at least not mentioned a chain of stores regarded as the choice of the affluent.

I was exhausted when, towards the end of the second day, my time in the witness box was complete and the tribunal moved on to the lawyers' submissions. I was relieved to have survived, albeit at the expense of critical comment in the media, and also relieved not to be personally slated in the tribunal's judgement when it appeared a couple of weeks later. They said 'We found him to be a candid and reliable witness on matters of fact... Where matters of judgment were involved, at times his answers were rather obviously framed to maintain and justify, or at least not to contradict, the line adopted by the House in response to the requests, rather than to give a direct answer to the question.'[25]

All of this made good media copy, but the case itself turned more on detailed legal arguments about the interaction between the Freedom of Information Act and the Data Protection Act, which entailed weighing up the public interest in disclosing details of MPs' claims versus MPs' interest in privacy for themselves and their families. The submissions and legal proceedings hinged on technical details. The tribunal accepted Eleanor Grey's submission (on behalf of the House of Commons) that MPs' claims to the ACA constituted personal data and that the key questions should be determined by reference to the tests in the Data Protection Act, and not subjected to an additional and higher-level test imposed by the Freedom of Information Act.[26] But her argument that MPs' privacy rights should protect them from further disclosure was not accepted. The various parties to the case proposed 12 legitimate public interests that would be advanced by public disclosure.[27] These included ensuring that MPs used public money wisely, providing the public with a useful way of assessing politicians' probity and measuring them against their public pronouncements, and maintaining and enhancing public confidence in the central political institutions of parliamentary democracy. The last of these would be proved wrong during the crisis that followed.

The tribunal published its judgement on 26 February. It found the ACA system inadequate, identifying a 'long-standing lack of public confidence in the system.'[28] The public interest in seeing the details of MPs' claims outweighed their wish for privacy. They overturned the Information Commissioner's decision that disclosure in broad categories would be sufficient to meet the public interest: '[We] conclude that full detailed information is necessary to meet these objectives. In our judgment these aims cannot be achieved by means that interfere less with the privacy of the MPs' personal data.' They said that while MPs must from the very nature of their functions be prepared to accept a greater degree of public scrutiny than the average citizen, this did not mean that they were entitled to no privacy. However, 'only the most pressing privacy needs should in our view be permitted to prevail', and such needs should be modest. They added:

> It was submitted that, perversely, the most conscientious MPs, who provided the most supporting information for their claims, would be exposed to the most public scrutiny. We would have thought that, subject to safeguards for any specially sensitive items of data,

the most conscientious MPs would have the least to fear from disclosure.[29]

One legal commentator has pointed out that the jurisdiction of the tribunal to review the operation of the ACA system was at least questionable, and that some of their findings of fact strayed into the realms of opinion, possibly influenced by the prevailing mood in the media following the SSRB report and the Conway report, which had been published the previous month (both were raised during the tribunal proceedings). But – whatever the rights and wrongs – the genie was out of the bottle and could not be put back.

Never knowingly undersold

It was not the detailed legal argument that grabbed the headlines. It was the 'John Lewis list' that took many – both the public and MPs – by surprise; and it gave journalists a field day. In 2003 when the Green Book was tightened, requiring officials to challenge MPs if they claimed for items that could be seen as extravagant or luxurious,[30] the Fees Office had started to compile a list of precedents on a spreadsheet. The intention was to ensure that if, for example, one Validation Officer had restricted MP A to £500 for a new television, another Validation Officer did not inadvertently allow MP B to claim £750 for a television the next week. Because John Lewis claimed to be 'never knowingly undersold', and carried their prices clearly on their website at a time when online shopping was in its infancy, the Fees Office chose John Lewis as a benchmark. They also referred to Argos, but it was the John Lewis name that stuck.

During evidence to the tribunal, Andrew was seeking to establish that the Fees Office had tightened up its scrutiny and did reject what they saw as inappropriate claims. To support that argument, he disclosed the existence of the precedent list and provided a copy to the tribunal. The list was quickly asked for in an FOI request, and was disclosed to the public soon after.[31] The details in the list, including £10,000 for a new kitchen, £350 for a washing machine and £90 for a dining chair, gave the media a field day and gave the public the first real taste of the kinds of things MPs could buy on expenses.[32] Members of the public asked why MPs could buy – and keep – items that they themselves would have to buy out of their own taxed income, or could not even aspire to afford. One MP told us how his wife met someone in the street who asked her how she was enjoying her Hygena kitchen.[33] The MP had not claimed for a kitchen on expenses, but their constituent had made the assumption that they must have done so, as it was on the John Lewis list.

Andrew in the doghouse

No one was happy. Andrew was blamed by the Speaker for the John Lewis list, and for not having circulated it to MPs. Many MPs took the same view. John Lewis were not happy either. Far from being pleased that their pricing policy had been used as a benchmark of good value, they wrote to Andrew to complain that they did not want their good name associated with MPs' expenses. And, in response to Sam Coates' *Times* blog about the tribunal evidence, one member of the public commented: 'Amazingly poor defence from Walker for a series of very poor decisions and apparent policies.'[34]

The Speaker was soon in the doghouse, too. Just over a week later, Michael Martin was accused by the *Mail on Sunday*[35] of using the air miles he had collected from his and his wife's weekly flights between Glasgow and London and from his overseas trips on parliamentary business for personal benefit. Unlike government ministers, who were not allowed to use air miles from publicly paid-for travel for their own personal use, there was no such rule in the House of Commons. The Fees Office, if asked, used to advise MPs that they could use the air miles they collected to pay for future parliamentary travel. But it was left to their discretion. The Speaker had allegedly used his air miles to fly his extended family from Glasgow to London the previous New Year.

The story was picked up by other newspapers. Then, the following week, the Speaker's media adviser Mike Granatt resigned.[36] Granatt had defended the Speaker the previous December when his wife was accused of running up £4,000 of taxi bills at public expense over four years. Granatt had said that the spending was justified, pointing out that Mrs Martin 'goes shopping for food and so on for entertaining official visitors'. In May, when he found out that he had misled the press, he resigned as a matter of principle. Although Mike Granatt said that this arose through no fault of the Speaker, calls grew for Michael Martin to resign.[37]

Appeal dismissed

The House had lost the tribunal case comprehensively, at a considerable cost in terms of public money.[38] The glimmers of hope that any further appeal would be successful were few, the legal team advised. But the Speaker and the MEC decided to find a new Counsel and appeal to the High Court, partly to buy time. Given the long delays endemic in the legal system, the case might not be heard for months. One MEC member, Nick Harvey,[39] recalled that their lawyers warned them of the problems, but they couched it in terms of possibilities: it might be a disaster but there was a possibility of success. He said that they only heard the second bit; their hearing was selective. It was a surprise when the High Court expedited the appeal.

There were in any event limited grounds for appealing. Nigel Giffin QC argued for the House that the tribunal had misdirected itself by failing to give appropriate weight to MPs' reasonable expectations about precisely how information relating to the ACA claims would be made available to the public. The grounds turned out to be thin. The case was to be heard by three of the country's most senior judges: Lord Justice Judge (President of the Queen's Bench Division), Lord Justice Latham and Mr Justice Blake. It would not be an easy ride.

The hearing was on 7 and 8 May. In court, Lord Justice Judge criticised counsel for repeating the same limited argument, and the court's judgement delivered on 16 May was damning:

Once legislation which applies to Parliament [i.e. the FOI Act] has been enacted, MPs cannot and could not reasonably expect to contract out of compliance with it, or exempt themselves, or be exempted from its ambit. Such actions would themselves contravene the Bill of Rights, and it is inconceivable that MPs could expect to conduct their affairs on the basis that recently enacted legislation did not apply to them, or that the House, for its own purposes, was permitted to suspend or dispense with such legislation without expressly amending or repealing it. Any such expectation would be wholly unreasonable.[40]

So, MPs could not be above the law.

A secondary appeal that the private addresses of MPs' second homes should not be disclosable also failed. The High Court concluded

we cannot interfere with the Tribunal's decision on the basis of what the appropriate outcome might be if the Tribunal were not addressing the deeply flawed system which the Tribunal believed had so convincingly established the necessity of full disclosure which included the addresses to which the ACA forms applied... The appeals by the Corporate Officer of the House of Commons are dismissed.

One MEC member told us that Mr Giffin did a very bad job, but that it was a steep hill to climb: maybe no other counsel could have climbed it either. But it does leave us with a question about whether or not the complexity of MPs being both public figures and private people was adequately explained or sufficiently understood.

The information requested by the three journalists about the 14 prominent politicians – redacted in line with the court's decision – was supplied to them on 23 May and placed on the House of Commons internet site. The BBC website headline was 'Blair was chased over unpaid bill'.[41] The MEC quickly decided to publish all MPs' claims, including receipts, in the autumn.[42] The government quietly introduced a Statutory Instrument on 23 July 2008 that amended the FOI Act to exclude MPs' residential addresses, regular travel arrangements and security information from disclosure.[43]

Root and branch reform

While the tribunal appeared to be influenced by other developments in January 2008, such as the SSRB report that recommended an external audit of MPs' claims, it did not accept the argument that the House of Commons was in the process of putting its house in order. They concluded, 'We cannot be influenced by the mere possibility that the House might at some future date introduce changes to the system, particularly when the nature of the changes is at present entirely undetermined.'[44]

The House of Commons authorities really were trying, by then, to reform the whole expense system. Three members[45] of the MEC started meeting regularly, advised by a senior clerk and by the Head of the Fees Office. They had frequent formal meetings,[46] as well as informal ones, and commissioned expert advice on a range of topics. In that time, they issued four reports, beginning with a proposal in March to cut the threshold for receipts (in future requiring receipts for all MPs' expenditure over £25), and canvassing views from Members, parliamentary committees, auditors, the Committee on Standards in Public Life, and others on all aspects of the expenses system, not just the second home allowance. Their report, published on 25 June, made recommendations for major reforms, both to the nature and value of a number of the allowances and – crucially – to the arrangements for audit and assurance.[47]

How would MPs react to such a radical agenda? The assurance proposals, in particular, would relinquish the House's normal self-governance in this area, and open up their claims to independent scrutiny. And some of the more egregious aspects of the allowances themselves would be removed, including claims for furniture, household goods and capital improvements to their second homes.

Backbenchers rebel

The proposals were supported by the whole MEC and the frontbenches. The media gave a guarded welcome. An experienced and influential member of the Parliamentary Press Lobby, David Hencke, wrote: 'This means the end of parliament as a "gentlemen's club" and ushers in modern corporate practices that belong in the 21st century.'[48] And Joe Murphy in the *Evening Standard* hailed it as the end of the John Lewis list.[49] But they spoke too soon. Many backbench MPs were not ready to agree to major surgery – or they viewed the proposals as the wrong form of medical treatment.

The MEC had tabled a motion to give effect to their report. Enter the Member for Islwyn, Don Touhig, a prominent Labour back-bencher. He was seen as a voice representing his colleagues' views. He told us that he had stuck his head over the parapet by tabling an amendment that would reject key elements of the MEC's proposal: it became a rallying point for many backbenchers.[50] The Touhig amendment was accepted by 172 to 144 votes.

The table below sets out what the House agreed to, and what they rejected.

MEC recommendation	House decision
Enforcement, accountability and audit	
A new system of external 'practice assurance' covering 25 per cent of MPs each year	Rejected
More rigorous and extensive annual audit by the National Audit Office	Rejected and replaced with 'a rigorous internal system of audit of ACA covering 25 per cent of MPs each year'.
Receipt threshold for MPs' claims to be reduced from £25 to zero: all claims to be backed by receipts.	Rejected
Green Book (setting out the rules on allowances for Members) to be revised to specify more detailed rules	Rejected
Rigorous enforcement of requirement for MPs to deposit staff contracts and job descriptions with the Department of Resources	Retained

MEC recommendation	House decision
Scope of overnight expenses	
With immediate effect, MPs should no longer be able to claim for furniture and household goods or for capital improvements (items on the John Lewis list)	Rejected
Outer London MPs to be eligible to claim only half of any overnight expenses allowance	Rejected
Constituency offices	
Constituency offices to be organised and paid for centrally by the House of Commons	Retained
Communications	
Rules for Communications Allowance to be tightened	Retained
Communications Allowance to be frozen for three years	Retained
Travel	
Car mileage allowance to be retained at HM Revenue & Customs rates	Retained
Separate mileage limits for small, medium-sized and large constituencies (Paragraph 164)	Retained
Overnight expenses	
Additional Costs Allowance (ACA) to become overnight expenses allowance, max £19,600 (compared with current ACA max of £24,006), *plus* a daily subsistence allowance of £30 for 140 days a year (=£4,200 a year)	Rejected
London Supplement (for London MPs not claiming ACA) to be consolidated into a taxable amount of £7,500	Retained
Resettlement	
The resettlement grant (money for MPs leaving the House at a General Election) should be reformed	Retained

MEC recommendation	House decision
Other SSRB recommendations	
The SSRB proposal that Incidental Expenses Provision should be abated for every workstation in London should not be implemented	Retained
There should be no increase in the Staffing Allowance for staff based in London	Retained
That the SSRB's proposal that partners of Members should be entitled to the same travel arrangements as spouses and civil partners should not be implemented	Retained

The amendments cut the heart out of the proposals. External audits and accountability, as well as an end to claims for household goods such as TVs, fridges and fitted kitchens as set out in the John Lewis list, might or might not have been enough to win the public round, but rejecting those proposals sent out a clear signal that many MPs had not heeded the messages. Don Touhig told us that it was right that MPs should disclose their expenses: 'Nobody makes you become an MP', he added, and he had never believed that MPs should have a say over their own pay. But he felt it was unnecessary to bring in an outside firm to audit MPs' use of paperclips. It would be a bonanza for big audit companies: the House should not be panicked by the media, he thought.[51] He said to Nick Harvey in the debate on the floor of the House at the time:

> Is it not a fact that it will cost £1,200 a day to bring in fat cats from the City accountancy firms to spend three days a year going around examining Members' office cost allowances? The hon. Gentleman is like Ethelred the Unready: pay them gold and they will run away. That is what he is trying to do: he is trying get rid of a bad headline by throwing public money at it, and thereby wasting that money... The amendment that I have tabled, with the support of others, supports the continuation of the principle of the ACA to meet the necessary costs of MPs living away from home. I think that most fair-minded people would accept that the extraordinary situation of an MP needing to live both in his or her constituency and in London requires an allowance to support those costs.[52]

One member of the MEC told us that most of the Conservatives and Liberal Democrats supported the MEC's plan, but Labour MPs did not. 'The [MPs'] reaction was hysterical', he added. Traditionally, votes on MPs' pay and expenses were not subject to the party whip – at least not formally. This was the case here, although there may have been behind-the-scenes pressure from the party leaderships. The parliamentary record shows that some Conservative MPs did vote for the Touhig amendment alongside Labour MPs, but that changed on the vote two weeks later (see below). The media response, too, was predictable. The *Telegraph* proclaimed 'MPs vote to keep John Lewis List', adding, 'MPs defied public anger over their generous regime of taxpayer-funded allowances last night as they threw out reforms designed to restore confidence in the parliamentary expenses system.' Similarly, the *Independent*'s line was, 'MPs... rejected calls for tough new external audits on their claims.'[53] How could the House of Commons come so close to addressing the challenges and perceptions that had been building up so inexorably, and yet pull back at the last fence? They probably had different reasons – some mostly self-interested, others mostly critical of modern corporate practices – but whatever the motives, in retrospect this may have been the last chance saloon.

Accountability to whom?

Would the MEC's proposals really have lanced the boil? When David Hencke commented that, if adopted, the MEC's recommended reforms would bring an end to the gentlemen's club and bring in 'modern corporate practices', he used a phrase suggestive of the New Public Management reforms that had swept through the UK public sector in the previous two decades.[54] One aspect of this more commercial approach to management in the public sector was the requirement for sound finances and audit of delegated functions. But is upward accountability via auditors sufficient or even beneficial? Some argue that relying too much on upwards accountability creates new problems. More attention should be paid to downwards or outwards accountability to the public, staff in organisations, communities and other stakeholders.[55] The expenses system was designed for upwards accountability, in that the National Audit Office might have been satisfied with the general system as long as MPs complied with it, but not for more participatory forms of outwards accountability, because as soon as the public saw the John Lewis list they were furious. Arguably the House of Commons was behind the curve not only in upwards accountability, but it had also not recognised at that stage the demand for downwards and outwards accountability. So, even if the MEC's proposals had been accepted, it might not have reversed the public reaction.

At the beginning of 2008, the parties had been on the same page. Party leaders and MPs involved in the governance of the House of Commons foresaw many of the dangers inherent in the developments, which they knew were inevitable – or at least likely – in the coming months. But by the summer the party leaderships were heading in different directions. In February, the Conservatives had announced a 'Right to Know' form: all Conservative frontbenchers were required to disclose their office expenses, their second home claims, and details of all the staff they employed, including family members. David Cameron announced that he was encouraging his backbenchers to follow suit. On the same day, Gordon Brown announced that Labour MPs should disclose their employment of family members. For the Liberal Democrats, Nick Clegg, too, encouraged his MPs to publish details of the staff they employed.[56]

These announcements had not made a big impact at the time, but when the House rejected important elements of the MEC's reform proposals, the Conservatives declared a universal tightening-up for their own MPs. Theresa May, then the Shadow Leader of the House, used an Opposition Day debate on 16 July to reintroduce the reform agenda. She moved a motion that would, in effect, restore most of what the House had rejected two weeks earlier: there would be regular reporting and auditing of MPs' expenses, publication of the names and salaries of relatives employed by MPs, and the abolition of the John Lewis list, so that MPs would no longer be able to claim for furniture and household goods. Labour MPs criticised the Conservative frontbench for using their Opposition Day to raise what they saw as House business rather than party business.[57] But it *was,* by then, party business. From now on, with a general election less than two years away, the parties needed to be seen to be taking action. The party battle lines were being drawn up. This time when the House voted, it was largely by party, with the Liberal Democrats and Conservatives voting for Mrs May's motion, and Labour MPs voting against it. Even the independently minded Ann Widdecombe, a Conservative who had argued forcefully that the House had been kow-towing to the media, did not vote against it despite saying:

> The rules say that one cannot whistle up a £10,000 kitchen from John Lewis, or a £5,000 bathroom. If a kitchen or bathroom is replaced, the rules say very clearly that those costs must be divided between genuine replacement and betterment, and the betterment element must be paid for by the Member. But out there, egged on by the press and by the silly, crawling, gutless response of the House, everybody believes that these things can be whistled up with no rules, restraints or accountability. We should have had the guts to defend ourselves.[58]

Using their inbuilt majority, however, Labour MPs defeated the motion.

Instead, the House agreed to a government amendment that provided for the Green Book to be rewritten by the Advisory Panel on Members' Allowances, which should 'advise on any further modifications, including in relation to reimbursement of reasonable costs of a second residence, to include abolition of the so-called John Lewis list', and provide for audit by the National Audit Office. The wording did not make it clear whether or not the abolition of the John Lewis list meant that MPs would be banned from claiming for furniture and household goods in future. The following month it emerged that – in the government's eyes at least – they would not.[59] The backbench rebels had won the day.

A watchdog watches

An external body with a supervisory remit also seemed to be sitting on its hands. The CSPL was looking on as the expenses affair developed. Sir Christopher Kelly had been appointed as its chair from 1 January

2008, and would play a key role the following year when the crisis blew up. He told us that, when he arrived, the CSPL had already had discussions about the expenses system. The three politicians then on the committee all felt that the arrangements needed looking into. In their discussions on expenses, CSPL members had been amazed at Parliament's and MPs' wishes to keep the whole thing hidden. He said that the committee predicted a car crash, and then watched it happen.[60]

In February 2008 Tony Wright MP, Chair of the Commons' Public Administration Select Committee,[61] wrote to Sir Christopher expressing concern that the CSPL had not announced an inquiry into the system of MPs' allowances. Kelly replied that, while the CSPL had not ruled out such an inquiry: 'We will want to be clearer about the nature and possible outcome of the various parliamentary and political party initiatives announced over the last few days before making a decision.'[62] As the in-depth MEC review got going (to which the CSPL submitted a paper), the committee decided not to launch its own investigation.

After the failure of the MEC initiative, pressure again mounted on the CSPL to launch its own investigation. Sir Christopher recalled a conversation with Harriet Harman, the Leader of the House and therefore a government minister, in which he had floated the idea of an inquiry into MPs' expenses. She suggested that the House ought first to be given the chance to sort out its own affairs as intended. Kelly agreed that it would be much better for public confidence if the House reformed itself, so they held back for a time. He announced that the CSPL would again defer a decision on an inquiry:

we have decided to take a pragmatic approach and defer a decision about whether to launch an inquiry until next year. Whether we do begin an inquiry then, and if so whether it takes the form of a relatively simple stock take or a more in-depth review, will depend on developments over the next 12 months or so.[63]

There were rumours that Harriet Harman had discussed the idea with Gordon Brown, who had vetoed it. He was having difficulty managing Labour backbenchers, who were sore about this issue. Ultimately, some months later in 2009, Gordon Brown did ask the CSPL to take up the challenge (see Chapter 5), but it was too late by then. It is tempting, with the benefit of hindsight, to suggest that the CSPL should have intervened sooner, but since we do not know what that would have produced, such hypothetical questions can never be conclusively answered.

By mid-2008 Michael Martin was looking more isolated. He had not been able to deliver the legal victory on FOI that his Tea Room friends had been promised.[64] If the MEC reform proposals had been accepted, it could have helped to restore his authority. But his former colleagues had voted down his plan for reform, and after that, according to Don Touhig, he distanced himself from them.[65]

Perhaps in an attempt to improve his image, Speaker Martin gave an interview to a journalist, Stephen Robinson, and he and his wife were photographed in the palatial State Apartments for the *Sunday Times Magazine* on 27 July 2008. The article charted his rise from humble origins in Glasgow, and set out his achievement in becoming the country's most senior commoner. But the second half of the article was a litany of criticism, ending with the quote, 'having achieved this great eminence, he's going to be remembered as the worst Speaker for 200 years.'[66]

Kicking the can down the road

On the face of it, the second half of 2008 was quieter. But the actions and inactions of those months would have a profound effect in 2009. With the economic crisis continuing, and the recent unsatisfactory debates on expenses, MPs had some respite when the House of Commons rose on 22 July. The House did not return until 6 October. Meanwhile, the US government had rescued Fannie Mae and Freddie Mac, and Lehman Brothers bank had been allowed to collapse on 15 September. In the UK, two days later, Lloyds Bank had rescued HBOS, the UK's largest mortgage lender, after a huge drop in its share price. The Irish economy collapsed. In comparison, the unresolved MPs' expenses affair must have seemed a relatively small matter.

What were the politicians doing on expenses during these crucial months? No consensus had been reached among MPs. There were two initiatives. First, on 5 August, Harriet Harman published a consultation document about audit and assurance of MPs' allowances,[67] which was hardly noticed as everyone was on holiday by then. It summarised the limited progress that had been made in agreeing a more robust system of expenses, and went on to launch a consultation on whether the amounts MPs could spend on furniture and household goods should be capped; whether receipts should be required for all expenditure, regardless of value; what the nature of a revised internal system of audit might be (given that the House had ruled out the MEC's proposal for external 'practice assurance'); and whether MPs' children should be barred from being employed by them. This went over some of the ground covered by the MEC proposals, but seemed more like a retrenchment rather than a clear way forward.

Harriet Harman issued a statement on 10 September,[68] requesting comments from MPs by 29 September, and the following month issued a further statement[69] extending the deadline to the end of October. Responding to the document, the CSPL found itself in a difficult position. It had been persuaded by the government to hold back in July, and defer any inquiry of its own until the following year. But the committee's frustration with what looked like kicking the can down the road was evident in Sir Christopher Kelly's letter to Harman on 30 September.

> You are, of course, aware from our previous exchanges of my Committee's deep concerns about the current arrangements for reimbursing MPs' expenses. We remain of the view that there should be a fresh and independent look at the complete picture of how MPs should be remunerated and supported in a modern system,

he began. The letter went on to list – and criticise or question – the Harman proposals, adding 'I am sorry to say that we are not convinced that the current proposals measure up to these [the CSPL's] principles in all respects, nor that they will address all the public's concerns about MPs' pay and allowances.' Thereafter, the Harman proposals disappeared from view. In parallel, the Members Estimate Audit Committee pressed ahead with agreeing alternative approaches on audit.

The second initiative was more productive, though ultimately fruitless. The government amendment on 16 July, which the House had agreed, said that the Advisory Panel on Members' Allowances should rewrite the Green Book, the expenses rule book. The latest version of the Green Book, published in July 2006, had been slated by the Information Tribunal for its 'laxity and lack of clarity'. The MEC had therefore proposed that the Green Book should be revised to specify more detailed rules.

Don Touhig, fresh from his victory on 6 July, was asked to take over chairmanship of the Advisory Panel on Members' Allowances, whose main task over the next six months was to redraft the Green Book entirely. The revised version began with key statements of principle: Touhig felt that it had been a good attempt to police the system.[70] But it did not come into force until a year later, well after the coffin of the expenses system had been nailed firmly shut. And while the principles it enunciated were unimpeachable (for example, 'claims should be above reproach', there should be no 'improper personal financial benefit', and so on), it had even less detail and precision than the previous Green Book that had been so heavily criticised.

Looking back, it might not be unreasonable to assume that MPs – or at least those involved in drawing up the new Green Book – were still in denial about how bad their expenses would look to the public.

5

The leak

An *Evening Standard* columnist, Nick Cohen, claimed to know a mole who was put into the Fees Office in 2007 and uncovered the Derek Conway affair. But that leak was microscopic compared with the shattering revelations that led to the crisis in May 2009. The impact of this storm of exposure might have been contained if MPs and staff hadn't become bogged down by a series of redaction battles.

A million documents prepared for release

Once the High Court judgement had been given on 16 May 2008, MPs decided quickly to publish full details of all MPs' expenses for all the years for which the House of Commons held historic records.[1] The problem was working out how this was to be done. Options included: (1) Continuing to publish summaries by category of expenditure in the autumn, and responding to individual FOI requests for receipt-level information on a case-by-case basis (a number of such requests had already come in); (2) Going straight away for full detailed disclosure of the information contained on MPs' claim forms and on the supporting documentation such as receipts. To comply with the court's judgement, there was no requirement to publish the claim forms and receipts themselves: the relevant information could be copied on to a spreadsheet; or (3) Publishing the claims and receipts themselves, editing to exclude a small amount of private information that the court had said need not be disclosed (such as security-related information).

A headache with the first option was that waiting for people to put in FOI requests for receipts whenever they wished would lead to a constant drip of disclosures, which might never end, and would also undermine the MEC's wish to treat all MPs similarly. So this was rejected. The second option would require a huge effort in copying and checking information from millions of paper documents. It would require a lot more staff, would take many months, and there would inevitably be errors in copying. This option was rejected, too. So the third option appeared the most doable – publication of scanned images of all MPs' claims and receipts for four years, 2004/05 to 2007/08. It seemed at the time that this approach could be achieved, provided that all of the documents could be successfully and securely scanned electronically, and that the redactions – the items blacked out because of their privacy and sensitivity – were not too extensive. The House authorities decided to go down that route. But the assumptions made turned out to be too optimistic. The process would be much more challenging, time consuming and risky than they imagined.

From the start, many MPs were, justifiably as it turned out, worried about security – both their own personal security if, for example, their home addresses were disclosed, and the security of the copying and redacting process. Trust in the Fees Office was low. Some suspected it of being leaky following the Nick Cohen article. Dr Julian Lewis MP tabled a Parliamentary Question to ask whether the staff employed on the redaction work would be permanent or temporary staff, and what security checks would have been carried out on them. On behalf of the MEC, Nick Harvey MP answered on 1 July:

> Quality assurance and editing will be undertaken by security-cleared permanent staff as will any further revisions after hon. Members have had an opportunity to check their information. However, the House does not itself have the capacity to carry out all the work required. It is therefore planned that the scanning of some 1.3 million documents and first stage redaction to remove details such as addresses, telephone numbers, banking details and account numbers will be undertaken under secure conditions by a contractor familiar with providing services to Government and Parliament whose staff have been security cleared... The Parliamentary Security Co-ordinator and the Serjeant-at-Arms have been consulted, and their approval of the arrangements will be sought before the work

goes ahead. Staff of the House will be involved in monitoring the whole process.[2]

The sheer magnitude of the task meant that it had to be undertaken externally, thus increasing the risks.

Earlier that same day, Andrew had been to see his boss about the challenge they faced to get the work done. It was proving difficult to find a contractor who was willing and able to take on such a huge task at such short notice. The House of Commons already had a contract for secure printing and publishing with TSO.[3] They were willing, they had the technical capability to scan large numbers of documents in secure conditions, and they were confident that they could employ sufficient security-cleared staff to carry out an initial redaction exercise. Given the MEC's wish for publication at the earliest date, that seemed the only viable option.

Mindful of the risk of leaks, the Serjeant-at-Arms and the Parliamentary Security Coordinator were dispatched to evaluate the security arrangements at TSO and declared the arrangement secure. When Andrew visited TSO's premises, he was relieved of his mobile phone and was security checked as he entered, just as you would be when you enter any secure government installation. He was shown the security measures taken in how the documents were carefully handled from the moment they arrived from the House of Commons to the moment they were delivered back to the Commons after being scanned. He was shown the computer security and how the workers were managed and supervised so that, for example, no single worker saw the whole picture. And he was shown the CCTV system that would identify any unauthorised personnel or unusual behaviour.

As a Fees Office insider recalled, the MEC had decided that as MPs were so concerned that no private information was disclosed by accident, each MP would be shown the exact proposed redactions so that they were carried out to their satisfaction.[4] To achieve this, the preparation was done in three stages. The first stage was to scan the documents as they were. Then the contractor's staff would identify what should be edited out on each form, based on guidance from the House of Commons. They then 'greyed out' all of the information they judged should be redacted on the basis of those criteria. This version of the scan was called the 'audit version', which was sent to Bob Castle's FOI team for quality checking. Then the redacted version would be shown to MPs for their comments.

On 3 April 2008, an announcement had been made to the House of Commons that summaries of MPs' claims for the past four years would be published the following autumn.[5] After the adverse High Court decision, the House was told on 20 May that 'the publication scheme announced for the autumn will now include information down to receipt level'.[6] On 12 September, the Fees Office wrote to all MPs to tell them about the plans for scanning and publishing their claims for the past four years 'later this year' and asked them to be ready to check for accuracy. A Fees Office leaflet for MPs said, 'The process of scanning and editing the large amount of information is being undertaken in secure conditions. The aim is to have this information ready by the autumn, with a view to publication in November or December.' But wrangling about what details were to be published would carry on for months, delaying completion of the work until the following summer, to the consternation of Heather Brooke and others.

The leak

The scanning and initial editing of more than a million documents – claims and receipts – was complete by mid-October. That would allow a month for MPs to check their own information on a secure website, and for any further redactions to be made before publication in mid-January. But, unknown to the House of Commons, the greyed-out audit scans were being copied. It must have been in October 2008 or shortly afterwards: before then, the documents that appeared in the *Telegraph* the following year had not all been scanned.

The *Telegraph's* Robert Winnett and Gordon Rayner tell a gripping story about the leak.[7] In order to employ sufficient security-cleared staff quickly, TSO had taken on soldiers who had served in Afghanistan, who, it is said, were incensed when they saw what MPs were claiming, particularly for their second homes, while they had been suffering privations and lack of equipment while on active service. But that factor alone does not fully explain the leak. No single squaddie had access to all the data they were editing, and any attempt by some of them to make unauthorised copies would have been recorded in TSO's computer logs and spotted on CCTV. And in any event, the million or so electronic images that had been scanned and edited added up to a vast amount of data. It would have required hundreds of CDs or memory sticks to copy and carry that amount of data. When the data reached the *Telegraph* it was on a high-capacity external hard drive. No one – in public at least – has satisfactorily explained the technicalities of how the leak was achieved. It was like carrying out a gigantic bullion robbery without anyone noticing at the time, or for several months afterwards. Two things are clear. First, the leak needed detailed and forensic planning: it was not a spur-of-the moment job. Secondly, it required deep technical knowledge of IT and the specific systems involved.

So who did it? Some MPs suspected the Fees Office. The Fees Office thought it was TSO, as Winnett and Rayner were later to write. The Speaker hinted that it was TSO: 'No one in that organisation, either for financial gain or any other reason, should be handing over information that has been put and safeguarded with it to do a certain job of work.'[8] A forensic review was commissioned, but the report was seen by only three people, and never published.[9]

Redaction battles

If only MPs or the Fees Office had known about the leak sooner, it might have led to a greater sense of urgency about getting the claims and receipts published. As it was, publication kept getting delayed: by late October 2008, the publication date had slipped to the following February, and by November it had been pushed back to mid-March. By December, publication was not envisaged before the end of March. In the months that followed, it was to be pushed back even further.

The MEC returned to the issue at most of its meetings over the winter of 2008/09, as the published records make clear:

20 October 2008   The Committee would consider a timetable for publication at its next meeting.

10 November	The Committee took note of the letter from the Chairman of the Advisory Panel on Members' Allowances.
17 November	The Committee noted with approval that the work on redaction of receipts was continuing.
15 December	It was noted that the process of redacting receipts was continuing.
26 January 2009	The Committee agreed that the scanning and redaction of receipts should continue.
2 March	The Committee considered the timetable for sending the scanned and redacted material electronically to Members for checking, for Members to respond with suggestions for further editing, for further editing to be carried out and for publication. The Committee agreed that... headline figures for 2007/08 should be sent to Members for checking as soon as possible and published before the Easter recess.
30 March	The Committee revised and approved the letter to Members about the scanned receipts and claims, and agreed that it should be signed by an official... It agreed that the timetable for the July publication should be communicated to the Information Commissioner.
11 May	The Committee agreed to bring forward the publication of the scanned receipts and claims for 2004/05 to 2007/08 by several weeks.
8 June	The Committee agreed that the scanned receipts and claims for 2004/05 to 2007/08 should be published on 18 June, if possible in the early morning to reduce the risk of a sudden peak in demand...

The records are brief, and show no hint that the meetings sometimes went on well into the evening, but the extracts tell their own story. A clue as to what was going on is in the record of 10 November 2008 – the Advisory Panel on Members' Allowances had made strong representations to the MEC that too little was being deleted from their expenses claims. It was suspected that the Fees Office were FOI 'believers', and would do their best to publish as much detail as they could. Many MPs, in contrast, felt that too much was being disclosed. After all, hadn't the High Court ruled that information that might affect their security should be withheld?

The MPs' concern that disclosure of their home addresses would make them vulnerable to unwanted attention or attack had been dealt with in July 2008, when the government amended the FOI Act to exclude their residential addresses from being published.[10] But there were other concerns too. Would the publication of parts of credit card numbers on receipts, possibly combined with additional information from invoices, lead to identity theft or other kinds of fraud? In the end, a financial fraud expert confirmed that such risks were very low, but more time was lost while this was explored. And MPs' unease did not vanish. Even the question of disclosing the identity of local traders who supplied their offices was raised – what if they were targeted, or what if they were reluctant to supply the MP in future if their identity was revealed?

MPs feeling exposed

What was at the heart of MPs' anxiety about exposure? Like many celebrities, politicians tend to crave attention – whether for personal or political reasons – but also loathe it. To understand the loathing, you have to fathom the craving. To realise their ambitions for themselves, their constituency, party or wider society, they need to build up their reputation. This is always the case with elected politicians, who depend on a huge range of support to get elected and secure impressive achievements once they have a seat, but the nature of reputation has changed over the years. In 1989, during the first televised speech to Parliament, in the days when the massaging of image was relatively new in the UK, Ian Gow told the Commons about a letter he had received from a PR company. It contained the following preposterous assertion:

The impression you make on television depends mainly on your image (55 per cent) with your voice and body language accounting for 38 per cent of your impact. Only 7 per cent depends on what you are actually saying.[11]

This provoked laughter, especially when the almost completely bald Mr Gow added that he was offered advice about hairstyling.

These days no MP ignores their own image or appearance. The late Paul Flynn MP advised: 'Be ubiquitous and ever present in the constituency. The drip feed of blog, tweets, early morning radio interviews repeated throughout the day, widely advertised surgeries, and attendance in the Chamber in a camera-exposed position, all propagate the message "Busy MP".'[12] As former MP Tony Wright told Emma, as soon as MPs ask a question in the Chamber, they then rush back to their office and instruct their staff to put out a press release or call the local paper.[13] Since that interview, MPs have had to adapt to the eruption of digital communication. The first thing many MPs do now is tweet about it, followed later by another tweet with a video clip of the exchange. So these days photos and reports on how MPs have raised constituency issues bloom all over MPs' websites, their campaign literature, in the local press and on Twitter.

Part of MPs' anxiety would have been about their reputation. How would the claims look to constituents? Even if their pleas for more redaction were about security, their general tendency to want to black out information may have been partly linked to a worry about appearances. However, the more serious problem with exposure for most MPs was probably about neither reputation nor security, but their privacy. Security is easy to explain, but privacy is far harder for MPs convey. These public figures feel owned within various relationships – by local party, by the whips, by other MPs, by journalists, by constituents – all demanding their political support, their actions, their time, and often in an antagonistic manner. Angie Bray MP (Conservative) told a journalist, 'You get emails from one side saying you're morally deficient if you vote no and emails threatening hell fire and brimstone if you vote yes.'[14] One MP told Emma a constituent emailed at 2.30 am complaining about a neighbour and then emailed again at 6.30 am saying: 'Why haven't you replied to my email? You are paid with our taxes.'[15]

Politics is partly about dealing with grievances and conflicts of interest, and elected politicians are not only caught in the middle of this, but also exposed to the attacks of their opponents (principally other politicians but also journalists and activists, and often in coalitions). When these attacks stray into the personal domain – most painfully about their family members – as a way of undermining their credibility or moral consistency, it becomes agonising for them. But that is the dramatic end of exposure.

There is also simply MPs' need for some respite, some quiet away from all the heat to remind themselves who they are in their private world. Human beings need some personal space for themselves and their families. Public figures are no different. The expenses claims threatened to reveal that private world, thereby obliterating a part of their private selves.

More blacking out

So the Fees Office was sent back to edit the claims more extensively. MPs were to be given more time to challenge the Fees Office proposals about what to redact. If MPs still did not agree with the Fees Office, then they could appeal to the Advisory Panel on Members' Allowances to adjudicate. While there were MPs and committees arguing for more time to edit and check, there were also MPs who were pressing for quicker publication. Nick Harvey MP, the Liberal Democrat representative on the MEC, was in a difficult position as he was also the MEC's official spokesman. Members of his own party, including Norman Baker, Jo Swinson and Simon Hughes, went public in pressing the MEC to get on with it, but it fell to him to present the MEC's agreed line in answers to Parliamentary Questions throughout this period. On 28 January he used the formula 'a date for publication cannot yet be set'.[16] In June he said to the House,

> appeals by Members about the precise scope of what is included in the publication scheme are due to be heard and determined by the Committee on Members' Allowances during the course of next week... Publication will follow as soon as possible after that.[17]

By the end of March 2009, the publication timetable had slipped by eight months to July 2009. Until, that is, the *Telegraph* started publishing its revelations in May. At that point the MEC decided to accelerate the publication, but by then little time could be recouped.

If MPs hadn't wanted more to be redacted, then perhaps the leak would not have happened, or it might have had less impact. Referring to the long delay in publication, Christopher Hope of the *Telegraph* said, 'the whistleblower got cross about that'.[18] So the delay itself may have been one of the causes of the leak. Without the further redactions, publication would at least have happened more quickly, with fewer blacked-out lines and pages. When the Fees Office started redacting MPs' claims, they had approached two MPs to act as guinea pigs. The team redacted private addresses, names, bank details and names of third parties. But the MPs were not satisfied, and wanted more deletions. Other MPs reacted in the same way, so the programme of editing took longer and longer, with robust discussions and disagreements needing time to resolve.

Various administrative headaches also got in the way – misfiled papers from five years earlier turned up in the wrong place, or could not be found at all; and misunderstandings and distrust between MPs and Fees Office staff dogged relationships. In the meantime, Heather Brooke couldn't fathom the delay, 'It was a PR disaster!', she told us, amazed that officials or MPs could be so foolish. Since no one knew what was causing the delay, and Parliament did not explain, it looked as if they were concealing wrongdoing rather than legitimately protecting MPs' privacy.

At sixes and sevens in Byzantine bureaucracy

Perhaps the biggest 'if only' was the increasing complexity of the governance arrangements. If only the House of Commons administration could have been simpler and more decisive. In the light of the complex governance we set out in Chapter 1, it might have occurred to MPs collectively that simplifying and streamlining the governance of the expenses rule-making and administration would have strengthened Parliament's capacity to deal with the developing crisis. The 2004 decision to introduce the Members Estimate Committee (MEC) had been an attempt to do just that. But during 2008 and the early months of 2009, the governance and supervision arrangements became more complex and – at least from the Fees Office perspective – less clear.

As we saw at the end of the last chapter, fresh from his leadership of the backbench victory over the MEC in July 2008, Don Touhig was appointed as Chair of the Advisory Panel on Members' Allowances (APMA). His job was Solomonic. While the resolutions agreed by the House in July gave APMA key tasks, it did not clear the ground of all the other committees that might take an interest. He told us that when he took over the APMA, he found that his committee and the MEC were pulling in different directions.[19] The MEC was firmly in the driving seat on the release of MPs' claims to the public; but the APMA had been given a remit to revise the Green Book.[20] There was no mention of it answering to the MEC. But at its meeting on 21 July 2008, the MEC said that 'any changes to the Green Book brought forward by the Advisory Panel on Members' Allowances would have to be considered by the MEC before implementation.'[21] There was no love lost between the two committees, which seemed locked in a power struggle.

Touhig told us that if the MEC had worked more closely with his committee and the Fees Office, it would have done better. He recognised that the Fees Office was under pressure trying to serve more than one master. His hand was strengthened the following January when the government was persuaded to transform the APMA – a mere advisory body – into the Committee on Members' Allowances (known as the MAC). Under his chairmanship, the MAC was constituted as a fully fledged select committee with considerable powers. If those had been the only two committees involved, it might have been relatively simple for the Fees Office to work with them both, or to act as go-between. But other committees were also engaged in this Byzantine bureaucracy.

The Members Estimate Audit Committee (MEAC) had been set up some years previously. It had two external non-parliamentary members and was traditionally chaired by the Shadow Leader of the House – Theresa May in 2008, who was also a member of the MEC. Alan Duncan took over the role in January 2009. The MEAC argued for stronger controls and audit, including the introduction of a 'full scope' audit by the National Audit Office, in place of the relatively limited annual audit that had been carried out hitherto. And in 2008 and 2009 it would flex its muscles further by proposing and monitoring a new system of audit and assurance. Its perceptive verdict in its 2008/09 annual report was that the committee 'was disappointed that various complexities in governance which remained to be resolved, together with logistical issues, meant the new system would not be in place from 1 April 2009.'[22]

Another member of the MEC, Sir Stuart Bell, chaired the Finance and Services Committee (F&S). The remit of this committee did not extend to MPs' expenses, but in March 2009 it asked Andrew to justify the proposed arrangements for an Operational Assurance Unit (one of the Audit Committee's recommendations). As F&S was responsible for administrative budgets, its interest in the administrative cost of the proposal was legitimate; yet its discussion of the issue was not limited to its cost, but also to the merits of the Audit Committee's proposal. Then there was the House of Commons Commission. To be fair, it had the same membership as the MEC, and many of the meetings were jointly held. The Commission was (and still is) the employer of House of Commons staff, so it was responsible for overseeing the staffing and administration of the Fees Office. The Administration Select Committee had no management responsibility for the Fees Office, but they saw themselves as having oversight of all services provided to MPs. So from time to time they called Andrew in to answer to them about the Fees Office's services. Committee members visited the Fees Office a couple of weeks before the *Telegraph* started publishing its revelations. Later in the year, one of its members proposed that the committee should review the Fees Office. It may have been no more than an expression of the committee's frustration with the House of Commons Commission or the MEC. The proposal came to nothing.[23]

Other committees of the House also showed an interest in the expenses system. For example, the Select Committee on Standards and Privileges got in touch with Andrew in early 2009, seeking a role in influencing practice notes[24] and guidance to the Fees Office on what goods and services purchased by MPs would be deemed to be extravagant or luxurious, and therefore not allowed under the rules.

Yet another committee, the Joint Committee on Security (JCOS), discussed the security arrangements for scanning and editing MPs' claims and receipts – justifiably so, as events would shortly demonstrate. The issue of expenses alone reveals the tangled complexity of the Commons' committees and how they related to one another. And aside from these committees, the Leader of the House, Harriet Harman, was exploring options for a more robust scrutiny and assurance regime through the summer of 2008 and the following winter.

Most of the committee activity was hidden from the outside world. Indeed, probably few, if any, MPs were aware of the extent of the activities of all these committees – until they talked to someone in the Fees Office, who would try to remember which committee had taken a particular decision. One of the strengths of the Westminster democratic system is the variety of committees with cross-party representation. They act as a voice in holding the government to account, exposing waste and challenging social injustice. Following the failure to reform the system of expenses in the summer of 2008, it was understandable that different MP groups would become frustrated. But the multiplicity of voices within the House of Commons – declaring their views on what needed to be done with the expenses arrangements, how and when expenses information should be published, how the Fees Office should be run, and who should be in charge of decision-making – resulted in confusion rather than clarity, and in disunity just at the time that the House needed to demonstrate to the media and to the public that it was united in addressing their growing concerns. As one official told us, it perhaps reflected the House's almost endless capacity to talk about and consider itself: the House and MPs are something that all MPs think they are experts on.[25]

The internal fragmentation had practical impacts. The main one was the sense of indecision and consequent delay, which risked Parliament appearing frozen like a rabbit in the headlights – or worse, as if it had something to hide. But there were further impacts, such as the Committee on Standards in Public Life (CSPL) not knowing who to approach in the House of Commons to hear their official position. Should they talk to the MEC, the Committee on Members' Allowances, or House officials? And who was authorised to brief the media? The internal disagreements between committees and the frequency of their meetings in the winter and spring of 2009 led senior officials to meet in order to discuss how best to handle the competing pressures and messages from the committees. The issue was raised as a concern at the MEAC meeting in March 2009. Committee members, particularly the external members, were sympathetic[26] but did not have the power to change the situation.

Committees involved with MPs' expenses

Acronym	Full name	Description
Admin	Select Committee on Administration	A 'domestic committee' of the House set up to oversee internal services provided for MPs.
APMA	Advisory Panel on Members' Allowances	Began life in 2001 as Speaker's Advisory Panel on Members' Allowances (SAP). Renamed in 2005. Replaced by MAC in 2009.
CSPL	Committee on Standards in Public Life	Set up in 1990s following the cash-for-questions scandal. Independent of the House of Commons, but two MPs appointed to it.
F&S	Select Committee on Finance and Services	A domestic committee of the House, set up to oversee administrative budgets and expenditure (but not expenditure on MPs' expenses).
HOCC	House of Commons Commission	Set up in 1978 and chaired by the Speaker. The main administrative committee of the House. Responsible for administrative expenditure and employment of House staff.
JCOS	Joint Committee on Security	Set up to advise on security relating to both Houses of Parliament.

Acronym	Full name	Description
MAC	Select Committee on Members' Allowances	Set up in January 2009 to replace APMA.
MEAC	Members Estimate Audit Committee	A sub-committee of the MEC, with both MPs and independent external members. Chaired by the Shadow Leader of the House.
MEC	Members Estimate Committee	Set up in 2004 to take responsibility for the House of Commons: Members Estimate (budget), which was the source of funding for MPs' pay, pensions and allowances.
PASC	Select Committee on Public Administration	The Commons committee that recommended that the FOI legislation should be applied to Parliament.

Esprit de corps

It would take six months for the leaked claims to be published. In the meantime, the work of preparing the documents for publication went forward. The Fees Office's workload had increased dramatically: it did not have enough staff to carry out all of its tasks. In addition to handling MPs' monthly claims as usual, the office was now dealing with more queries from MPs, particularly as parties increased the pressure on them to ensure their claims were in order. And work was being carried out to explore further reforms to the rules and to produce an entirely new version of the Green Book under the supervision of the APMA.

Terry Bird, the Fees Office's Director of Operations, had been working flat out in the first half of 2008 on the MEC's reform proposals, which the House had rejected in July. Now he had the seemingly impossible task of asking his staff to take on significant extra work. The House of Commons Service came to the rescue. Gradually, over the winter, staff from other House of Commons departments volunteered, or were volunteered, to help: library researchers, clerks and others sat alongside Fees Office staff. A senior clerk, Paul Silk,[27] was drafted in to lead the work on the new Green Book; and volunteers from all over the House Service came to help with the work of redaction. The *esprit de corps* was palpable. Bob Castle, who was in charge of the FOI releases, told us how he had a whole room of senior clerks reviewing MPs' requests for further redactions.[28]

When MPs received the data and saw what the House proposed to publish, many became angry. One threatened to take Bob Castle to court if he didn't make the alterations he'd asked for. But officials had to stick to the High Court ruling and the instructions on redaction agreed by the MEC. For example, if an MP had claimed for something and later paid it back in a subsequent year, the records of the original claim could not be expunged, much to the irritation of those MPs who had made repayments in the hope of wiping the slate clean.

Once the Fees Office's original proposals for redactions were rejected by the MEC, additional redactions were made. Repeated attempts to edit the claims and receipts to the satisfaction of individual MPs resulted in much to-ing and fro-ing, thereby increasing delay in publication. Bob Castle and his team found themselves under increasing pressure from MPs. Some Members would simply not agree with the proposed deletions; one MP jokingly told a staff member that if he was ever to take refreshment on the Terrace, he should not stand too close to the wall. In early 2009 the Committee on Members' Allowances (MAC) was asked to arbitrate in the most difficult cases.

The new Green Book

The old Green Book had been criticised by the Information Tribunal in February 2008 as being insufficiently clear, precise or detailed. In its report to the House in the summer, the MEC had proposed that a more comprehensive and authoritative guide should be written. But, as we set out in Chapter 4, the APMA took the view that the new Green Book should be simpler and based on principles rather than rules. That was the basis on which Paul Silk was asked to lead the drafting. The Fees Office and the Audit Committee thought that – on its own – a new Green Book drafted in this way would represent a step backwards. At the very least, unless supplemented by detailed specific instructions, the Fees Office would struggle to apply it fairly or consistently. What would happen, for example, if an MP disagreed with a junior member of the Fees Office on how to apply the Green Book principles? Who would win the argument?

The message from the Speaker in the new Green Book was also noticeably watered down. Whereas in the 2006 Green Book Michael Martin had reinforced 'the Department's [i.e. the Fees Office's] authority to interpret and enforce these rules', his Foreword to the 2009 Green Book used milder language: 'the Department... has the task of administering the rules, of ensuring compliance with them and of giving help and advice to Members. I urge Members to make use of that advice in any case of doubt or difficulty.'[29]

In parallel, the audit arrangements were reconsidered. In the summer of 2008, Harriet Harman had proposed a new approach to audit and assurance (as mentioned above). The consultation period on these proposals was pushed back to the end of October. Andrew wrote back to her with comments and questions from an operational perspective; but her initiative was by then being overtaken by other events, and petered out. Following consultation with the National Audit Office (NAO), the Audit Committee, chaired by Theresa May, made a report proposing: strengthening audit of the allowances; a significant reform of assurance work in the Fees Office, with a stronger emphasis on senior staff helping Members while at the same time ensuring compliance and maintenance of standards; and clear governance arrangements and escalation routes.

In particular, because the Green Book was an insufficient basis for operating the expenses system, the Audit Committee proposed – as the Fees Office and the NAO had suggested – that there should be clear guidance and detailed practice notes to interpret the new Green Book.

The MEC put the revised Green Book along with the Audit Committee's proposals to the House on 15 January 2009.[30] Following a debate the following week, the House agreed to the Green Book and the audit proposals. But it also endorsed the Leader of the House's proposal to convert the APMA into a select committee (the MAC), thus giving it more powers. A government proposal to remove MPs' expenses from FOI altogether for the future, so that they would be published on a *voluntary* basis, was withdrawn at the last moment. But Dr Tony Wright MP commented in the debate:

> My understanding was that the dark forces on both sides of the House had conspired— *[Interruption.]* Well, my colleagues on both sides of the House had come together to persuade the Government to remove the House and Members of Parliament from the scrutiny of the Freedom of Information Act in relation to detailed spending.[31]

Maybe he was right.

The leading edge of the storm

Despite Dr Wright's forebodings, it looked like progress was being made. Potential conflicts between the key committees involved in MPs' expenses seemed to be settling down. The media was fairly quiet, though the *Mail on Sunday* had another pop at Michael Martin on 25 January 2009,[32] this time accusing him of wasting money in requiring the new version of the Green Book to be reprinted. All that was needed was a period of calm for the Fees Office to complete the job of preparing MPs' receipts for publication, and setting up the arrangements to introduce tougher audit and assurance of their future claims. Maybe the House of Commons had turned the corner, and the problems and disagreements of 2008 would be left behind.

But within days, rumours of a major leak began to circulate around the Westminster bubble. On 8 February 2009, the *Mail on Sunday* published its first exposé of the Home Secretary Jacqui Smith's expenses for the previous four years. The key allegation was that she had nominated as her main home her lodging arrangement with her sister in London, and was therefore able to claim expenses on the family home in the constituency as her second home. A London neighbour, Mrs Taplin, said, 'I would estimate that she's here about a third of the time' – implying that her London lodgings were not her main home, and adding that she had written to the Fees Office to complain.[33] 'Jacqui has documentation to prove that everything is completely above board. It has been cleared by the Commons Fees Office,' said her spokeswoman.[34] The following month, the *Sunday Express*[35] ran a story that Smith had claimed for two pay-per-view pornographic movies on expenses. Her husband took responsibility, but the damage was done. She had also had the temerity to claim reimbursement of 88 pence for a bath plug. Gordon Brown backed her,[36] but Smith returned to the backbenches on 5 June. And the further information that the *Express* was able to disclose subsequently showed that they had got hold of detailed and accurate information.

Meanwhile another government minister was targeted. On 22 February, the *Mail on Sunday* revealed that Tony McNulty, an outer London MP, had his main home three miles from Westminster, and his second home in his Harrow constituency some 11 miles further away. He used the second home when in his constituency but it was also occupied by his parents as their main home, rent-free. The Parliamentary Standards and Privileges Committee decided that, although he followed the advice of the Fees Office, it had been mistaken in advising that this fell within the rules, and further, that McNulty himself had also been remiss in failing to put in place a formal agreement with his parents. He was required to apologise to the House of Commons and make a repayment.[37]

It was beginning to seem likely that more information had been leaking out. 'It was only when the *Sunday Express* approached Jacqui Smith about the porn films that it became clear that actual documents might be finding their way into journalists' hands,' comment Winnett and Rayner.[38]

Andrew got an early taste of popular disapproval when he received a letter from a member of the public: 'I was having a clear out at my home and I came across a spare bath plug. I wondered if Miss Jacqui Smith could make use of it.'[39] Later letters he got would not be so gentle.

Gordon Brown calls in the cavalry

After the government had twice discouraged the Committee on Standards in Public Life (CSPL) from launching an investigation into the arrangements for MPs' expenses,[40] its chair Sir Christopher Kelly again approached the Cabinet Secretary, Gus O'Donnell, in early March 2009 to propose an inquiry. The Prime Minister replied on 23 March that he would welcome such a review, and the CSPL announced that it would start its inquiry towards the end of the year. Gordon Brown wrote again to Sir Christopher asking him to speed up the review. Having been lobbied by the government not to launch a review the previous year, the Prime Minister now pressed the CSPL to carry it out as a matter of urgency. So on 31 March the CSPL said it would try to report by the end of 2009.[41] Sir Christopher told us that the CSPL was determined to go through a proper process, and that would take time.[42] The announcement persuaded a retired top Commons official to break cover. The next day, 1 April, the *Guardian* printed a letter from a former Clerk of the House of Commons, Sir Roger Sands, which pointed out flaws in the system of governance of MPs' pay and expenses, because MPs had 'the ability to overturn, or covertly sabotage' the findings of independent review bodies such as the SSRB and the CSPL.[43] The letter was prescient. It would take more than another review to put things right.

On the same day at Prime Minister's Questions, David Cameron, the Leader of the Opposition, said,

> the problem is that we do not need another review. Let us be clear: this is exactly what happened last time. The Prime Minister supported a review, he sent it a letter and when it came up with conclusions, he did not vote for them. [*Hon. Members: 'Nor did you.'*] I did vote for them. The public are sick and tired of this situation, and it requires political leadership.[44]

The suspicions that there had been a major leak were confirmed on Monday 30 March, when the *Daily Express* ran a further story about Jacqui Smith, with additional information about her expenses. They released copies of some of her receipts, clearly showing her husband's name. The disclosures in the *Mail on Sunday* and the *Express* were, according to various journalists, tasters in advance of the sale of the full electronic file of information to the *Telegraph* towards the end of April.[45] On 30 and 31 March, Andrew's phone was busy with calls from journalists. The realisation that something big was ready to break seemed widespread among the media. The Fees Office was being asked for all kinds of information about the expenses system and its operation.

On 1 April, Sam Coates of the *Times* reported that expenses receipts were being hawked by a City businessman, who had offered his newspaper 'details of every expense claim made by MPs over the past five years' for £300,000.[46] A member of the MEC, Sir Stuart Bell, was quoted as saying, 'We have a pretty good idea of not the person but the source, and that is a subject of a House of Commons investigation.' MPs were putting their heads in the sand, still hoping that it would come to nothing.

A broth in danger of spoiling

Despite the Smith and McNulty revelations, the atmosphere in the House of Commons calmed down, and MPs went home a day or two later for the Easter break. Business in the House of Commons carried on as normal when MPs returned on 20 April. The main preoccupations on expenses within the Commons still seemed to be about the process of redaction and the publication of claims and receipts, which was by then scheduled for July, and about the drafting of practice notes and reorganisation of the Fees Office to manage the stronger checking and monitoring. A new unit was to be created, the Operational Assurance Unit, which would check MPs' claims, but also that the items purchased through the expenses system were used only for parliamentary purposes. This became known as 'checking behind the MP's signature'. No longer would the word of the MP be the final say. It remained to be seen, however, whether this would come to pass. Fees Office insiders doubted whether MPs would accept more thorough checking and challenge by House of Commons officials, particularly given the often frosty reception they were becoming accustomed to when they were summoned to answer to the various committees of MPs. The phrase 'rough ride' was at this time used frequently by staff reporting on their experiences.

Andrew had got used to negative references about him in the media, particularly during the Information Tribunal hearing a year previously, when he had disclosed the existence of the John Lewis list. But he was unprepared for the broadside from Peter Oborne on 11 April, in the wake of the Jacqui Smith revelations. He was described as the real culprit: 'if only Walker... had done his job with proper integrity and fastidiousness, the expenses fiasco would never have occurred... Is it simply that Walker is useless at his job? Or is something more sinister at work?', he asked.[47] This was, however, a single straw in the wind. Once the scandal itself broke, the brickbats came thick and fast.

Progress on reforming the expenses system in the House of Commons was snail-like. The Speaker's credit was running short, and his authority was waning. There was no longer party unity on expenses, and different factions in the House of Commons were straining to take different paths. The government's decision at last to support a review by the CSPL would not yield results until late 2009 at the earliest. And a general election was now only a year away.

Gordon Brown decided to launch a new initiative: 21 April was the day chosen for an announcement and a charm offensive. Harriet Harman announced to the House of Commons, 'The Prime Minister has asked Sir Christopher Kelly and the Committee on Standards in Public Life to look at all of the relevant issues involved in MPs' allowances as speedily as possible. In the meantime, the Government thinks it is right to bring forward reforms that can be enacted sooner.' She called for immediate abolition of the second home allowance, to be replaced by a daily flat-rate attendance allowance,[48] and that all future MPs' staff should be employed directly by the House of Commons. In addition, receipts would be required for all expenses claims, no matter how small. The reforms would be made the following week. The Fees Office had not been consulted, nor – seemingly – had any other authorities in the House of Commons. The ideas came out of the blue.

Gordon Brown made a personal announcement via an online video on the same day.[49] It went viral, not because viewers liked the reform proposals, but because they were entertained by the video itself. It became known as the 'Smile' video, and was later caricatured by the impressionist Rory Bremner.[50] Fees Office staff were amused by the apparent gaucheness of Brown's performance and in equal part appalled at the seemingly off-the-top-of-the-head ideas now presented as government policy.

What had caused the Prime Minister to take this initiative? His memoirs shed no light on the episode; nor do Harriet Harman's.[51] The *Guardian* heralded it as a reversal of policy, 'The announcement marks a significant U-turn by Brown, who until today had resisted calls from David Cameron and Nick Clegg for reforms of MPs' expenses to be introduced quickly.' It reported a measured, but perhaps irritated, statement from Sir Christopher Kelly of the CSPL: 'Sir Christopher Kelly... said it would be a mistake to think the expenses problem could be solved by "a quick fix"... This issue needs to be dealt with properly so that the public can have confidence in the integrity and probity of the system.'[52] On 23 April, Sir George Young, Chairman of the Standards and Privileges Committee, asked why the government could not wait for the outcome of Sir Christopher Kelly's review. On behalf of the government, Harriet Harman responded,

> The point is that we have to take action. Public confidence has been draining away. We do not want Sir Christopher Kelly to have to truncate his work and complete it in an unsatisfactory way – obviously, he would not be prepared to do that anyway. He has to take some time to deliberate, but it is not acceptable to leave the present lack of confidence to continue until after Sir Christopher has reported.[53]

The party leaders met and did not reach agreement. On 27 April the *Times* announced, 'Gordon Brown's YouTube plan for MPs' £150 a day expenses collapses'.[54] The same day, Harriet Harman tabled motions to give effect to the Ministerial statement. The idea of an attendance allowance had been dropped. Backbench MPs objected to 'clocking in', saying that they were just as much at work when they were in the constituency or visiting another town as when they were in Westminster.[55] Instead, the government proposed that MPs' attendance at Westminster should be 'taken into account'. But in the face of an amendment tabled by Sir George Young, the government backed down, and the initiative to introduce an attendance allowance in place of the second home allowance was effectively at an end.[56] It had been, literally, a nine-day wonder. Some other aspects of the government's proposals were, however, accepted, though with modifications.

With so many cooks in the kitchen, the broth was in danger of spoiling. There were many players in the House of Commons taking different positions, but not operating as a cohesive team – always the challenge in politics. The main hope at this point was that, given a clear enough run, Sir Christopher Kelly's committee, the CSPL, would be able to come up with a set of proposals that would unify the whole House and command public respect. That was a big ask, and the required clear run already looked unlikely.

The scene was set for the *Telegraph*'s bombshells.

6

'A tempest dropping fire'

What was about to break forth on the UK political world was to be worse than many imagined. As Shakespeare expresses it on the lips of Casca on the eve of the Ides of March:

> *I have seen tempests, when the scolding winds*
> *Have riv'd the knotty oaks, and I have seen*
> *The ambitious ocean swell and rage and foam,*
> *To be exalted with the threat'ning clouds*
> *But never till to-night, never till now,*
> *Did I go through a tempest dropping fire.*[1]

The Bunker

Towards the end of April 2009, an American former taxi driver, a PR man called Henry Gewanter, introduced *Telegraph* journalists to an ex-SAS man John Wick. They were offering revealing data about MPs' claims for sale as long as the political parties were treated equally in any exposé. The amount of information on offer was vast, but would it turn out to be a pig in a poke? Robert Winnett (Deputy Political Editor of the *Telegraph* in 2009) and William Lewis (Editor) had to take a huge gamble. At least two newspapers had already turned down the offer of the information. There were unanswered questions. Had the data been acquired by legitimate means? What was the risk of prosecution for receiving stolen goods, or the risk that the purported scans would turn out to be fake? How would the *Telegraph* exploit the data without other newspapers spiking their guns or beating them to the draw? And was the information on offer worth the huge sum of money that was being asked for?

The *Telegraph* journalists swallowed hard and agreed to the conditions. They stumped up more than £100,000 to clinch the deal. They put together a team of seven full-time reporters in 'the Bunker', telling other *Telegraph* staff that they were on a training course to conceal their work on this major scoop until the story broke. Winnett told us that he had no idea at the outset that the *Telegraph*'s story would become as big as it did.[2] But as experienced journalists, he and Lewis must have had more than an inkling of the potential of the story.

Most previous media stories about MPs had been one-off, running for just a few days. What the *Telegraph* was now preparing for was a summer blockbuster that would overshadow other political stories for weeks. Winnett and his colleagues realised that in journalistic terms, the fact that the House of Commons was planning to publish scans of both claims and receipts meant that the stories would come to life with lurid details about MPs' lives and spending, about bath plugs and moats, duck houses and gardening. He said that part of their problem was that MPs were being caught in the attempt to clean up. He remembered thinking, 'What must this have looked like beforehand?' Yet ironically, as he says, it was the details resulting from the attempts to clean up in 2003 and 2004 that filled the newspapers for the next few weeks. As one former MP pointed out, it was the receipts that allowed the journalists to paint the story so that they could catch readers' prurient imagination, either because they were humdrum (we all use bath plugs) or extraordinary (most of us don't own houses for ducks).

Meanwhile, in Downing Street, Gordon Brown asked his Cabinet colleagues to publish their own expenses.[3] This failed when two or three objected, so he decided that it was impossible to go ahead. Back in the House of Commons, the new Head of the National Audit Office,[4] Amyas Morse, paid a visit to the Accounting Officer and Clerk of the House, Malcolm Jack. In future, starting that summer, the National Audit Office would conduct a more rigorous audit of the House of Commons accounts from which MPs' expenses were paid. For the first time, they would 'go behind the MP's signature' – they would test the validity of MPs' claims, and how they had used the goods and services they had paid for with their expenses. This would later result in the annual accounts being qualified by the NAO.

Political bombshells

On Thursday 7 May, the *Telegraph* dropped a bombshell on the most important politician in the land. The Prime Minister's office received an email from the *Telegraph* saying that they were going to publish details of Gordon Brown's expenses the following morning. Other cabinet ministers got similar emails during the afternoon. The *Telegraph* waited for the expected legal injunction which would stop them publishing. But it never came. According to Winnett, Gordon Brown held an emergency meeting that afternoon in his office. But in the end each minister who had been approached gave their own defence.

In the House of Commons, Sir Stuart Bell, a senior Labour MP and member of the MEC, had got wind of the story. An emergency internal meeting was called that evening. Unlike cabinet members, the House of Commons insiders did not know exactly what was going to be revealed the next day. Until they saw what was published, they wondered whether the *Telegraph* would just rehash earlier material. But, given the possibility of something bigger, they would have to prepare for the worst, seeking to protect the privacy of third parties such as MPs' staff and suppliers, as well as the security of MPs themselves. Much would turn on how the *Telegraph* presented the information.

They did not have to wait long. On 8 May the *Telegraph* was head-lined, 'The truth about the Cabinet's expenses'. The front page showed a photograph of a receipt for cleaning in Gordon and Sarah Brown's Westminster home. The receipt was from his brother, who had apparently arranged the cleaning. Over nine pages, thirteen other ministers were covered in that day's newspaper. Hazel Blears was accused of 'flipping',[5] and thereby claiming expenses on three different properties in a year; John Prescott was ridiculed for having had a toilet seat repaired twice in two years; Andy Burnham was quoted as asking the Fees Office to reimburse him quickly or he might face divorce. The Fees Office had responded to him along the lines, 'that may be so, but you must still send in a receipt'.[6] The 8 May edition promised more revelations over the coming days. In fact, the revelations went on for weeks. Circulation figures for the *Telegraph* jumped immediately by 87,000.

The next day, Saturday, there were further revelations about ministers, and on Sunday it was Sinn Fein's turn. On Monday the broadside against the Shadow Cabinet began. David Cameron got off relatively lightly, as he had used the lion's share of his second home allowance to pay for mortgage interest on his constituency home, leaving little over to buy other goods and services. The following days it was the turn of Tory grandees, including Douglas Hogg. The paper pointed out that he had included the cost of clearing his moat in the overall accounts he submitted to the Fees Office. Hogg is quoted as telling the Fees Office:

> Whilst some items may be disputable as to whether they do or they do not fall within the allowance, I would suggest that it is certain that allowable expenditure exceeds the allowance by a sizeable margin and consequently we need not spend too much time in a debate.[7]

The Fees Office did not pay for the moat cleaning, and Hogg hadn't asked them to, but it quickly emerged as a totemic symbol in the media of how out-of-touch MPs were. No political party was exempt – all were targeted.

Although the leaked disk contained details of the whole range of expenses that MPs could claim, it was the expenses claimed for second homes that provided the journalistic bonanza – enabling readers to peep behind MPs' front doors in the interests of public accountability – precisely the kind of exposure that many MPs feared most.

The *Telegraph* got into a daily rhythm. The reporting team had not had time to investigate all the leaked data before the story launched. So they would select who they were going to target for each day's edition a few days before. Having prepared their story, the journalist concerned would then get in touch with the MP they were writing about during the afternoon before publication, giving them a couple of hours to comment. In total, the story ran for six weeks, from 8 May to 20 June, and covered 646 MPs.[8]

Apparently at the height of the coverage the resolve of *Telegraph* editor William Lewis was fortified by a conversation with the Queen at the Chelsea Flower Show,

> When a man came scuttling along and whispered in my ear that Her Majesty was on her way... and we had a very nice conversation and I was able to afterwards hotfoot back to my office even more resolute and even more robust in my desire to continue with our investigative efforts.[9]

The alleged abuses reported by the Telegraph[10]

- *Flipping:* changing the designation of the MP's second home to maximise the amount of expenses they could claim, for example on their mortgage or on household goods. Under the rules, the identification of the main home was one of fact: where the MP's main base was, and where they spent most time.
- *Climbing the property ladder:* this was the allegation that MPs had done up their second home at public expense in order to make it more valuable before selling it.
- *Phantom mortgages:* claiming for mortgage interest after the loan had been paid off. Elliot Morley and David Chaytor had done this.
- *Capital Gains Tax avoidance:* the allegation that MPs had told the tax office that their second home was really their main home (main homes are exempt from CGT, whereas second homes are not). This oversimplification did not take account of the fact that the Commons rule was that what was the second home was a matter of fact, whereas for CGT the second home designation was a matter of choice for the taxpayer. The *Telegraph* admitted that 'MPs may not have done anything illegal'.
- *Claiming for the 'wrong' address:* nominating their family home as their second home so that they could claim more mortgage interest or claim for more household goods there.
- *Last-minute repairs:* MPs claiming expenses to do up their second home to increase its value just before they planned to leave Parliament. The Fees Office routinely challenged such expenditure where an MP had announced an intention to stand down, but inevitably did not know about undeclared intentions to leave Parliament.

- *Maxing out:* MPs claiming amounts just below the thresholds above which receipts were required (e.g. items just below the £250 lower limit). Many MPs claimed this practice was to save bureaucratic paperwork and often led to them claiming less than they were entitled to.
- *March madness:* MPs rushing to spend money in the last month of the financial year to use up spare allowances. This feature of most annual budgeting systems will be familiar to many people who work for organisations that budget in this way.
- *Long distance shopping:* having furniture or other household goods delivered to the main home rather than the second home, raising the question of whether the item was really intended for the second home at all.
- *Keeping it in the family:* the allegation that MPs financed and/or improved their second home in order to pass it on or sell it at a discount to a family member. One ex-MP told the authors that the *Telegraph* had accused him of selling his second home cheaply after doing it up at public expense. The allegation was untrue, but his lawyers advised him against suing the *Telegraph* for defamation.[11]

Did all of these happen, and were they all wrong? Some of these practices were clearly against the Fees Office rules set out in the Green Book, for example claiming for a phantom mortgage. Such claims were also fraudulent, as the courts later decided in some cases (e.g. Morley and Chaytor). Buying goods or services for a home other than the MP's main home was also wrong and did occur (e.g. Margaret Moran wrongly claimed for a damp proof course in her family home, which was not her second home). Some practices were against the spirit but not the letter of the rules. This could be true in the case of an end-of-year spending spree, if MPs were tempted to buy or renew items when it was not strictly necessary. Checking on genuine need was not something the Fees Office was empowered to do: the MP's signature that the item had been purchased 'wholly, exclusively and necessarily' for a parliamentary purpose had to be accepted. But other aspects of these practices could be proper and acceptable. For example, switching the designation of homes between main home and second home often genuinely reflected a change of circumstances. This could happen when an MP was appointed as a government minister, and had to spend much more time in their ministry in London, and therefore moved their main base from the constituency to London. A problem for MPs was that, given the public mood, defence of what they had done was often impractical, even if they had done nothing wrong. Many MPs paid back money voluntarily even when they were in the right. The Fees Office investigated all the *Telegraph* reports. Where they found that MPs *had* broken the rules, they were required to pay money back.

'Your mum is going to prison'

Malcolm Jack, the then Clerk of the House and Chief Executive, had to decide quickly whether or not to call in the Metropolitan Police to investigate the leak. He kept the Speaker in the picture, but the decision was his, as data controller for the House, rather than Michael Martin's. That decision was taken swiftly and the police were invited to investigate, as there was *prima facie* evidence that a criminal offence (at least of theft and of handling stolen property) might have been committed.[12]

Following the initial publication, the Speaker had the weekend to reflect. There would be a joint meeting of the House of Commons Commission and the MEC on the evening of Monday 11 May. But, given the widespread concerns, he needed to make a statement to the House of Commons about the leak before that. He told the House about the Clerk's action in informing the police, and his decision not to seek an injunction. He also said he was writing to the *Telegraph* telling them of 'the serious security implications if personal data that might expose Members and others to risks to their safety were to be published.' In fact, as Dr Julian Lewis MP pointed out, the *Telegraph* had taken some care to protect such information.

But it was the next exchange in the Commons that helped to seal Michael Martin's future. Kate Hoey MP challenged the wisdom of seeking to bring in the Metropolitan Police when they had other, much worse, problems to deal with. The Speaker responded,

Let me answer the hon. Lady. I listen to her often when I turn on the television at midnight, and I hear her public utterances and pearls of wisdom on Sky News – it is easy to talk then. Let me put this to the hon. Lady and to every hon. Member in this House: is it the case than an employee of this House should be able to hand over any private data to any organisation of his or her choosing? [...] I just say to the hon. Lady that it is easy to say to the press, 'This should not happen', but it is a wee bit more difficult when you have to do more than just give quotes to the *Express* – or the press, rather – and do nothing else; some of us in this House have other responsibilities, other than just talking to the press.[13]

When Michael Martin laid into Hoey he lost the confidence of many of his remaining supporters, a number of MPs told us.[14] One thought his tone was sneering.

When the MEC met that evening, it decided to try to accelerate the publication of redacted scans by the House. Andrew was asked to write to MPs explaining to them the implications of the leak, for example what to do about the risk that information about their staff or their credit card details might become public. The Fees Office set up a helpline for them. Some MPs were merely distressed, others extremely anxious. Many phoned the Fees Office for help and advice, or to complain. Don Touhig MP told us that the party whips supported MPs who were on the edge of breakdowns or whose families were targeted in their constituencies.[15] He related one instance where the child of an MP was told, 'Your father's a ****ing crook'. The son of one MP was told by a school friend, 'My mum says that your mum is going to prison.' For another, the accusations were far worse than an earlier false newspaper story claiming that it was no surprise that her husband had left her.[16]

On Tuesday 12 May, Malcolm Jack and Andrew Walker were summoned to appear before the Committee on Members' Allowances. Andrew recalls that the atmosphere was hostile. One MP in particular was trying to bully him into admitting that the leak had come from the Fees Office and was therefore his fault: it seemed probable to a number of MPs that a mole was to blame. Andrew refused to agree with the implication that his staff were at fault: it very much reminded him of the hostile cross-examination he had had the previous year in the Information Tribunal – not an experience he wanted to repeat.

Another official who was present told us that the MPs on the commit-tee were furious with officials.[17] The MPs had a feeling of being perse-cuted, the official said, but no one was saying 'Gosh, we've got to get this right.' The feeling of persecution was understandable; the search for an internal scapegoat to persecute in turn was not.

As the *Telegraph* stories began to appear, MPs had to prepare for the possibility that they would be next in line. There was a daily sense of foreboding among MPs who had not yet been 'done'. Nausea hit them each afternoon as they waited for the email or call that would turn their lives inside out and give them very little time to respond. Some MPs decided that the best thing for them to do was to get ahead of the game and publish their own claims in order to pre-empt the *Telegraph*. The parties jumped into action. One senior Conservative told us that his party asked all MPs to report in as soon as they heard from the *Telegraph*.[18] In parallel, the party set up a 'star chamber' to look at the validity of their MPs' claims, and to start publishing the information on the Conservative Central Office website. The Shadow Cabinet felt it had to look as if it was doing something. Following this, the Fees Office found that more and more MPs started to make 'vol-untary' repayments of what had been judged excessive claims. This was to prove a challenge to an already overburdened Fees Office, whose systems were already close to breaking point.

The Fees Office reviewed the *Telegraph* stories each day. Many MPs were within the rules as the Fees Office operated them, but there were cases where the journalists had uncovered further information of which the Fees Office had been unaware, which altered the picture. Individual MPs asked the Fees Office for reassurance, or arguments to support their position, so that they could respond to the journalists' questions. But it was rarely possible for the Fees Office to check over four years of claims in the timescales allowed by the *Telegraph*'s publication sched-ule. And some MPs (at least a handful) were well outside the rules, and knew it. For example, Elliot Morley MP had continued to claim for a mortgage after he'd paid it off, as the *Telegraph* revealed on 14 May.

The pressure built in the media and within the Commons during that week. By Friday 15 May, the storm had become a deluge. MPs from all parties were on the back foot. Morley was suspended from the Parliamentary Labour Party.[19] On 16 May, the *Telegraph* targeted

David Chaytor MP for continuing to claim expenses on a mortgage he had already paid off. He, too, was immediately suspended from his party. Morley and Chaytor were both prosecuted. The Conservatives were not exempt from blame either. The following week the Tory grandee Bernard Jenkin was accused of renting his second home at public expense from his sister-in-law just across the road from a large home already owned by his wife. Renting from a family member had been banned since 2006 and the policy was published in the Green Book, but Jenkin blamed the Fees Office for not alerting him that his own arrangement no longer complied with the policy.[20]

By now, the Speaker's position was precarious. Calls for his resignation grew over the following weekend, and it was rumoured that Gordon Brown's support for him had been exhausted.[21] He made a statement to the House of Commons on the afternoon of Monday 18 May,

> Please allow me to say to the men and women of the United Kingdom that we have let you down very badly indeed. We must all accept blame and, to the extent that I have contributed to the situation, I am profoundly sorry. Now, each and every Member, including myself, must work hard to regain your trust.[22]

He went on to say that he had called an emergency meeting with the Prime Minister and the party leaders to discuss reforming the expenses regime. He acknowledged the review currently being undertaken by the Committee on Standards in Public Life (CSPL), but said that there was a need to deal with the immediate situation. Meanwhile, MPs were asked not to submit any more expenses claims. The House of Commons was truly in crisis mode. He concluded,

> I say again that we all bear a heavy responsibility for the terrible damage to the reputation of this House. We must do everything we possibly can to regain the trust and confidence of the people.

But the House was not satisfied. In the points of order that followed, MPs from all the main parties weighed in to support a motion of no confidence in the Speaker, and to ask him to jump before he was pushed. One MP summed it up:

The statement you have made would have been extremely welcome had it been made a few weeks or months ago but I have very grave doubts, given the appalling situation in which we find ourselves – this midden of the House's own making – that any action taken by Members of this House will restore the trust that we need.[23]

It was too late. The House, led by the Speaker, had wasted its opportunities to put things right, and had to accept the consequences. Gordon Brown is said to have met Michael Martin privately later that afternoon and advised him to go.[24]

The next day, Tuesday 19 May, the Speaker made a statement to the House of Commons as soon as it convened at 2.30 pm:

Since I came to this House 30 years ago, I have always felt that the House is at its best when it is united. In order that unity can be maintained, I have decided that I will relinquish the office of Speaker on Sunday 21 June. This will allow the House to proceed to elect a new Speaker on Monday 22 June. That is all I have to say on this matter.[25]

His resignation statement had taken just 33 seconds to deliver.

It was a sad end to Michael Martin's speakership. The last Speaker to be forced from office had been Sir John Trevor in 1695; he had accepted a bribe of 1,000 guineas – a huge sum in those days. Martin's failure was not venal, and in some respects he was the fall guy for a collective failure of the whole House of Commons, as Matt, the *Telegraph*'s cartoonist, commented the next day: [*One MP to another*] 'As soon as I saw what I'd been up to, I knew the Speaker had to go.' Shirley Williams was sympathetic to Michael Martin. He was a 'warm and kindly man', she wrote. But then she summed up what other MPs must have come to feel:

I suspect he had little idea how crudely the moth-eaten expenses system was being milked by the MPs who had voted to make him their Speaker. But that he continued to see himself as their champion rather than as the champion of the people who elected them is undoubted. It means that he cannot be the person charged with the reform of expenses, let alone with the reform of Parliament itself.[26]

He was made a life peer some months later.

Desperate measures

A finger was urgently needed in the dyke to stop the flood of criticism that would engulf the House if nothing was done. But a quick and dirty fix would not solve the problem for the longer term. And, sadly, none of the changes adopted would have the effect of restoring public confidence in Parliament and politicians. Fundamental damage had already been done.

The MEC met on the Wednesday afternoon and decided on emergency measures. The Prime Minister and the other party leaders, plus Don Touhig, the Chair of the Members' Allowances Committee, joined them. In the early evening, following this meeting, the Speaker made a further statement to the House.[27] The next morning the MEC met again to put the announcements of the previous day into effect. Instructed by the MEC, Andrew wrote to all MPs the following day with the details. The Fees Office was to reject all claims it felt were not reasonable. There would be no appeal against their decisions. Basic housing costs would be allowed, but purchase of household goods would not. 'Flipping' would be banned. MPs would have to pay capital gains tax on any profit from a property on which they had claimed the second home allowance. MPs who were married or in a civil partnership could claim only one second home allowance (ACA) between them. Finally, ACA claims for past years would be re-examined.[28] The new rules had immediate effect. MPs were given a week to put in claims for past spending under the old rules. These changes were ill thought through, and some were impractical, but the pressure to be seen to be taking action was intense.[29]

The MEC meeting on 19 May had also looked at more radical measures. The Prime Minister submitted a paper proposing major changes. All the main parties had now agreed that radical reform was needed: given the intensity of the crisis, they could wait no longer. They decided that the House's self-determination of their own pay and expenses had to be ended completely. Harriet Harman announced this to the House on 20 May, 'We are... proposing that this House moves from a system of self-regulation to a system of statutory regulation', she said.[30] There would be urgent consultation on a proposal to legislate for a new and independent Parliamentary Standards Authority, which would replace the Fees Office. The new authority would implement the findings of the Kelly Committee when it reported later in the year.[31]

In the debate, Shadow Leader of the House Alan Duncan accepted the proposals on behalf of the Opposition, as did David Heath for the Liberal Democrats. Don Touhig also welcomed the proposals and added,

> I hope the Government will consult and involve the staff of the Fees Office. They have served this place very well indeed. They help us in every way possible in trying to give us information and advice. Although we may feel bruised, they, too, feel somewhat bruised at present.[32]

John Prescott's tonic

The expenses scandal was to have a profound effect on MPs, Parliament and on democracy in the UK more generally. News of it even rippled throughout the world.[33] As Touhig had said, Fees Office staff were bruised. In the debate following the Leader's statement, Diane Abbott MP said that Fees Office staff should be treated with respect:

> Does she agree that it would be wrong for this House to deflect blame for the current crisis on expenses on to ordinary members of the Fees Office on average salaries, many of whom have served this House with great dedication for many years? There may be questions to ask at the very top of the Fees Office, but the ordinary staff are not responsible for the culture around expenses that has flourished for too long.[34]

Andrew recalls how one of his team in the Fees Office had already told him of the extreme pressure staff were under earlier in the year, working late and not taking leave. The *Telegraph* revelations increased the pressure further. Stressed and anxious MPs brought their problems into the Fees Office, or phoned up in distress. They sometimes boiled over. One member of staff felt there was a universal impulse to blame officials; others used the Fees Office as a shield. Bob Castle and his team withstood terrible pressure as the finger of suspicion was pointed at them: 'my team and I went through hell', he told us, until it was discovered that others were to blame.[35] But not all MPs blamed them. Andrew bumped into John Prescott in the street outside Parliament at the height of the storm. Prescott said he was sad to hear his MP colleagues blaming the Fees Office. 'Have you got five minutes?' asked Andrew, 'If so, the staff would love you to pop in and have a word with them.' 'I'll come in right now', said Prescott. They entered the Fees Office together. The staff gathered round him, and he gave an extempore five-minute speech. Staff members remembered it years later – one recalled Prescott saying, 'Don't you lot feel guilty, it's their own bloody fault.' The Fees Office was at a low ebb, and Prescott's visit was a much-needed tonic.

When the Leader announced a new Parliamentary Standards Authority to take over the Fees Office's work, staff had a new worry: would they have a job in a few months' time? No one could tell them the answer.[36] There were other pressures on staff too: the name of one who had been challenging MPs' claims was made public. She was then doorstepped by a reporter. Other staff received hate mail. The police were informed. The House's consultant occupational physician, Dr Ira Madan, got in touch. Could she help to support staff? She'd be happy to see staff who were worried or anxious. A number took her up on her offer.

A memorable house

The most memorable house of that week of crisis was not the House of Commons but Sir Peter Viggers' duck house. It became the most enduring icon for the whole episode. This was ironic, because no money was ever paid to him for this pond feature, and it was doubtful even if it had been claimed for. Like Douglas Hogg, he had got into the habit of submitting to the Fees Office information on the upkeep of his second home that far exceeded the amount of allowances available. He had

'Make the most of this. Our man is being forced to stand down at the next election.'

asked the Fees Office to determine what was allowable, and restrict his payment to that amount. Thus, the Fees Office paid £10,769.94 out of the total bill of £18,522.59. The £1,645 for the pond feature was marked 'not allowable', and was not paid. The *Daily Telegraph*'s report on 21 May by Nick Allen was mostly accurate (unlike other newspapers that followed up the story). But the *Telegraph* could not resist milking the story with its implicit ridicule. Later that day, the *Telegraph* published a piece by Alastair Jamieson, 'So just what is a duck house?' The following day, Bryony Gordon provided a whole page piece on a Lincolnshire duck breeder's views on duck houses; Nick Allen followed up his article by asking where the duck house was now, as recent aerial photographs showed it had gone; and Matt's cartoon on the *Telegraph* front page showed two ducks eyeing up the duck house and saying, 'Do you think we could fit a plasma TV in there?' Despite the careful words in the original article, readers were left with the impression that expenses for the duck house had been claimed and paid.

SPEAKER'S SCAPEGOAT

Official who signed off MPs' expenses didn't even have a qualification in accountancy

By **Simon Walters**
POLITICAL EDITOR

THE row over MPs' expenses intensified last night as it was revealed that the parliamentary finance chief who signs off their claims had no formal accountancy skills – and that he feared he would be sacked when he warned the Commons Speaker the system was being abused.

Andrew Walker, who runs the Commons Fees Office responsible for MPs' wages and expenses, told Speaker Michael Martin more than five years ago that he must act to curb excessive claims. But Westminster sources say the Speaker told him not to meddle, and 'punished' him by refusing to speak to him for weeks at a time.

It is understood that Mr Walker felt he could be dismissed from his £125,000-a-year job as director general of resources at the Commons after issuing

Turn to Page 6 ⟩⟩

Rehashing news

In the face of the *Telegraph*'s scoop, what were the other newspapers to do? They still had back stories that they could rehash, but that would not compete with what the *Telegraph* was running. Andrew's phone was hot with calls from the media on 8 May and for the next few days. Even Ben Wicks, producer of the news quiz show *Have I Got News for You*, phoned to ask about gardening, but unfortunately Andrew did not have time to watch the next episode.

Most newspapers tried to follow up the same stories, but without adding much that was new. On 8 May, the *Guardian* ran a story about the leak itself. But they did not have a great deal to go on. The *Mail on Sunday*[37] ran stories about Commons staff, headlining Andrew as the 'Speaker's scapegoat' – a double-edged piece alleging that he was not professionally qualified, but that he had been told by Michael Martin not to meddle, who then punished him by refusing to speak to him.[38]

Malcolm Jack, the Clerk of the House, was targeted for having homes in three countries. The Speaker's Secretary wrote to the *Mail*'s editor later that week denying that the Speaker had bullied Andrew.

The difficulty faced by the *Telegraph*'s rivals was illustrated one week after the first revelations. On Friday 15 May, the *Telegraph* triumphantly announced a circulation boost of 220,000 copies and ran a story about the justice minister Shahid Malik's expenses. He immediately stood down from his role, although he was later exonerated.[39] In contrast, the other titles had to make do with other news items. The *Guardian* ran a four-page spread on Heather Brooke (including two full-page photos of her) entitled 'Unsung Hero', while Sam Coates in the *Times* rehashed his blog about Andrew's evidence at the Information Tribunal 15 months before.[40]

Unsung hero

The only reason we know anything about all those claims for light bulbs and moat cleaning is that campaigning journalist **Heather Brooke** has spent the last five years fighting tooth and nail for MPs to come clean about their expenses . . .

Other newspapers were less scrupulous than the *Telegraph*. For example, the *Independent* accused Sir Peter Viggers of 'spending' £1,645 on the duck house. Of course he had indeed spent that money on it, but it was his own money, not public money. Some of the reporting in other newspapers was even more inaccurate. The Fees Office started compiling a list of claims they had turned down in relation to items mentioned in the press, in order to demonstrate that there was proper scrutiny and that the Fees Office was not simply in MPs' pockets.

Many MPs at the time felt that the media reporting was unfair. Don Touhig, previously a journalist himself, had reservations about the standard of reporting. He told us, 'I think the *Telegraph* did the right thing',[41] but he felt that sometimes other media outlets had scant regard for the facts. He recalled that there had been a witch-hunt of Sir Peter Viggers, with his local paper doing a countdown: 'X days until Viggers goes.' He said that journalistic standards had dropped, but that politicians were partly to blame for getting into the habit of giving anonymised briefings themselves.

An ex-minister told us how he had previously cultivated the press; he described himself as having been a bit of a 'media tart'. He developed

lots of relationships that had helped him to explain government policies and put out messages through journalists he trusted. There was a
mutual benefit. But this did not help when the expenses crisis broke.
At that stage, he said, there was no point in talking to journalists –
they just wanted 'heads on spikes. They wrote inaccurate nonsense'.

MPs did not sue for defamation even when stories about them
were untrue, as they were sure to lose out in the eyes of the public. A
Liberal Democrat ex-MP told us how a newspaper had criticised him
for selling his constituency flat to his daughter after he had allegedly
done it up on expenses.[42] The allegations were untrue. He had consulted a prestigious law firm who had advised him not to sue: in the
febrile political climate he was likely to lose irrespective of the facts
and a lawsuit would be likely to damage him more than the newspaper.
His honesty had been challenged unfairly, but he felt powerless to do
anything about it. He thought that many MPs in the scandal felt the
same.

Some people felt that, by starting with Labour ministers, and
dubbing David Cameron as 'Mr Clean', the *Telegraph* was showing
evidence of a bias in favour of the Conservatives. Valentino Larcinese
and Indraneel Sircar examined whether media reporting had been fair.
After researching the coverage in seven newspapers, including the *Telegraph* from 8 May 2009 onwards, they found 'only limited evidence
of partisan coverage of the expenses scandal across newspapers'.[43] In
general the media did not appear to favour one party over another.

Greater attention had been paid to frontbench MPs and other senior
MPs from the two main parties, but women MPs were mentioned
more frequently. Was this because women MPs were more greedy or
less trustworthy than male MPs? A study by Georgina Waylen and
Ros Southern found that women MPs' behaviour in expenses claims
was similar to that of male MPs.[44] They were neither more nor less
corrupt. But women MPs were punished more than male MPs by both
the media and the electorate for any perceived wrongdoing. Somehow,
societally we *expected* women MPs to behave better than male MPs,
and were disappointed when they did not.

Parliamentary Lobby correspondents hardly contributed to the
coverage. Had they been asleep on the job? Many of them spend
their working hours in Parliament rather than in newspaper offices,

occupying the 'Burma Road' corridor in the Palace of Westminster. One correspondent we interviewed said that most lobby correspondents had been aware of issues bubbling around on expenses during the mid-2000s but did not have hard evidence.[45] Another speculated that they were fearful of antagonising their informants or even, in the case of older journalists, deferential to them.[46] But they did not realise the scale of the issue until the *Telegraph* story broke. That might have been partly because some lobby journalists were close to MPs. Some were *too* close, one journalist told us.[47]

A new Speaker

The newspaper revelations continued. Some accused the *Telegraph* of artificially prolonging the stories. But Robert Winnett pointed out that the newspaper had a vast amount of data to review. By the end of May they had many MPs' expenses still to examine, so the project carried on. The revelations continued until 20 June, when they published the complete list.

Following Michael Martin's resignation, the process of electing a new Speaker began.[48] There were many candidates to begin with from both sides of the House, who set out their platforms and held hustings. The eventual winner, John Bercow, was a Conservative whose right wing credentials had been impeccable some years earlier, but he was now widely perceived as moving towards the centre left. In 2008 he had written the Bercow report, commissioned by the Labour government, which argued for better coordination of services for people with speech, language and communication needs. The report was widely welcomed by the educational special needs community. He told us that his decision to stand as a candidate for the speakership had been the result of a long-standing ambition in preference to pursuing a ministerial course. He stood on a parliamentary reform ticket. He favoured reforms to the House of Commons that would make the government more accountable to Parliament and give backbenchers more say in setting the House of Commons agenda. At his first hustings he addressed the issue of expenses. His pitch was 'It has been overgenerous, but we have to live in two places. Therefore there will have to be an

THE  TIMES

Max 21C, min 6C   Friday June 19 2009 timesonline.co.uk No 69666   Newspaper of the Year **90p**

Freedom of information

● Shame of MPs after release of expenses   ● Officials black out many crucial details

Philip Webster Political Editor
Dominic Kennedy, Francis Elliott

MPs were shamed yesterday after the much vaunted opening of their expenses files produced a humiliating cover-up of the most serious abuses.

Parliament and its officials were accused of colluding in a £2 million operation to protect the greedy as the supposed new era of transparency was drowned in a sea of black ink.

More than a million pieces of paper — bills, receipts and claim forms — were posted on the House of Commons website shortly before 6am, but thousands of them were indecipherable. Much of the information was blacked out as the MPs, helped by the authorities, censored incriminating material, citing security and privacy.

The redactions included addresses, making it impossible to tell from the official version which MPs "flipped" their second homes to maximise returns from the taxpayer or changed the designation of their homes to avoid paying capital gains tax.

Even so, the exposure produced more dramatic developments in a saga that has shaken politics to the core.
⬧ It was slipped out last night that about 200 MPs had rushed to pay back nearly £500,000 because of public outrage over their claims.
⬧ In four years Labour MPs have channelled £235,000 of taxpayers' money to a computing consultancy that operates from party headquarters. Several Cabinet ministers have used their Commons allowance to pay Computing for Labour to manage communications in their constituency offices.
⬧ The papers revealed that Alistair Darling, the Chancellor, asked his accountants to change the wording of an invoice for tax advice before he submitted it to the fees office and controversially claimed it back on expenses.
⬧ David Cameron said that he would repay almost £1,000 in overpayments on mortgage, electricity and phone bills. He blamed the overpayment on an "inadvertent administrative error."

The expenses scandal has already ended the careers of 20 MPs, and more are expected to follow.

The cover-up shocked campaigners. Commons officials had removed references to previously revealed absurdities such as the cleaning of moats and the purchase of houses for ducks. The names of companies providing goods and gardening services were also blanked out to avoid having to show where the work was done.

Without earlier disclosures no one would have known that Hazel Blears claimed second home expenses for three different properties in a year, or

that the second home of Margaret Moran, who claimed £22,000 to treat dry rot, was in Southampton, 100 miles from her constituency.

The official record would not have exposed the Labour MPs David Chaytor and Elliot Morley, who claimed thousands of pounds against mortgages that had already been paid off. This only emerged after their addresses were cross-checked against Land Registry records.

Nevertheless, the political establishment was smarting as the full tawdriness of its claims was laid bare to a public audience. By 4.30pm 250,000 people had visited the website and clicked on 15 million pages.

The receipts revealed that the Conservative MP Graham Brady claimed £71 to get back into his house after being locked out and that the former minister John Reid claimed £29.99 for a book explaining basic economics.

Tony Blair, the former Prime Minister, spent £260 on shredding as he wound up his parliamentary affairs, and claimed £6,990 for repairing the roof of his constituency home two days before leaving No 10. The fees office reduced his claim to £4,453. Others spent a fortune on paper clips, matches, milk frothers, assertiveness training courses and the Racing Post.

MPs themselves were hugely embarrassed by the cover-up. Vince Cable, of the Liberal Democrats, said: "If people had had to rely on this information to find out about their MPs they would have been faced with swaths of black ink rather than information about the flipping of homes and the avoidance of capital gains tax. It took a huge amount of effort from campaigners, my Liberal Democrat colleagues and other independent-minded MPs to get even this much information released. It's a shame that it is still far less transparent than it could have been."

The Commons authorities spent more than £140,000 trying to avoid publishing the expenses before being defeated in the High Court in May last year. The process of scanning and editing all the receipts from 2004-08 has cost a further £2 million and taken 13 months to complete.

Sir Stuart Bell, of the Commons Commission, described the disclosure as unprecedented and said that it was right that information was blacked out to protect MPs' privacy and security.

Maurice Frankel, of the Campaign for Freedom of Information, said: "The mood of the House of Commons was that they did not want any of this information to be published and, failing that, as little as possible."

Leading article, page 2
Reports and analysis, pages 4-11

RECEIPT / INVOICE

CUSTOMER RECEIPT

FOR: 2520.00(GBP)

Please keep this copy

Part of a receipt for furniture submitted by Hazel Blears for November 2004. She also claimed £1,812 for a TV, radio and bed. The files show she spent £2,673 on furniture and bedding in March 2005 but not which home she furnished

---

independent body to devise, implement and oversee a new system.'[49] He thought there should be accountability for expenditure, so he did not support the idea of a *per diem* system or an attendance allowance as Gordon Brown had earlier proposed. Instead, accountability would be secured by the system being both devised and managed externally. He was duly elected Speaker, and took up office on 22 June.

Meanwhile, on 18 June the House of Commons published the long-awaited scans of the expenses of all MPs for the past four years online. On the face of it, MPs' expenses had already been done to death in the press. But once the data had been released at 6 am, public access skyrocketed. By 4.30 pm that day there had been a quarter of a million visits to the website and nearly a million page views. The majority of visitors had been referred from the *BBC News* website. While the public had already seen the *Telegraph* reportage, including a few photographs of scanned expenses claims, many were unprepared for the fully redacted versions that now appeared. First, the House of Commons versions had many more items blacked out than they had seen in the newspapers. Secondly, everything was obliterated in heavy black, not just masked in grey. The volume of redactions had grown over the months as MPs had sought to have more items hidden, so the impression was again that the House of Commons had still not listened to public concerns.

On 19 June, there was a knock on Dr Richard Walker's front door in the town where Andrew Walker lived. A dark-haired reporter and cameraman were looking for Andrew Walker of the Fees Office. Did he live here? No, said Dr Walker. After he'd shut the door on the TV crew, he phoned Andrew Walker (no relation) and left him an answerphone message: 'I suspect this happens all the time to you at the moment,' he said. Andrew was in another part of town having a check-up on his teeth. Never before had he been so grateful that he was visiting the dentist.

Three Herculean tasks

The scene was set for major changes. The crisis in public confidence generated by the *Telegraph* stories forced the House of Commons to coalesce in a way it had not been able to a year earlier. The election of a new Speaker helped, although a number of the reforming steps now taken were actually decided in Michael Martin's final month, after he had announced his resignation. After the confusion, misunderstandings, internal wranglings, distrust and crossed wires of the previous 18 months, the solutions adopted were straightforward, if not entirely plain sailing.

First, the Parliamentary Standards Bill[50] went through Parliament at breakneck speed. This legislation set up the Independent Parliamentary Standards Authority, IPSA, to decide on MPs' pay and expenses.

IPSA would also administer the system and investigate possible wrong-doing by MPs. The bill also introduced the new criminal offences of knowingly providing false or misleading information in a claim for an allowance; failing without reasonable excuse to comply with the rules on registration; and breaching the rules that prohibit paid advocacy. Given that it made an important constitutional change in taking away part of Parliament's self-determination, it was important to get the new law right. It was introduced on 23 June with a view to complet-ing all of its parliamentary stages in just over a week. Some expressed concern at the speed,[51] recalling the ill-fated example of the Dangerous Dogs Act where Parliament had acted in haste, but repented at leisure.

The Clerk of the House, Malcolm Jack, quickly reviewed the bill. Some aspects of it concerned him, particularly those which could have an adverse impact on parliamentary privilege, notwithstanding the constitutional provisions of Article IX of the Bill of Rights of 1689, which says, 'the freedom of speech and debates or proceedings in Parliament ought not to be impeached or questioned in any court or place outside Parliament.' Clause 6 of the Parliamentary Standards Bill as published would have given the courts powers to make deter-minations in respect of parliamentary proceedings and would have impeded the freedom of speech in such proceedings. The Clerk also raised concerns about other clauses of the bill. He wrote rapidly to the House of Commons Justice Committee and he, the Speaker's Counsel and another senior clerk gave evidence to the committee at a hearing. The committee in turn made urgent recommendations in a report on 1 July.[52] The government made alterations to the bill as a result. The Clerk of the House's courage, perspicacity and quick reactions had averted a constitutional blunder. The bill received Royal Assent on 21 July.

Urgent steps were taken to set up IPSA. By the autumn a chair-man (Sir Ian Kennedy) and chief executive (Andrew Macdonald) had been found, and they began the daunting task of setting up IPSA and getting it operational in time to hit the ground running from the general election in May 2010. There was much criticism by MPs about the cost of IPSA – it was inevitably more expensive to run as a stand-alone organisation than the Fees Office had been. And the service it provided in the early days fell well below many MPs' needs. This was a

major challenge for new MPs, as IPSA was initially slow to pay (grap-
pling with the huge challenges of setting up a new body), meaning that
MPs who had used up all their ready funds on their election campaign
ran up large debts to set up their new offices. Andrew recalls MPs
coming to see him in a furious rage about what they saw as IPSA's poor
performance and lack of sympathy for their needs, while IPSA junior
staff felt helpless and bullied.

Secondly, the Committee on Standards in Public Life review, led
by Sir Christopher Kelly, would be completed and published later in
the year. Sir Christopher told us that when it launched the inquiry in
2009, the CSPL recognised that there had been false starts in 2008,
and therefore saw the need to produce something substantial.[53] It also
wanted to build consensus and to help people reach conclusions. But,
by the time it reported, some key decisions had already been taken
(for example, the setting-up of IPSA), so it was focusing on a moving
target. Its report was published on 1 November.[54] It made 60 recommendations, covering not just second homes (the public purse should
not help MPs to *purchase* a second home), but also the employment
by MPs of family members, the abolition of the Communications
Allowance, and ensuring that the expenses system did not subsidise party political activity. It recommended that IPSA should be
given enforcement powers to ensure that MPs complied with their
decisions.

Reflecting on the experience, Sir Christopher said that if the decision to set up IPSA had not already been made, the committee would
not necessarily have come to the conclusion that an external organisation was needed. Looking back at the scandal, he said that outright
fraud had been a relatively minor element. But he felt there was 'something about what you have to be to be an MP' – for example, MPs
needed to be risk-takers – that may have spilled over into their use of
expenses. In his view, MPs were not paid enough relative to alternative
occupations if the House of Commons was to continue to attract good
candidates with wide experience, though he saw that the public would
never accept this. At the same time, the regulatory regime was inadequate – it was too lax: he referred to the 'feebleness of the Fees Office'
for encouraging MPs to claim, rather than acting as guardians of the
system and the spirit of its rules. Finally, problems arose because living

"YOU CAN'T   "OH YES I CAN!"
CATCH ME!"

costs were met on an individual basis (for example, second homes), rather than the Scandinavian system of state provision in kind.[55] MPs still made the mistake of allowing practices to continue that people outside Parliament would find unacceptable.

The third task in cleaning the Augean stable fell to Sir Thomas Legg QC. Sir Thomas had been recruited as an external member of the House of Commons audit committees some years previously, and had more than once raised concerns about the audit and accountability of MPs' expenses.[56] In early June 2009 the MEC, still under Speaker Martin, decided in the light of the *Telegraph* stories that MPs' second home allowances since 2004 should be re-examined. The newspaper stories had raised allegations about misuse of public funds. The police were investigating a number of suspected crimes by MPs. Six MPs were prosecuted. Three of them tried to argue that the prosecutions would infringe parliamentary privilege.[57] The three took their case to the Court of Appeal and ultimately to the Supreme Court. They lost.

The courts ruled that the claiming of expenses by MPs was not a proceeding in Parliament, so parliamentary privilege did not apply. In its summary, the Supreme Court said, 'Scrutiny of claims by the courts will not inhibit freedom of speech or debate. The only thing that it will inhibit is the making of dishonest claims.'[58] The MPs' case was not supported by Parliament, which did not see the administration of MPs' expenses as protected by privilege. All six were found guilty of false accounting. Five were sent to jail.[59]

But how were all the other allegations to be resolved? The MEC wanted to deal with the matter quickly, and identified Sir Thomas as a trustworthy and credible person who could hit the ground running. On 10 June the Legg review of MPs' use of the Additional Costs Allowance was announced.[60] On 23 June Harriet Harman announced his appointment to the House.[61]

The MEC felt that it would be unfair to judge MPs' use of the ACA against an entirely new set of criteria or rules, so the terms of reference stipulated that they should examine payments against the rules and standards in force at the time. This was later to become a point of contention.

Sir Thomas told us that when he began his investigations he felt, as a former civil servant, that MPs did not seem to share the same public service ethic. (He told a story of how, when he had started as a junior in 1962, his boss always tried to use second-hand envelopes, saying 'We must remember, Tom, it's not our money'.) He formed the impression that, while most MPs were not especially greedy or profligate, there did seem to be a sense among some of them that because they were elected they could do what they wanted.[62]

He built a team of Commons insiders as well as outsiders, led by Edward Wood, an experienced senior manager from the House of Commons Library. MPs began to be concerned when the team started to show that it was independent of the Fees Office. He told us his most difficult task was the interpretation of the existing rules, which he was bound to apply. Understanding what these rules were and how they should be applied was very challenging. He took the view that he had to infer detailed criteria, such as monetary limits for cleaning and gardening, which looked to some MPs as if he was changing or introducing new rules retrospectively – something he felt emphatically that he was not doing. He understood that some MPs felt that this was unjust, and that if a public authority (in this case the Fees Office) had agreed a claim then it should be regarded as approved. But this, he said, ignored the fact that many such approvals by the Fees Office had been plainly incorrect. When the direction of the review became clear, Labour MP Tony Wright commented,

> My worry is he's gone for the easy stuff. He's not asked questions about MPs with vast mortgages or who have been doing property deals or haven't paid proper capital gains tax. My question is how have they passed his test of reasonableness when others with cleaning or gardening bills have not?[63]

Sir Thomas went before the MEC and was given a critical reception. He speculated to us, 'I think they may have expected me to let them off more lightly than I did.'

The review went on for longer than had been hoped. When it appeared in February 2010, the report ran to 237 pages, covering hundreds of MPs, many of whom had to repay money.[64] Sir Paul Kennedy, a former senior judge, had been asked to hear any appeals on equitable grounds against Legg's decisions. Some MPs did appeal, and 44 had their penalties adjusted. In total, £1.2 million was paid back, though the review itself had cost more than that. But as one insider explains: 'The audit wasn't a debt-collection exercise: it was intended to identify any expenses which MPs had been paid but were not entitled to, as part of the long road to rebuilding credibility and trust.'[65] Legg argued, and explained in his report, that it could not be acceptable under the rules as they stood for an individual MP to pay the whole of the £24,000 allowance to a cleaner. His decisions were based on the rules at the time, he said, as they had to be interpreted in the light of the decisions and declarations of the House itself.

Many MPs were exasperated by the review. Some felt that the outcome was unfair. Former MP Ann Widdecombe wrote, 'Rumour had it that Legg, far from applying the rules prevailing at the time, chose to impose retrospective limits for gardening and cleaning. It was both unjust and illogical.'[66] One MP told us that not only had Legg, in his view, made up rules retrospectively, but he had also said that some people had spent too much on cleaning, which amounted to punishing those MPs who paid cleaners a generous wage.[67] Others were concerned that the time it took to finalise the review and the subsequent appeals would affect their electoral chances. From the MPs' point of view, it was the damage to their reputations that was more painful than paying back money.[68] That said, a subsequent study found that while the expenses scandal had a *general* effect on the public's perception of MPs as a group, the fact of whether Legg had required them to pay back money or had exonerated them made no discernible difference to whether or not electors voted for them in the May 2010 Géneral Election.[69]

MPs did have a point. While they were collectively responsible for a system of second homes support that appeared over-generous, at the same time many individual MPs found that they were required to pay back money that had been claimed and paid in good faith within the rules set out in the Green Book. But whether it was Legg's intention or not, the *realpolitik* of the situation was served by his review: it was perceived by the media and public as having teeth (the *Telegraph*'s leading article on the day the report was published was headed 'a damning indictment of brazen dishonesty'). The media seemed satisfied, but many MPs were not.

Were the six MPs found guilty in court the only criminals? Negatives are difficult to prove, so it would be impossible to say for certain whether or not there were others who got away with it. But the *Telegraph*'s investigation was wide ranging and extensive. Subsequently, thorough reviews by the police and Sir Thomas Legg did not throw up further cases for prosecution. It seems likely therefore that the criminals who had committed fraud, false accounting or forgery were identified, dealt with and paid the price.

The 2010 general election was looming. The timing of the Legg report ensured that the expenses issue was still in the public mind in the run-up to the election. It almost certainly affected some MPs' decisions to stand down. The reputations of politicians in general had been damaged for years, as the Hansard Society's annual audits of political engagement would show over the years that followed.[70] But the shock of the crisis also created opportunities. As John Bercow told us, the atmosphere of the crisis was helpful in the wider reforms that he and others in the House of Commons would now pursue. In the wake of the scandal, the Wright Committee made recommendations in November 2009[71] to reform management of the business of the House, to reform select committees and to involve the public more. That, at least, was a positive.[72]

Black humour

Amid the vituperation and accusations against politicians and parliamentary officials, the British spirit succeeded in throwing a few shafts of humorous light on the scandal. During 40 years in the public service, Andrew Walker received few letters of a personal nature. But 2009 was an exception. Of course there were deeply unpleasant missives, such as the one he received following Peter Oborne's piece in the *Daily Mail* on 11 April, which had described him as the 'the real culprit in the scandal of MPs' expenses'. The anonymous correspondent had cut out the article and scrawled across it in capitals 'YOU ARE AS CORRUPT AS THE MPs YOU TOADY UP TO'. But the scandal gave the British public an opportunity to show some wry humour, too.

```
Mr Andrew Walker
Director General of Resources
House of Commons
London
11th April 2009

Dear Sir

I was having a clear out at my home and I came
across a spare bath plug. I wondered if Miss Jacqui
Smith could make use of it. I also have fridge and
television, both in excellent condition, which I no
longer require. Could Miss Jacqui Smith or any of
her colleagues make use of these? I could deliver
them free of charge either to their main home or
second home
```

If they are of no use, then I will donate them to a
charity for the homeless.

I look forward to hearing from you.

Regards

Mrs [Name]

[Bath plug and two pence coin taped to letter]

16th May [2009]

Dear Fees Office

Please remit my £10 from Tesco and also £23,400 of
other expenses and £14 million for my new house.

Thanks

[Name]

[Tesco receipt for £10 enclosed]

1st June 2009

Dear Sir

Please find my bill for lawn seed and duck tape
enclosed to be paid from the money pot.

I'm not an MP according to the rules but I don't see
why rules should matter. I have the necessary brass
neck and thick skin and if there are any complaints
from people who fail to appreciate my shallow and

unfettered ambition for social status, I shall 'tough it out' and blag my way to the next election.

Yours faithfully

[Name]

[Homebase receipt attached for £14.76]

15/5/09

I would like to enclose my expenses for your perusal.

Mortgage	£350 per month
Gas	£25 per month
Electric	£40 per month
House insurance	£30 per month
Television licence	£17 per month
Catalogue for clothes	£30 per month
Food varies say about	£50 per month
Car insurance	£17 per month
Petrol	£40 month varies
TOTAL	£559
Water rates	£35 per month
TOTAL	£694 per month

As you can see I pay out a lot on just basic things and I get £80 per week pension = equals £320 per month.

So ask yourselves 'how pensioners manage' or 'PERHAPS' you all do not live in the real world because pensioners and a lot of ordinary people do not live, but try to exist!

I await my cheque for all these expenses, please
send it as soon as possible.

[…]

Your 'untrusting' voter

[Name]

P.S. I have not claimed for the hanging baskets
or the sink plugs, broken vase or computer that
accidentally got wet, so my needs are very simple as
are my expenses, 'except' I do not have the money
to pay them

As you can tell I can't afford proper writing paper.
Should I claim for some?

P.P.S. Would it be possible for me to apply to
become an MP. At least I would be true to the cause
i.e. running our country, by respect, conviction
and honour.

Forgot

£2000 overdraft

19th May 2009

[prison number redacted]

HMP [location redacted]

I hope this letter finds you well. I am shaw you must
be bizy. But please can you anser a question which
I am shaw you are asked every day?

Please can you tell me why [location] Prison + all
other prisons all over the UK are full of ofenders
that have committed deception/theft for stealing
money from campany's that thay have workd for some
relativy small amounts 1k ect and thay have receve a
prison sentence. When a MP steals from the tax payers
pot that's OK becos it wos a mestak/oversite "O I am
sorry" is exceptabl and that mak's things all OK.
Brush under the capet. Lost in the old by sistam. Dus
this mean pepol that have dun the same as MP's will
thay naw be relecd Looking forward to your reply?

[Name]

[Spelling as in the original letter]

23rd May 2009

Due to the recent unforeseen announcement that the
'Speaker' Michael Martin is to resign, I would like
to take this opportunity to put forward my formal
application for 'Speaker of the House of Commons'.

Hopefully, by the time you receive this letter, the
position will still be vacant as I imagine you will
be inundated with speakers talking/writing to you.

With the role predominantly requiring vocals, I
thought it would be better to phone you instead of
writing. Unfortunately I was unable to source a
telephone number, as the 'men with moustaches' were
intolerant of my stammer.

I am confident that I have the credentials to achieve
the roles requirements……. And then some. After 15
years in the building trade, and occasional weekend/

bank holiday work at Sotheby's, using a hammer is
like second nature to me. Tying that in nicely with
my experience as a self-employed fast food trader
you'll have the perfect combination. Ok I know
shouting 'Hotdogs' is not quite the same as shouting
'Order!' but both words contain two letters which
are <u>exactly</u> the same (O and D). So I'm halfway there!

The only reservation that I have is regarding the
dress code. I've tried tight pants and a wig before,
but they really don't complement my blue eyes. As
a solution (rather than discarding my application
altogether) would it be possible to wear a baseball
cap and a kilt? (My mother's father was Scottish).
From my research I realise that I would be sat down
most of the time so I'm sure no one would notice my
leg wear anyway. Or failing that maybe tartan pants?
(My mother's father was Scottish).

I trust you will speak to Gordon and the guys about
my application to see what they think, and I'll look
forward to your reply.

Got to go now, I've got the plumber coming round to
fix a leak. Think it's coming from the tennis courts
or something.

Keep that seat warm!

Kind regards

[Name]

P.S. Just to rectify when I said I was halfway
there, I should have said $^2/_5$s as O and D are only 2
of the 5 letters of the word 'Order', not 2½ of the
5 or 40% instead of 50%, whichever you prefer.

Good job the role doesn't involve looking after anyone's figures!

19/6/09

Sir

My local MP, [xxx], has claimed £1,500 for bedroom decoration, despite earning £64,000 a year. I have an income as a pensioner of £10,499.81 p.a. I wrote to [my MP] recently to see if I was eligible for Warm Front assistance for double glazing.

He hasn't replied, so I've had to fork out for it myself, and will be in hock for the next 5 years as I repay the loan.

I'm enclosing a copy of the bill for you to refund to me.

Yours truly

Mrs [....]

"the unredacted life is one worth living", if Socrates were alive now, I'm sure he would echo this

7

Aftershocks

Owing to the expenses scandal the public fell further out of love with MPs, or at least had a new potent way to express it, and have remained out of love with them ever since. Politicians have always been loathed as a group but their constituents and local party members tended to love them; as individuals they were often put on a pedestal and treated as special. For a time after the expenses scandal, this special relationship nose-dived. MPs were spat on in supermarkets, sworn at in the street and attacked on the TV and the web. For MPs this was the worst media coverage of their lives: it went to the heart of their political identity by attacking their honour.

MPs' pain

The damage to MPs' reputations lived on. Women MPs were vilified more than men, and with the same amount of media attention were more likely to stand down.[1] One MP pointed out that women were attacked especially if they (or their relatives) were pretty; it was an excuse to have a photo of a pretty woman in the newspaper. There is nothing new here; the misogynistic treatment of women by the press has a long history. A woman MP was depicted some years earlier by a tabloid newspaper looking frumpy because she was pregnant, along with a caption implying 'no wonder her husband has left her for his secretary', but the story of her fiddling her expenses upset her far more.[2] One MP wrote on her blog at the time that the atmosphere in Westminster at the time was unbearable; everyone feared a suicide or at least that colleagues were at breaking point.[3]

The journalist who broke the story, Robert Winnett, was mindful of this impact at the time. He thought about how the revelations might impact on individual MPs' lives and their families; he was conscious of whether, for example, some might harm themselves. If representations were made by an MP that a story would be damaging, the *Telegraph* might delay publication or remove details, but they never pulled a story entirely. It was reassuring to the journalists that the political parties were there to support some MPs. But in practice there was little their party could do. One Labour MP whose expenses became national news was told by a colleague, 'this little poison will hang around your head for ever'.[4] Although it was more intense at the time of the scandal, the thought that people might remember them as 'disgraced' haunted MPs. One said that every time he walked into a room during the scandal he thought it fell silent, or it did not, and he wondered whether people were thinking/talking about his expenses story. For many MPs and their families, the emotional and political costs were severe. Even relatives were hounded by the more ruthless journalists – in one case an MP's father in the middle of treatment for cancer. MPs were mortified and although they felt a terrible sense of injustice, they could hardly defend themselves – that merely brought more opprobrium on their heads.

The impact on MPs' sense of identity was irreparable. According to one, the expenses scandal destroyed a generation of MPs.[5] If the public hated them, perhaps many MPs couldn't help but at least in part feel self-loathing; after all people are created through their interaction with others. One long-standing MP explained how the public's hate is hard to talk about: it is painful but it also sounds as if you are moaning.[6] MPs often talked more about the injustice done to their colleagues than themselves. On the Labour side, David Taylor MP was vilified by the *Telegraph* for expenses claims, but in that case his colleagues felt it was totally unfair and believed it contributed to his early death the following Boxing Day.[7] On the Conservative side, Emma was told that Douglas Hogg was a completely honourable man. His policy was to send all receipts to the Fees Office and to leave it to them to judge what could be covered. 'Of course he did not expect to get moat cleaning refunded,' said his former colleague.[8] Another MP, a former GP, highlighted the impact of public loathing by comparing how people relate to MPs in comparison to GPs. Whatever a GP does, they are seen by patients through a benign lens, so you are always good – as a consequence, you feel good about yourself. Whatever an MP does, in contrast, is viewed through a filter of distrust and suspicion, so whatever happens you are bad in both their eyes and to some extent your own.[9]

The psychological impact of the expenses scandal arose because MPs lost control of events and, in particular, the public reaction to the crisis. Lack of control over our working conditions is a good predictor of poor mental health, especially depression and anxiety.[10] A psychological study of MPs comparing their mental state in 2003 with 2010 showed a much higher proportion reporting poor mental health and well in excess of the working population. Half of the MPs in the sample stood down in the 2010 election, 27 per cent of them owing to the expenses scandal, according to their own explanations.

MPs' perceptions of the impact of the expenses crisis (percentages)[11]

Aspect of functioning	High negative impact	Moderate negative impact	Low negative impact	No impact
MP view of the job	58	22	11	9
MP view of the House of Commons	51	38	9	2
MP's ability to do the job	9	29	36	27
MP's health	9	11	31	49
MP's family (*n* = 14)	29	21	14	36

Percentages may add up to greater than 100 due to rounding.

For MPs it was undiluted pain, and for many it was long lasting. A number of MPs and ex-MPs we interviewed had not come to terms with how they had been treated. Some still felt the party bosses had been unjust in forcing them to pay back claims or stand down as MPs when they had kept within the rules from their own point of view. To some it seemed like an unnecessary act of self-humiliation in the name of party political advantage-seeking. Others felt the press had been cavalier and in some cases downright meretricious. Ten years on Ann Cryer, MP for Keighley until 2010, said, 'It just broke you up, just awful – a dreadful situation to be in. I've never really got over it', when she appeared on a BBC radio in April 2019, blaming the *Telegraph*'s reporting of her own expenses. She demanded an apology from a *Telegraph* journalist on the programme.[12]

Reputation: the loss of political capital

The wise man said: 'A good name is more desirable than great riches; to be esteemed is better than silver or gold.'[13] MPs' pain went beyond damage to their sense of themselves as moral beings. It ripped into the most precious political capital for elected politicians: their reputation. When Hazel Blears resigned due to pressure caused by the expenses scandal, a Labour colleague told the BBC,

> It's fine for people like myself to forgive Hazel. But it's not me who she's got to apologise to. It's the people of Salford and all the candidates that were standing on election day and the activists who were knocking on the doors. It's the upset that's caused there.[14]

The standing of MPs in the eyes of others, especially those who might vote for them or give other kinds of support, is not just about appearances. Reputation requires the endless renewal of relationships. To discern its importance, you merely have to follow MPs around as they go about their work. When Emma followed MPs in their constituencies as they knocked on doors and attended meetings in churches, community centres, business parks, housing associations or schools, they nearly always took photographs and emailed them to their staff or put them on Twitter themselves.[15] They do this partly so as to canvass with next election in mind, and they are becoming increasingly sophisticated in their election tactics. Stephen Pound, MP for Ealing North, calls on every newcomer to the constituency and all the estate agents let him know when new residents move in, even if they can't provide the names. He introduces himself, says, 'By the way the library is over there...', and offers other useful local information. He also sends letters to all his constituents, both old and new, and delivers them by hand – 150–200 a month – reaching all of them at least once between elections.[16]

For Richard Fenno, a political scientist, the magic ingredient in US politicians' relationships with their constituents is trust. 'If people like you and trust you as an individual, they will vote for you,' members told him.[17] US politicians and their constituents talk less about politics, and more about whether the representative can be trusted. Trust depends on moral approval, which takes time to nurture; it means getting close to people or giving the illusion of closeness. One US representative told Fenno that no one will vote against you if you are on a first-name basis; and if you chew their tobacco, then they will even fight for you. Another representative put it,

> The best way to win a vote is to shake hands with someone. You don't win votes by the thousands with a speech. You win votes by looking individuals in the eye, one at a time, and asking them. Very rarely will anyone ask you about how you stand on anything.[18]

So according to US Members of Congress, it is often not policy agreement that voters demand but a shared feeling of belonging.

Fostering trust to win political support is equally vital to UK politicians and they too believe 'there is no better alternative to pressing flesh and looking people in the eye.'[19] Repeatedly when Emma asked which part of the job MPs enjoyed, they brought their constituencies into the conversation: a place you can knock heads together, or convene critical meetings, and hurry along the progress of development. It brings with it a huge sense of satisfaction, a feeling that you are a person who can cheer people up or even sometimes totally transform their lives.

Caroline Lucas (@CarolineLucas)
01/02/2013 17:20
RT @ExeterStHall: Breaking News! We've done it!! Exeter Street Hall saved for the community. You are all AMAZING!!
Caroline Lucas, an MEP, Leader of the Green Party since 2010 and the UK's first Green MP, shows her support for a local community organisation

Despite their fears, curiously, the fury at politicians did not translate into a huge impact on the 2010 election. Voters did not appear to punish MPs severely through the ballot box; in fact, scholars have estimated the electoral cost of the expenses scandal at only 2 per cent.[20] Voters knew about misconduct in general – via the media, campaign groups and from politicians themselves – but did not have the details about their candidates or did not believe them. But even those that did refrained from punishing them; those who knew about misconduct were only 5 per cent less likely to vote for them. Turnout went up from 61 per cent in 2005 to 65 per cent in 2010, but this may have been because the expenses scandal was less of a shock to voters than it was to people inside the Westminster bubble. As we mentioned above, it possibly played into an existing narrative of corruption. If you think all MPs are corrupt, then voting against one on grounds of corruption might leave you with no one to vote for.

If MPs and the House of Commons had been guilty of hubris, then the nemesis of public exposure and vilification was, when it came, swift and severe. But was there a cathartic effect? Did MPs and onlookers learn from the experience?

Partial recovery

Robert Winnett told us that the political parties reacted to the scandal in different ways. Labour, especially the No 10 Downing Street machine, was hung up about the Prime Minister. Gordon Brown even took them to the press regulator.[21] That had clouded their wider response, and No 10 seemed to pay less attention to other Labour MPs. In contrast, he told us that David Cameron jumped immediately into reform mode – but then as Opposition leader rather than PM, he had fewer other concerns at the time. There had been a discussion among Conservative MPs about taking a class action against the *Telegraph* but they decided against it, whereas the pressure was on the government to change the system of expenses.

The two largest parties tried to distance themselves from the scandal and continue to do so, often digging MPs deeper into an over-simplified narrative. MPs were lumped together as a group exhibiting general immorality; as typified by the then leader of the Labour Party, Ed Miliband in August 2011:

> It's not the first time we've seen this kind of me-first, take what you can culture. The bankers who took millions while destroying people's savings: greedy, selfish, and immoral. The MPs who fiddled their expenses: greedy, selfish, and immoral. The people who hacked phones to get stories to make money for themselves: greedy, selfish and immoral. People who talk about the sick behaviour of those without power, should talk equally about the sick behaviour of those with power.[22]

However, the impact of the scandal on the institution of Parliament itself was restorative, at least to an extent. As one Labour MP put it, 'there have been some silver linings after the expenses nightmare. Everyone wanted to demonstrate that they were reformers.'[23] As a consequence, one political journalist has claimed 'We now have a different kind of politician.'[24]

Speaker John Bercow has talked about how the House of Commons has experienced a Doctor Who-like regeneration since 2010 for three reasons, arguably all helped by the expenses scandal.[25] First, the Coalition challenged both Westminster and Whitehall to devise new norms and opened up space for backbench ingenuity. They had to be seen to be taking drastic action towards reform to recover the reputation of Parliament. Secondly, the large intake of new Members arriving in 2010 into the two main parties was not only more diverse than ever before, but determined to bring about change. Many stood for Parliament because of the unprecedented resignations of so many MPs, stung by the expenses scandal. Finally, changes in the rules of the game transformed the way business was conducted. This came about under the leadership of a reforming Speaker who stood on a platform of recovery, sending a reform prospectus to all MPs just before the Speaker's election process,

> The next Speaker faces an unprecedented challenge – to help clean up politics, to place Parliament at the centre of an effective democracy and to build a relationship of mutual respect with the electorate.[26]

He was going to stand in any case to promote deeper scrutiny, more backbencher involvement and greater diversity, he told us, but the expenses scandal meant that all candidates had to address the crisis and need for reform. He was elected for a variety of reasons, but one Tory told him his greatest asset for the times was that 'You're splendidly ordinary', meaning he was a state school boy. The Speaker and those supporting reform, both officials and other MPs, were able to bring about change partly because the reputation of Parliament was at an all-time low, so anything that sounded as if it might strengthen it was difficult for the government to block. As Bercow put it, 'the lion was out of the cage', and no one could put it back in.[27]

In 2009 Parliament threw out the old expenses system and created a new body to regulate MPs' pay and allowances – the Independent Parliamentary Standards Authority. In record time this new body was established outside Parliament and processed MPs' claims, putting them all on the internet for everyone to see. The teething troubles, which meant that some MPs got into terrible debt, are now over and this works reasonably well, with the potential at least for transparency, accountability and a restoration of the public's trust in MPs' probity.

Of course it hasn't panned out quite like that. The media obsession with expenses continues because it is marvellous ammunition for the local press to write scurrilous reports about MPs. Making fun of MPs spending money on toilet paper or on sugar to sweeten their constituents continues in a formulaic fashion. Take the example of a newspaper story published in September 2012.[28] Journalists studied expense claims and complained that there were increases between 2010/11 and 2011/12, despite the fact that 2010 would have been a shorter year because MPs were only elected in May and took some time to (re) establish their offices. The press picked out specific expenses from the information about each MP, implying that some wrong had been committed, including: two computers (£1,900), stationery (£638.92), newspapers (£23.30), sugar (61p), recycling bags (£2.40), a bus fare (£1.60), advertising an MP's surgery to constituents (£1,710), desk and office chair (£330.95), a Dictaphone (£52.99), cork boards (£17.46), and food and drink for an intern (£3.85). Wouldn't most offices have these or similar items? The whole article gives the impression that MPs are continually extravagant with taxpayers' money, whereas in reality many subsidise constituency costs, knowing that all claims are made public. MPs now mostly pay for anything that is likely to be picked on out of their own pocket, such as taxis or toilet paper. Such reports resonate with a now deeply entrenched narrative of MPs as corrupt, greedy and venal, but if MPs earn money on top of their salaries it is not through allowances – it is by having a second job outside Parliament.

The rise of the backbenchers

MPs also introduced reforms to the way Parliament works in order to create a good news story about parliamentary business. This came about because in 2009 Tony Wright (then a Labour backbench MP) wrote to PM Gordon Brown with some suggestions. Nine days later, on 10 June, Professor Wright was sitting in the Chamber and Jack Straw came up to him and asked: 'Did you know that the PM is about to announce the establishment of a committee on reform and you will be Chair?' He didn't.[29] The Wright Committee, as it came to be known, worked at tremendous speed with the guidance of the then Clerk of Committees, David Natzler. The Wright Committee members were champions of the backbencher at a moment when a new Speaker was clearly taking their side as well. Most of the committee members were approaching retirement – they had nothing to lose by opposing the whips and the interests of government. They came up with a series of proposals to challenge the dominance of the executive, even if only mildly. Mindful that whips favoured loyal party members on committees, and even tried to remove two troublesome committee chairs in 2001 – Gwyneth Dunwoody MP and Donald Anderson MP – only for them to have been reinstated by backbenchers, the Wright Committee recommended that the whole House should elect chairs to committees.

The other main proposal was for a Backbench Business Committee to plan the use of backbench time and a House Business Committee, with backbenchers represented on it, to agree government time.[30] Most of the time allowed for debate in the House of Commons is allocated to government business, and is largely under the control of the government's business managers. In contrast, the Backbench Business

Committee has only a limited allocation of time outside government control in which it can schedule subjects for debate suggested by back-bench MPs. The idea of a Backbench Business Committee came from Australia via the committee's Specialist Adviser (and later academic) Meg Russell.[31] The committee also encouraged action on the stalled process of introducing an e-petitions system. They had not forgotten how such reforms had been sabotaged in the past by whips, who saw them as anti-democratic, weakening party accountability and giving too much clout to whimsical backbenchers. So some Members sought support from party leaders and they went along and prepared themselves for a struggle. The Wright Committee managed to bring about a second debate before the General Election but the frontbenches conspired to try and water down some of the proposals.[32] The elections to committees were secured but frontbenchers colluded with pro-whip backbenchers to defeat reform without appearing too obstructive. So the 2005–2010 Parliament dissolved with no Backbench Business Committee.

At the 2010 general election, the turnover of MPs was greater than in the two previous general elections. There were 227 (35 per cent) new MPs, compared with much lower turnover in the previous elections. The demography of the House changed: more MPs than before were women (143, 22 per cent); 27 were from minority ethnic groups; and the average age of MPs was slightly younger than in the 2005 Parliament.[33] These changes, and the fact that no one party had an overall majority in the House of Commons, gave an opportunity for the reformers.

Many of the new MPs were intent on healing Parliament and politics after the expenses scandal. Former members of the Wright Committee, including Graham Allen, kept working away behind the scenes to make it happen. A group of NGOs working on governance – including the Hansard Society, Democratic Audit and UCL's Constitution Unit – had written in March that year to all MPs arguing for change.[34] The new coalition government had promised to implement the Wright proposals and some of the anti-reformers left the House at the election. New MPs were desperately trying to get to grips with the onslaught of being MPs and the Leader of the House, Sir George Young, was a reformer and even sat briefly on the Wright Committee

"Take me to your backbenchers."

(before being promoted). So, the proposal for a new Backbench Business Committee was passed in the new Parliament without a vote.

One of the most significant results of this committee was that MPs developed a new habit of working across parties outside of select committees. According to the committee's rules, when backbenchers propose debates they have to have cross-party support (including the main opposition) so there is an opportunity to express at least two sides to an argument. MPs and journalists agree that some of the backbench debates have been among the best of the 2010–15 Parliament and the public like them too. Typical viewing figures for BBC Parliament are 120,000 but backbench debates have attracted far more: 330,000 for Hillsborough and as much as 480,000 for the debate about holding an EU referendum.[35] In Sir George Young's words, backbenchers have gone where angels fear to tread, choosing topics that the government would prefer to avoid.[36]

Recovery from mistakes in politics always demands reform. According to many observers, since 2010 the select committees have been more impressive and the quality of scrutiny in Parliament has become stronger than it has ever been. But public ratings of politicians have continued to bump along the bottom, according to the Hansard Society.[37] One MP said to Andrew in 2009: 'It will take years – and maybe decades – for Parliament to recover from this disaster.' But it also depends on when you look and on what you perceive as a disaster – the challenge of any form of evaluation. When former MP David Heathcoat-Amory was asked about the scandal ten years on he told the BBC:

> If the expenses scandal did start to undermine people's faith in a political elite thinking that it had all the answers, if it undermined that and that led or fed the feeling that the European Union was a kind of bureaucratic racket at their expense and led to the referendum result then it was all worthwhile. Because I certainly always believed that we were better governing ourselves. And if so, my own loss of seat was not in vain.[38]

Officials and politicians

The expenses scandal dealt a serious blow to the relationship between MPs and officials. To understand how it changed, we need to explain how they got along in the first place.[39] The House of Commons service comprises several staff groups, analogous to but not quite civil servants. They include clerks, librarians, serjeants, caterers, official reporters, financial and administrative staff, and others. Many specialist roles are unique to Parliament and some – in particular clerks and serjeants – go back centuries. In the 1990s, each of these groups had its own culture and ethos. The clerks did not *run* the House of Commons administration, but the chief Clerk, the Clerk of the House, was accepted by all as the lead official.

Even though the large majority of House staff are not clerks, until recently it was primarily the clerks who used to set the tone for managing officials' relationships with the Speaker and with MPs more generally. They see themselves as serving Parliament through MPs or 'Members', as staff call them, and it is a matter of some importance that the Clerk of the House is appointed by the monarch, so that they can't be sacked by the government or MPs unless both Houses agree. One clerk told Emma she thought of the servants in the television series

Downton Abbey – a portrayal of a wealthy family and the servants employed by them – as she sat in attendance on MPs at a committee. Aristocrats and politicians will speak candidly in front of servants or clerks, as if they were not there, because they know that those serving them are utterly discreet. Like servants, clerks gossip about the Members among themselves, and perhaps a few trusted associates, but almost never to the media or to MPs. Clerks go out of their way to help Members to frame an effective motion or parliamentary question, but MPs understand that in the hierarchy of 'servants' it is the clerks' job occasionally to say 'no' to a Member who wants to break accepted parliamentary procedure without ensuring that it is the will of the House. The clerks' skill is to do this with great politeness, and MPs still expect more junior staff to do as they are told. Clerks have developed an influence and authority of their own, characterised by staff in other departments as 'the clerks' dark arts.'

There is generally a relationship of trust between staff and MPs but also, at times, this is abused by the politicians.[40] In contrast to the exquisite politeness reserved for potential supporters, MPs can be abrupt, even ill-tempered, to those closest to them: parliamentary staff, their own staff and other MPs whom they deem to be obstructive. Staff sometimes witness MPs at their worst and they are inclined to see some of them as self-important and ill disciplined. Their stories to illustrate this are not in short supply. They put up with this partly because it is a persuasive logic of democracy that the power of elected representatives must be respected for their office, if not their behaviour. An essential element of the culture in the Commons is the recognition, forcefully socialised in new recruits, that 'election' confers a power and authority that mere appointment can never achieve. Elected Members are, through the anointing of the polls, fundamentally different beings. There is, inevitably, a contradiction between this deeply held ethos and the realities of daily human contact with the individuals, who can never live up to these democratic ideals. In 2018 MPs and staff publicly called for more action against bullying and harassment, so there are future signs that it will be less easy for MPs to take advantage of officials' tradition of discretion.[41]

Staff stress the diversity of manners among MPs. Some are thoughtful and considerate while others are demanding, irrational and inclined to talk at great length during political debates or committees about their pet issue or constituency matters, ignoring the concerns of other committee members. They reserve thorough irritation for those Select Committee chairs and members who grandstand, divert a course of questioning to pursue their own personal political agenda or grab attention in the media for themselves rather than the whole committee or the issue, or those that bully staff (especially junior ones). If a junior member of staff is bullied, a senior official will speak to the Member about their behaviour. The morally reprehensible MPs leave some staff, and especially the longer-standing ones, somewhat disdainful (if not cynical), even if they remain fiercely loyal to Parliament. For the younger ones, the experience can be bruising. Staff remind themselves continually that they serve Parliament not individual MPs: 'It is to the office that I must give my loyalty, not to the individual', in the words of one, but the sense is conveyed by many.

On the other side of the coin, how do MPs view officials? Their respect for the intelligence and efficiency of parliamentary staff is nearly universal, but some MPs' evaluations are coloured by their politics. Critical MPs on the left tend to see clerks in particular as privately educated, privileged and conservative, while those on the right complain that clerks are bureaucratic, rule bound and risk averse. Modernisers perceive them as an impediment to change. When a clerk was once travelling with a very senior MP, the latter introduced the former to his wife saying, 'This is X, my wife. She is a Labour supporter, which you are probably not.'[42] The clerk was roughly on the left but kept quiet because as a clerk, his views had to remain unknown, even if those ascribed to him were the product of prejudice rather than observation.

Impartiality does not mean that staff have no political opinions; they collectively probably span the whole political spectrum, with a tendency towards being reform oriented. If anything, most staff complain about the innate conservatism of Parliament itself, especially when the Commons and Lords try to work together. But at the same time, as procedural specialists, the role of clerks in particular is designed to point out hazards when MPs seek advice on a plan or tactic; the senior ones have seen the results of so many ruses that it is hardly surprising they are disposed to warn about unintended consequences. Some MPs interpret this as caution or even resistance to change.

Ken Clarke MP, the Father of the House (a title bestowed on the longest-serving MP), has been a Member for nearly 50 years. But in comparison, most MPs come and go much more quickly with the ebb and flow of national politics. Most staff, however, stay for many years and collectively represent a continuity and institutional memory. They are as much part of the UK's parliamentary system as MPs are, playing a constitutionally important but different role from elected representatives.

Relatively few parliamentary staff are now clerks; none of the staff dealing with expenses in the Fees Office was a clerk, for example, but all staff are influenced by clerkly culture.[43] So as a consequence, the relationship between MPs and non-clerk staff was similar but also subtly different. Their knowledge was less esoteric – for example, the auditing of expenses claims would be recognisable to people in most organisations, and their self-confidence in standing up to MPs may have been wobblier. But they too would have withstood the irritation and sometimes fury of MPs when they had to block their wishes and demands. In an already sometimes tense set of relationships, the expenses scandal ratcheted up the potential for conflict.

MPs and staff accuse one another

During the expenses crisis MPs and staff blamed each other, although the latter could not do so publicly. MPs felt that staff devised and policed the system, so they should take the rap for all but the criminal cases. Staff did what they could to block abuse and reform the rules, but since they worked for Parliament through MPs, there were limits to their authority, as we have illustrated in earlier chapters. Since MPs were superior in the political hierarchy, they should have taken responsibility, the staff felt. Parliament is inevitably a strange institution because MPs are a collection of small enterprises with many bosses and none – but the institution itself also needs to get practical things done as a collective (like HR, finance, etc). When it is a popular service (library, catering, etc) then it is uncontentious because there is no conflict. But as soon as there is a conflict between the institution and MPs (or between MPs), then it can be difficult to resolve disagreements.

In 2009 and 2010, the question of who was to blame for the scandal was asked and discussed in the House of Commons corridors continually. Some MPs told us they blamed the party leaders for losing their nerve, and demanding that MPs should wear the hairiest of hair shirts, thus ensuring that more and more MPs were pilloried in public. Others – some MPs and clerks – blamed Andrew and the Fees Office managers. Some non-clerk staff saw clerkly disinterest in audit as part of the problem. Andrew felt that he and his staff should aim to police the system properly, but were prevented from doing so by MP committees and the Speaker, while some junior Fees Office staff felt that there were occasions when it was pointless to try to enforce the rules because their decisions would be overturned by more senior staff or by politicians. And yet policing and maintaining standards should not in itself have been an impossible task, as the clerks have demonstrated for many years in the field of parliamentary procedure.

The uncomfortable truth is that all of these internal players bear some responsibility: they needed to coalesce in designing, managing, explaining, monitoring and policing the system of expenses if was to prove possible for self-determination to be sustained. As we have demonstrated in this history, the seeds of the crisis had been sown decades earlier and the lack of cohesiveness between House departments and between MPs, their committees and House staff proved a fatal weakness.

Reforming administration

Following the expenses scandal the MPs, especially the Speaker, and staff were in agreement that Parliament needed reform – to be more outward facing and change the rules of debate in favour of backbenchers – but the administration of the House remained contentious. Both MPs and staff were split in their attitude towards whether the House should introduce more 'business-like' approaches to management. Many clerks, as well as either traditionalist MPs or those who saw Parliament as unique, portrayed the management of the Commons as flexible and creative, unlike many organisations plagued by the bureaucratic demands and inefficiencies of some kinds of managerialism.[44]

The usual public sector audit bureaucracy was encroaching, but it was against the will of many clerks. While the dominant management discourse elevates outcome above process, clerks focused on high quality process as much as outcomes because in a democracy due process is in itself a key outcome in earning the trust of the governed.

Some senior staff, and either modernising MPs or those who were determined that the Commons should be treated like other organisations, aimed to increase efficiency, value for money and the ability to prepare better for the future. Their view was that more modern processes would further this aim. Furthermore, some felt change was necessary due to dissatisfaction with accommodation for the growing numbers of MPs' staff, unhappiness about changes to on-site catering, and a sense that the clerks had taken on too much power for themselves.[45] One ex-staff member told us that the expenses scandal 'gave the clerks a good kicking' by making them feel less proud to say they worked for Parliament.[46] Some clerks countered that managerialism in the Fees Office was partly responsible for the crisis; but other clerks took the opposite view, and subsequently adopted more managerial approaches, such as performance management.

Partly in response to MPs' criticisms, the Clerk of the House and the Management Board launched a new corporate strategy in 2010 aimed at reform, renewal, unification of the House Service and improvements in services for MPs. An important element was to be an ethos of 'service rather than subservience' (also referred to as 'stewards not servants') – an attempt to restore the self-confidence of the administration following accusations that staff had been too compliant over expenses. But Speaker Bercow decided that the role of Clerk of the House should be opened up to outsiders, and new blood brought in. When Sir Robert Rogers[47] announced in 2014 that he would step down as Clerk of the House and Chief Executive later that year, Bercow recruited an Australian public sector executive, Carol Mills, to fill the role. Although Mills had worked at a senior level in the Australian Parliament, she was not a clerk or even an expert on procedure. A campaign opposing the appointment was launched in both Australia and the UK. The recruitment was abandoned.

Jack Straw, a trusted parliamentarian with consummate diplomatic skills, was asked to chair a committee that was set up to tackle the problem of governance and leadership of the House of Commons administration. Andrew gave evidence to the committee in favour of taking non-parliamentary expertise seriously; Emma argued that Parliament should be run by someone with deep knowledge of procedure and politics. Both argued that, whatever happened, clear lines of management responsibility were essential.[48] The committee's report, published in December 2014, proposed splitting the Clerk of the House role into two – Clerk and Director General – on a broadly equal basis, against the advice that Andrew and Emma each gave to the Straw Committee.[49] The Straw Committee's recommendations were accepted and implemented the following year. Its words on governance were seminal:

> Governance arrangements... must enable an organisation to meet its primary purposes: they must always be a means to an end, and not an end in themselves. They must deliver clear decision-making, with a high degree of transparency and clarity, whilst incorporating appropriate levels of oversight, challenge and effective personal accountability. They must be practicable and resilient under pressure, taking account of how people behave. They must also have the support and confidence of those who operate within them.[50]

It might have helped if the House of Commons governance had met those criteria in the years running up to the expenses crisis.

Rebellion rising, deference declining

When we asked Robert Winnett why the story became so big, he replied that it touched people's mood. People were discontented with the idea that politicians were out of touch with ordinary citizens and it was arguably an early warning of the kind of discontent that has become evident in Brexit, he elaborated. Perhaps links can be found between the expenses crisis and Brexit through a series of transformations in the relationships between MPs themselves and between them and others in society.[51] The expenses scandal happened partly because Parliament and parliamentarians were slow to catch up with a cultural

and political transformation that resulted from a decline in deference to authority, the Freedom of Information Act and the expectations of the public towards their leaders. Through the period leading
up to the scandal, MPs were becoming more attuned to changes in
society in some ways – for example in being early adopters of Twitter
and Facebook for communicating their political opinions. But at the
same time, MPs still felt a sense of privilege and entitlement, whereas
entitlement (if not privilege) had transferred to the public without
them noticing. The magic of elections, conferring on Members of Parliament an identity that matched their sacred duty as representatives,
no longer worked in the same way. As Heather Brooke said, 'where
people used to have to rely on an elected representative to have their
views made apparent, they don't need them any more and in fact they
feel they are incredibly ineffective.'[52] Once-extraordinary politicians
were becoming more ordinary and so their attitudes towards expenses
should have followed suit.

The relationship between party political leaders, whips and backbenchers has also changed quite dramatically since the expenses
scandal. It was already under strain.[53] Backbenchers have been rebel-
ling against the whip in larger numbers in every parliament since 1945.
The reasons for this, and the acceleration of this pattern since 2009,
are multiple: the election of select committee members and chairs has
given them more clout;[54] Speaker Bercow's reforms have strengthened
the position of backbenchers; deference to leaders has been collaps-
ing; and public support for political parties has been plummeting
(although Jeremy Corbyn reversed that for a while). Before the 2015
election, David Cameron was trying to hold his party together in the
face of this fragmentation and the threatening popularity of UKIP,
and duly put a referendum on European membership into his mani-
festo to keep some Tory MPs quiet. The then President of the European Council Donald Tusk reported that Cameron told him he did
not think in 2015 that they would win the election outright, and if
they did, that 'Remain' would easily win the referendum.[55] If true, he
was wrong on both counts. He did not put a threshold on the referendum because it was 'advisory' not decision-making. Referendums in
the UK tend to be treated as binding, even when they are not in a legal
sense: arguably politicians, already weakened by the expenses scandal,

were terrified of falling out with the public still further, so had even less choice about this one than usual.[56]

The final thread in the imaginary rope that ties the story about expenses to Brexit is money. During the campaign, the Brexiteers claimed that the money saved by leaving the European Union would be spent on the NHS. They declared on their slogan written across a big red bus that an additional £350 million a week would be invested in health. This caught people's attention. The financial cocktail may have been like this in some people's minds: the financial crash, in which many lost savings, was followed by the bankers awarding themselves bonuses nonetheless; then it was found that MPs were claiming thousands on flat screen TVs, flipping their houses to play the system and covering their tracks by refusing to publish the details; austerity followed for over ten years with cuts to benefits, legal aid and much besides; and now the EU was continuing to demand millions every week for the privilege of 'ordering us around'. The millions splashed across the big red bus seemed to be the final straw – people voted to take back control of our money and our government.

A mix of the expenses scandal, Brexit and even more recently climate change appears to have galvanised people to engage in politics with a new form of vigour and scepticism. As De Tocqueville argued in his book *Democracy in America*,

> Democracy does not confer the most skilful kind of government upon the people, but it produces that which the most skilful governments are frequently unable to awaken, namely, an all-pervading and restless activity, a superabundant force, and an energy which is inseparable from it, and which may, under favourable circumstances, beget the most amazing benefits. These are the true advantages of democracy.[57]

This restlessness can act as an antidote to the complacency and corruption of those wielding power for too long. As a democracy plunges into a crisis, citizens and those they elect are galvanised into creating new ideas, activities and alliances to restore some kind of equilibrium. The expenses crisis caused a major upheaval, with a negative impact on British politics, but it also provided opportunities for reform, as we have seen in this chapter. The dangers it exposed within Parliament – especially a serious misjudgement of the public mood – may not have been fully taken on board, as the subsequent Brexit affair has shown. Only time will tell whether the expenses scandal damages or renews the UK's democracy in the long term.

8

Ordinary MPs in an extraordinary scandal

In 2009 Members of Parliament in Westminster were caught over-claiming their expenses just as the country was reeling from the worst financial crisis in decades. Five went to jail and many more had to pay back thousands. Mostly these over-claims were either errors or within the rules but were over-generous, sometimes wildly so. The popular perception of 'snouts in troughs' was true of some, but unfair to many. MPs' sense of deserving generous expenses was greater than it should have been, but not as bad as the public now assume. What made this scandal extraordinary was not the scale of the money involved, which in most cases was small, but the response to it and what it revealed about huge but invisible changes in our political world and UK society at large.

MPs' salaries in 2009 were more than double the size of the average in the UK; they lost sight of how the public might react to their generosity towards themselves. They looked over their shoulders at the more generous salaries and expenses enjoyed by legislators in the US, Canada and Australia,[1] rather than at the financial problems faced by their constituents during the economic crisis. The most difficult aspect to explain is not why they were so relaxed about expenses – this is probably common in many professions if people can get away with it – but why they thought they could keep their claims private once they passed the Freedom of Information Act. One answer lay in their feeling of entitlement, of being out of the ordinary: placed in a sacred spot by democratic election, but also extraordinarily exposed. MPs have almost no privacy – they feel owned by their constituents, their parties, and one another in the endless demands made on their time and on their willingness to support various causes – so they jealously guard the small pockets of privacy they can find, mostly in their own homes.

So which are MPs – ordinary or extraordinary, like us or not like us, or is it possible that they are both?

Are MPs like the rest of us?

Representative democracy in modern times is based on the idea that elected representatives are like the rest of us: ordinary people. John Dunn writes,

> in human political communities it ought to be ordinary people (the adult citizens) and not extra-ordinary people who rule. This is not a very plausible description of how things are in the world in which we live. But it has become the reigning conception today across that world of how they ought to be. The idea itself is devastatingly obvious, but also tantalisingly strange and implausible.[2]

His point is that we no longer want to be ruled by super beings – deities, kings or leaders born to rule – we want to be governed by people like ourselves. Stephen Coleman puts it like this, 'In an age where authenticity and ordinariness are valued more than prestige and expertise, the challenge for democratic politicians is to be seen as ordinary enough to be representative, while extraordinary enough to be representatives.'[3] Making democracy work in the face of change, difference and disagreement is such a struggle that exceptional qualities *are* required in our leaders. We want to trust them, look up to them and rely on them to make wise judgements, but the inevitable antagonism and confusion caused by the struggle for democracy have often exposed politicians' weaknesses as a collective.

Our perception of MPs, and whether they are like us or not, is of course influenced by what we know about them. With the collapse of clear boundaries between public and private domains – thanks to 24-hour digital media and Freedom of Information – we know far more about them than we did. This causes its own problems. German minister Hans Eichel may have been telling the truth when he explained that he used a ministerial jet to attend a private party in 2001 because his work was 24/7, so private versus public distinctions shouldn't apply.[4] However, the image of him jetting around to parties then became the problem – it inevitably inspired irritation (if not anger) in those of us who struggle to pay for rail or bus fares. This is amplified even more if politicians have been increasing our taxes or reducing our benefits. So MPs are not like us in the sense that they are more powerful and wealthier[5] than the vast majority of those they work for.

It used to be the case that people overlooked the disparities of wealth or even took them for granted. Virginia Woolf sounded quite relaxed about the privilege of politicians in the 1930s when writing about how they are both like us and different from us:

> to look at, they do not differ much from other people. The standard of dress is perhaps rather high. We look down upon some of the glossiest top hats still to be seen in England. A magnificent scarlet button-hole blazes here and there. Everybody has been well fed and given a good education doubtless. But what with their chatter and laughter, their high spirits, and impatiences and irreverence, they are not a whit more judicious, or more dignified, or more respectable-looking than any other assembly of citizens met to debate parish business or to give prizes for fat oxen. This is true; but after a time some curious difference makes itself suspected. We feel that the Commons is a body of certain character; it has been in existence for a long time; it has its own laws and licences. It is irreverent in a way of its own; and so presumably, reverent too in its own way. It has somehow a code of its own.[6]

But in the last hundred years citizens have looked to democracy as an opportunity to demand that their interests are better represented and the privilege of the few surrendered or at least challenged.[7] If MPs are privileged people furthering their own personal interests and ignoring those of their constituents, then the betrayal is felt acutely. In 1952 Aneurin Bevan argued

> In one sense the House of Commons is the most unrepresentative of representative assemblies. It is an elaborate conspiracy to prevent the

real clash of opinion which exists outside from finding an appropriate echo within its wall. It is a social shock absorber placed between
privilege and the pressure of popular discontent.[8]

Since Bevan's time, ideas about privilege and class have changed in
the UK. Deference has declined and people have become more willing
to challenge class hierarchies, but at the same time historians have
argued that a mix of growing individualism and a huge increase in ine-
quality since the 1970s has left us with many angry citizens.[9] Some even
claim that the Labour Party has become so middle class that people
who define themselves as working class are no longer adequately politically represented. Florence Sutcliffe-Braithwaite makes an interesting
argument about this in England: a complex cultural shift in the second
half of the twentieth century elevated the value of authenticity and
ordinariness above privilege and snobbery.[10] Particularly during the
1960s and 70s, with social movements, environmental protests and
feminism, politicians tried to respond and democracy was reimagined
as more inclusive and participatory. Although this did not entail the
death of class, it did mean that people drastically changed their attitudes towards identity, tradition and elites.[11]

As a result of these shifts, to take popular discontent seriously as an
MP you have to remain in touch with your ordinary side. Labour MP
Jack Ashley told Emma that everyone is ordinary and that even developing a field of expertise and becoming a Lord can't change that – 'a
peerage leaves ordinary men ordinary'.[12] In some ways citizens want
MPs to be like them. One of the most inexperienced candidates at a
by-election in Eastleigh in 2013 responded to this sentiment when he
said during a hustings, 'If you want to speak to Westminster then I
am your chance. I am you. I'm not a party person. This would be true
democracy, I will speak for you. I am one of you.'[13] Most of us are not
particularly party political, and are getting less so, but we see ourselves
as belonging to a particular locality so, unsurprisingly, many voters
want their MP to hail from their local area and they mind less about
their individual background or social attributes such as their gender.[14]
A shared identity in the minds of constituents often means belonging
to the same place. When Emma conducted research with MPs during
the 2010–15 Parliament, a sizeable minority stood not to promote

the policies or their political party, but to champion the interests of their locality. Sarah Wollaston, the first MP to be selected by an open primary rather than her political party, took her mandate from constituents not her party.[15] (In 2019 she even left the Tories and created a new party with others from both sides of the House.)[16]

But politicians and activists seem to have broader priorities than voters when thinking about the shared characteristics between elected and elector. One reason the selection of MPs can provoke such tensions is because the whole concept of what representation signifies is contested between and even within political parties. Almost everyone agrees that the under-representation of women in the Westminster Parliament is a scandal of its own and that increasing the number of women MPs is overdue. Class, race and ethnicity are more contentious. In the summer of 2013 one of the architects of New Labour, Peter Mandelson (a former Labour MP), worried that the unions would give mass backing to Old Labour candidates and lose Labour the 2015 General Election. The General Secretary of one of the unions involved, Unite, explained why they had encouraged people to join the party and vote for union-nominated candidates: 'Labour MPs look less and less like the people they seek to represent. The big strides made in securing more women Labour MPs have also, unfortunately, been paralleled by a decline in those from working-class backgrounds'.[17] Conservative MPs now worry about the appearance of privilege too. Gyles Brandreth (former MP) recounted that fellow Tory Ann Widdecombe marched him out of a first-class train carriage to second class, advising him sternly that MPs should not set themselves apart.[18] But there are divides between those who want to be seen as accessible and those who see accusations of privilege as the indefensible envy of those who don't have the talent or energy to work themselves out of disadvantage.

Some may demand that MPs are accessible, even ordinary, but they can only survive by becoming extraordinary. We require our politicians to be different and set apart from us in at least two senses. First, we want politicians to be authentically themselves, less eager to please and bend towards us, saying whatever they think even if we don't agree. Both politicians and journalists speculate that MPs need to relearn authenticity and become less like those smooth, media-trained politicians who give a robotic, impersonal and flawless performance. We want them to speak from the heart and we love it when they speak against their own party line. The philosopher Harry Frankfurt wrestles with an epistemological problem in this attitude to authenticity.[19] On the one hand, if we want authenticity there is an increased expectation that politicians should have knowledge on a wide range of topics. But we also live in a time of scepticism, so we rarely believe what we hear, with the result that we are more often seeking sincerity rather than truth. 'Rather than seeking primarily to arrive at accurate representations of a common world, the individual turns toward trying to provide honest representations of himself', Frankfurt points out.[20] Politicians can't be experts on everything so inevitably they have to rely on their party machines to supply 'lines to take' (or messages on specific policy issues), but this reliance contradicts the demand for politicians' authenticity to be individually based.

Secondly, and again somewhat contradictorily, we want MPs to be different from us in the sense that they are career politicians whose job is to represent the diverse interests of up to 100,000 people. We want them not to voice their own opinions, but to reflect *our* views; so unlike us, they are not expected to have their own. Our views fracture into many perspectives. A politician needs to respond to endless requests from constituents, whips, interest groups and local supporters, as well as to proactively find out what they think and need, without having enough time to do justice to any of these demands. According to one: 'It feels like Genghis Khan attaching four horses to your limbs and you are pulled in four directions.'

The more inclusively you listen, the more directions you will be pulled in. The better you represent, the more you sink under the weight of many voices. One increasing feature of the painful parliamentary Brexit process in 2019 has been MPs saying 'I'm going back to my constituency over the weekend to get instructions.'[21]

What are they supposed to do when they disagree with the majority of their constituents – when the ideological differences between elected and voters just can't be reconciled? One Labour MP wrote in the *Times* in the middle of the Brexit crisis:

IT FEELS LIKE GENGHIS KHAN ATTACHING FOUR HORSES TO YOUR LIMBS AND YOU ARE PULLED IN FOUR DIRECTIONS

I am a Labour MP who voted Remain, representing a constituency that voted heavily to Leave. I'm torn in two. I wanted to be accountable, I want to be involved, but I sit uselessly and helplessly, trapped in a Commons that's falling to pieces at a time of national crisis. This diary is my silent scream...[22]

On the other side of the argument, Brexiteer MPs in Remain constituencies had no easy answer to the question about how they were representing them. Prominent hard-line Brexiteer and former chair of the Conservative European Research Group Jacob Rees-Mogg upset a number of his own constituents – who voted 58 per cent Remain in the referendum – when he was quoted by a local newspaper as calling Remainers 'cave dwellers'.[23] The inevitable multiple binds created by democratic politics – whereby supporters pull you in different directions, let alone constituents who didn't vote for you but whom you still represent – mean that politicians have to be selective about the truths they tell. Notice that the Labour MP above did not reveal their name.

There is no escape from hypocrisy in democratic politics, as David Runciman points out, but those who pretend to be immune from it through their superior knowledge and morality are indulging in a far more dangerous kind of deception than the everyday twists and turns made by MPs.[24] Whether people admit it to themselves or not, Runciman explains, politics demands some element of hypocrisy (or politicians pretending to be something they are not). It is an inevitable part of political performance to win support and cover over flaws. But when MPs are perceived to be hiding things from their electors, they are seen as hypocrites even when they are not. Professional politicians, who often go almost straight into politics when they are young, tend to understand this. And in yet another contradiction in our attitudes towards politicians, MPs and observers alike express wistful comments about how we lack specialists who have had a non-political career before standing for Parliament, who bring their own ideas and views. The increasing number of people who go straight into politics by working as local councillors or MPs' researchers and advisers alarms us. After all, how can they truly represent ordinary people if they have never had an ordinary, non-political job?

However much we may wish our elected representatives to be like us, we will always be disappointed. They may be in ordinary in a human sense – vulnerable, flawed and subject to the same emotions – but their jobs are different, with the result that in other senses they will always remain different from us. So even if we vote for them because they are ordinary, and we feel we can trust them to symbolically embody our community, that job of embodiment makes unusual demands. Each small element of politicians' work may be found elsewhere. Like politicians, senior leaders in any profession are interviewed by journalists and campaigners represent the interests of others. Celebrities can be even more exposed to the prurient gaze of the media and public, while charity workers have to be loyal to their cause in the same way as political party members. Politics can be found in all organisations – in the sense of alliance-building, winning support, power struggling and battling over resources – but politicians do all these activities, and politics itself, in a more concentrated, shape-shifting and exposed way than any other group.

So MPs are both ordinary and extraordinary.

An extraordinary scandal?

What implications does this have for their expenses? How serious was the hypocrisy of MPs caught over-claiming expenses? Was it ordinary or extraordinary? As Runciman argues, ideas about hypocrisy change over time:

> Dealing with political hypocrisy is a question not just of recognising that politicians wear masks, but of recognising that the masks they wear must suit the age in which they find themselves. Politicians find themselves in an age in which it is best to put on the mask of sincerity, in order to appear as though they are not wearing a mask at all.[25]

The problem was that no sincere soundbite on expenses was bearable once the media had determined the framing of the story as undiluted wickedness by MPs. This was particularly true of the *Telegraph* coverage, partly because of its repetitive intensity; but the rhetoric about snouts in the trough had begun much earlier, as shown in Chapters 3 and 4. So what might not have been viewed as hypocritical 50 years earlier was exposed as intolerable after our expectations of politicians had changed. We used to find it unsurprising that our leaders were privileged – male, pale and wealthy – whether inherited, earned or acquired as a Member of Parliament. Gradually it became seen as iniquitous that only the wealthy could sit in Parliament and salaries were introduced to make it possible for anyone. A problem arose when it became clear that it was no longer only established elites that were winning seats: it was people from a wider background entering Parliament who wanted enough resources to become the new elite.

'If you pay peanuts, you get monkeys' – so goes the proverb. But MPs were not paid peanuts. At nearly £80,000 a year, their basic pay is currently approaching three times the national average. On the face of it, that looks very generous. But it can be also argued that, contrary to how it must seem to most hard-working employees in the UK, MPs are under-remunerated for the responsibilities and challenges they face.

In 2011 56 per cent of new MPs (65 per cent Conservative and 39 per cent Labour) took a pay cut when they went into Parliament, and for one third it was £30,000 or more.[26] One staff member who had worked in Parliament since the scandal told us that since the tightening-up of the pay and expenses regime in 2010, including more control on expenses and a ban on employing family members, more MPs are struggling to make ends meet, though their constituency workloads have continued to grow. So MPs have started to employ younger and more inexperienced staff at lower pay just to cope with work volumes. This has had adverse impacts – for example, employing people with limited previous work experience exacerbates the power imbalance between the MP and their staff, leading to more bullying, perhaps because there is no longer an experienced office manager in-between them. This was often traditionally a role previously carried out by the MP's spouse or partner.[27]

The flexibility of the old system has gone, with some unintended consequences. That is not an argument to return to allowing the abuses that were highlighted in the 2009 scandal, but it does suggest that the hair shirt of the new regime may be too hairy. There is danger in returning to a world where only those with independent means of their own, or those with funding from third parties, can afford to seek political office – the very problem that the pay and expenses system was introduced to combat.

To decide whether the scandal was extraordinary or not, we have to take a step back to look at the wider historical and cultural patterns. The expenses scandal came about because the relationships between MPs and others in society were changing and MPs did not notice fast enough. First, it was in the area of the extraordinary and changing nature of MPs' work that expenses emerged as a problem. The relationship with constituents had shifted from remote to intense, from an occasional visit to showing their faces at a weekly or fortnightly stay packed with meetings, surgeries and functions. As the volume of constituency work skyrocketed, so too did the financial needs of MPs. Those living in constituencies outside London couldn't travel back and forth at the strange times that MPs start and finish work – indeed there wouldn't have been enough hours in the day to do so. So they needed two houses. The second home allowance was the mechanism through which many of the controversial claims were made. One of the critical and fatal moments in the expenses story was MPs' foolish manoeuvre to increase this allowance from £13,628 to £19,469 in 2001: it paved the way for over-generous claims for flat screen TVs, hanging baskets and glittering loo seats.

The revelation of MPs' claims wouldn't have happened in the way it did but for the moves towards transparency that radically changed their relationship with both the public and the media. In the private world of the Commons, a pro-transparency MP insisted on new rules to make MPs submit detailed schedules and receipts for their claims. It was this that exposed the lurid trove of information many years later. These supplied the gritty detail that gave the journalists a field day and caught people's dark imagination: it was the ordinary and the extraordinary fragments of MPs' lives that really got to them. On the one hand, the claims for bath plugs, talcum powder and toilet paper reminded people that MPs were *ordinary* people with ordinary bodily needs, claiming for household items that the rest of us have to pay for with hard-earned cash. The irony that these items were claimed because MPs were working harder and harder in their constituencies, thereby requiring a second home, was lost on most journalists and their readers.

On the other hand, the *extraordinary* claims provided shocking evidence of the privilege of our leaders. Two stuck out like sore thumbs: the duck house and the moat cleaning. In neither case were these claimed – they were merely lumped into a large pile of items from which these two MPs expected the Fees Office to pick those that were eligible – but that wasn't really the point. How could we trust people to rule us if they lived in such luxury? How could MPs appreciate the struggle to pay bills in the face of debt and devise appropriate policies and laws for the majority, if they were enjoying such benefits? Worse still, they seemed to be oblivious to their staggering assumption of entitlement. One Conservative MP, Anthony Steen, who had claimed thousands for gardening, notoriously said,

MP: I think I behaved, if I may say so, impeccably. I've done nothing criminal, that's the most awful thing, and do you know what it's about? Jealousy. I've got a very, very large house. Some people say it looks like Balmoral. It's the photographs, it looks like Balmoral, but it's a merchant's house of the 19th century. It's not particularly attractive, it just does me nicely – it's got room to actually plant a few trees...

Journalist: So you don't think any of the information should have ever been released?

MP: No! What right does the public have to interfere with my private life? None. Do you know what this reminds me of, this whole episode? An episode from *Coronation Street*. Do you know what Members are doing now? They are waiting by their phones between three and four o'clock in the afternoon because that's the time the Prime Minister used to ring you if you were going to get a job, and now it's a question of whether the *Daily Telegraph* are going to ring you because that's the time they will ring you. 'Is it the Prime Minister?' 'No, it's the *Daily Telegraph*.' They just know this is a kangaroo court going on.[28]

His constituents made their anger plain. So did his party leader, David Cameron, who announced to the BBC's *The World at One* on the following day, 'One more squeak like that and he will have the whip taken away from him so fast his feet won't touch the ground.'[29] He stood down at the 2010 election. The details may have been a revelation but it has been argued that people were already primed to think of MPs as corrupt. 'The *Telegraph*'s allegations slotted very easily into an already established narrative in which politics and corruption were close bed-fellows.'[30] Even before the expenses scandal, the idea of MPs as being self-interested, venal and power-hungry was well established. The main difference since then has been that the expenses scandal is perceived as the main episode that offers concrete, shocking and graphic proof.

More publicly, the fundamental move towards transparency meant that the Freedom of Information Act whetted people's appetite for juicy information and gave journalists the mechanism for demanding the release of documents produced by public bodies. Of this act, brought into law while he was PM, Tony Blair wrote:

The truth is that, for the most part, the FOI isn't used by 'the people'. It's used by journalists... The information is neither sought by the journalist because the journalist is curious to know, nor given to bestow knowledge on 'the people'. It is used as a weapon.[31]

Andrew's suggestion at the Information Tribunal that the public interest in seeing MPs' detailed expenses might have had an element of nosiness about it was – literally – laughed out of court. From the citizen's perspective, making MPs accountable for their expenditure of taxpayers' money – just as senior managers are in most public organisations – was entirely logical and good for democracy. From the viewpoint of MPs, however, the nature of their political office required special treatment. To strip away their last shred of privacy would make it more difficult to survive the emotional rigours of being an MP. These conflicting viewpoints could only be resolved by setting up a completely new transparent system (IPSA), which reveals MPs' spending but allows them the privacy of their own homes.

Attack dogs and spin merchants

The expenses scandal was partly a symptom of the changing relationship with journalists. Contrast the current scrutiny of politicians by the media – hostile, attacking, suspicious – with 50 years ago. There is a newsreel in black and white from the 1960s showing PM Harold Macmillan and Foreign Secretary Selwyn Lloyd coming down off a plane from an overseas trip. A BBC journalist greets them and asks, 'Prime Minister, have you got anything to say to the BBC?' Macmillan replies, 'No, I don't think so. Selwyn, have you got anything to say to the BBC?' 'No, I don't think so.'[32] For the PM to have 'nothing to say' to the BBC today would be unthinkable – political suicide. Although some say that Bernard Ingham was the first press secretary and spin doctor, Margaret Thatcher was the last PM who did not obsess about media reaction, according to former Cabinet Secretary Robin Butler.[33] She listened to the *Today* programme while having her hair done, but did not pay too much attention and used to say she planned to lead not follow. If you give people what they want, they want something different five minutes later, she quipped.

Tony Blair's Press Secretary Alastair Campbell took spinning to a whole new dimension. He told the Leveson inquiry that they did not lie, but in managing thousands of stories every day, he acknowledged that they made mistakes.[34] Combine that with the digital revolution, which brought with it 24-hour news and social media, and you have a complete transformation of the relationship with MPs and various forms of mediated communication. Political spinning soured the relationship as news journalists became increasingly suspicious of politicians, and their job morphed into purely catching them out rather than the old mix of education and scrutiny. Changes within the media world contributed to the incentives to attack as well. Newspapers were – and are – dying as their commercial basis crumbled with the advent of free news on blogs, Twitter, Facebook and news sites. Instead of only writing for their papers, journalists have faced far greater pressure to produce copy at speed for all these channels, looking for stories that would attract attention and that were inexpensive to research. Even if the leak and analysis of a mountain of information by the *Telegraph* entailed good old-fashioned investigative journalism, when the other outlets mined this without leaving their offices it was fantastic for business.

Arguably the harshness of some journalists towards MPs was influenced by the decline of regional papers, which meant that fewer journalists had contacts with backbenchers. By 2009, most of the Parliamentary Lobby were from national and Sunday papers, who focused their attention on the PM, ministers and only the influential backbenchers, so they scarcely visited constituencies where much of the expenses action was taking place.[35] Local and regional newspapers have receded from the Lobby, partly for commercial reasons but perhaps also due to devolution. Some Lobby journalists did not realise about MPs' over-generosity with their expenses, others did but felt sympathy. Ben Leapman of the *Sunday Telegraph* was one of these:

> Following my conversation with Mr Wilkinson five years ago, I knew that there were plenty of scandals locked away in the expenses files, and that their publication would end a few careers. But having spent five years in the 'Westminster village' as a lobby correspondent, I feel an instinctive sympathy with politicians, and I underestimated the level of public anger that the revelations would unleash.[36]

Some journalists had heard about MPs' greed, and them using expenses to compensate for poor salaries; some thought this went back to Margaret Thatcher but one claimed that it was Michael Foot who talked about generous pensions and expenses as compensations. When one Labour MP asked Foot to introduce decent pay, he allegedly replied, 'No can do. We have a generous system so fill your boots.'[37] But either the Lobby did not want to alienate the contacts they depended on for stories, did not have proof or did not think it was much of a story. Another collusive side to their relationship is explained by the political commentator Lance Price: 'Lobby journalists who enjoyed generous expense accounts were undoubtedly too close to those MPs and ministers that they took out on those very same accounts. So in a sense they were all in it together.'[38] In their silence the Lobby (and even academics who knew the stories about compensation too) colluded in the expenses system, not because they thought there was a huge secret to cover up, but because they didn't see the story.

The reporting of the expenses scandal was not predominantly in the hands of the Lobby journalists – who knew about MPs' compromises and pressures and even sympathised – but news reporters who were less familiar with Parliament. The TV journalists were under particular pressure to tell a compelling story. The TV coverage, according to Peter Bull, Ralph Negrine and Katie Hawn,[39] followed a pervasive shift from fact-based to a more interpretative style of reporting that involved adding their own 'contextualisation' and creating their own storylines with imaginary dialogues. Some tabloid newspapers went far further than reinterpretation and wrote scurrilous stories while hardly checking their facts. When MPs read false allegations about themselves, some phoned their lawyers to instruct them to sue for defamation. But they received the same kind of answer, which was something like: 'It is not worth it. The fact that what you say is true is not relevant. You will lose in this febrile climate. Forget it.'

Just as the MPs ranged from criminal to honourable, journalists varied between sloppy and impeccable on how they treated the facts. Robert Winnett, the journalist who broke the story for the *Telegraph* and its deputy political editor, was scrupulous about accuracy. We asked him for his reflections on the crisis after ten years.[40] Before the *Telegraph* had been offered the leaked disk, he had been aware that

MPs' expenses had in some ways been seen by them as compensation for stingy pay rises, but he did not have more than a cursory understanding of the system. Although individual cases had come to light, they had not really taken off as stories. When the *Telegraph* started publishing its revelations, other newspapers were trying to catch up. There were many rumours flying around, so newspapers could argue that if people had said it, it could be reported, at least as hearsay. At the *Telegraph*, Winnett told us, they did correct copy to ensure their facts were robust: editors would ensure that facts were checked, and that adjectives like 'disgusting' were deleted.

A culture of blame

The expenses scandal reveals what our political world is becoming. It is a place of blame: when anything goes wrong, the first reaction of press and public is to find the villain in charge. In the case of the expenses scandal, the media and the public blamed MPs, while many MPs felt that the Fees Office had let them down. After all, hadn't they examined and passed their claims month after month? And hadn't they encouraged them to claim the maximum possible? 'Just take the annual allowance, divide it by 12, and claim that amount each month,' they'd said for many years. The media, too, gunned for the Fees Office, saying they should have acted as watchdogs over untrustworthy MPs but instead colluded in the scandalous system. The John Lewis list, they said, illustrated just how much MPs were encouraged to claim for furniture and luxury goods in their taxpayer-funded second homes. How could they allow MPs to claim mortgage interest and then keep the house the taxpayer paid for?

Heather Brooke, and maybe others, assumed parliamentary officials had the kind of power that government civil servant Sir Humphrey had in the TV series *Yes, Minister*. Since Parliament had been reluctant to explain its own inner workings, and how different they are from government, journalists outside the Westminster bubble knew little about those working in the House of Commons. How could they know that while civil servants run government departments and account to ministers who set policy, the power of officials in Parliament is limited by their proximity to 650 MPs who assert that they are in charge? In a culture of blame, secrecy – or even the failure to communicate effectively – becomes dangerous. As we pointed out in the last chapter, one of the features of this story was the lack of cohesiveness within the administration of the House of Commons – both between officials and Members. It was an endemic weakness that contributed to the crisis.[41]

In a world where blame presides as a dominant theme, it is difficult to write about the expenses scandal without taking a position on who was responsible. Not to comment implies that we might think there was no wrongdoing. What emerges from our version of the story is a critique of those involved in the expenses scandal, but it is a complex one. Pointing the finger at only one part of Parliament is invidious. Collective responsibility – and with it blame – lies with Parliament as an institution. MPs, the Commission, various committees, the Fees Office, the Speaker and top officials must all share the main responsibility, while observers in the know colluded; after all, institutions can't have agency, only people can.

So where are our fingers pointing? MPs should have realised that they needed to be more like others and accept their ordinariness in the sense of accounting for reasonable expenditure of taxpayers' money. As the tribunal concluded, 'The laxity of and lack of clarity in the rules for ACA is redolent of a culture very different from that which exists in the commercial sphere or in most other public sector organisations today.'[42] Or, as Speaker Bercow put it, 'MPs had collectively perpetuated a system that did not pass muster in the court of public opinion.'[43] Some MPs did what they could to distance themselves from the system. As examples, Norman Baker MP campaigned for more openness, as we point out in Chapter 2; Adam Afriyie MP did not claim expenses at all; and Dennis Skinner MP took pride in claiming as little as possible. But this was rare.

Those who accuse the officials of colluding with MPs also simplify a complex story. The more accurate version we have related goes like this: from the late 1990s the Fees Office did see the importance of a tighter, more robust system of expenses that would stand up to the full glare of public scrutiny, and pressed for that internally. At the same time they tried to help MPs to get the best out of the system, to be seen as 'on their side'. With hindsight, it was a fatal flaw to try to carry out both of those functions, seeking to be both servants of MPs and watchdogs over them, and ultimately not to succeed fully in either.

The media, the fourth estate in our constitution, played a key role in bringing wrongdoing to light; but loose and sensationalist reporting also pilloried some MPs and their families unjustly, and contributed to lasting damage to Parliament. Did they think enough about the impact they might have on democracy? At the time of the crisis, the then Archbishop of Canterbury tried to warn about the possible political harm of focusing on MPs' expenses without caution. He wrote that MPs who claimed that all was well because rules were not being broken were clearly morally wrong, but care should be taken. The daily humiliation of MPs could permanently damage our confidence in democracy.[44] And Runciman warns that

> in an age of an almost limitless capacity for scrutiny of the political class... it is reasonable to hope for some restraint from the scrutineers, in their own interests as well as ours, to prevent the cycle of masking and unmasking from collapsing into farce.[45]

Journalists need to emulate the best of their group and return to their ethics of strict truth-telling.

The courts might have taken greater account of the extraordinary work of MPs and their need for flexibility, privacy and efficiency. The Information Tribunal's finding was that, while MPs must from the very nature of their functions be prepared to accept a greater degree of public scrutiny than the average citizen, this did not mean that they were entitled to no privacy; however, 'only the most pressing privacy needs should in our view be permitted to prevail' and such needs should be modest.[46] They added that conscientious MPs who provided more information had no reason to worry about disclosure because they had nothing to hide. But privacy for MPs is not about concealment of wrongdoing in general, even if it is for a few. The more people know about them – which type of pizza they like and what time they normally take the train home – the more they feel owned by the public. Privacy is guarded by public figures out of exhaustion with exposure, fear of yet more demands, verbal abuse or even physical attacks. Or they don't want their home addresses publicised so they can spend time by themselves or with their family without interruption in those moments out of the public's gaze. The tribunal's lawyerly understanding of MPs' fears seems to be making the false assumption that disclosure would only be a worry if MPs were acting improperly. It shows little understanding of the work of MPs and how exposed they are in every corner of their lives, or of the oversimplified discourse in the media.

As far as individual MPs are concerned, most were mainly guilty of ordinarily trying to do a decent job and in many cases getting into a spectacular ethical muddle. Some showed richer or poorer judgement than others. Michael Martin was chief among these ordinary culprits, in trying to protect his Members and losing sight of his and their responsibilities to ordinary citizens. The anthropologist Michael Lambek has written about how a theory of ethics has to take account of the endless contradictions we all face in everyday life:

> Ordinary experience encompasses the inevitable cracks and ruptures in the actual and the ubiquity of responses to the ever-present limits of criteria and paradoxes of the human condition, hence the attempts in everyday practice and thought to inhabit and persevere in light of uncertainty, suffering, injustice, incompleteness, inconsistency, the unsayable, the unforgivable, the irresolvable, and the limits of voice and reason.[47]

Ethics can't be judged in isolation. To understand the nature of the muddle that individuals, and therefore groups, get themselves into, you have to delve into both culture and history. This account has looked at the cracks and the ruptures, the contradictions and half-hidden aspects of expenses, in order to work out not just *what* happened but *why* it happened.

A few of the characters in this story were more extraordinary. Six MPs were caught and found guilty of false accounting. Given their position of power and responsibility, such villainy should be recognised in the strongest terms. But in some ways most extraordinary of all was the shy but determined outsider. Heather Brooke, the American feminist campaigner and investigative journalist, deserves far more recognition for heroism than she has so far received. Neither of us agrees with her unqualified enthusiasm for transparency and lack of sympathy for MPs' desire for privacy. But she is a hero of this tale for sure. She came to this country and was infuriated by its culture of secrecy and male entitlement, which she found so alien that she campaigned for half a decade to make UK politics more transparent. With no backers or patrons, she took on the establishment and beat them in court. When the *Telegraph* broke their story, they did not initially acknowledge her role in forcing Parliament to publish MPs' expenses, and yet if there was one person without whom this scandal could not have happened, it was Heather Brooke.

The wonder and tyranny of light

Mostly we have tried to resist the temptation to structure this book around judgement and put the emphasis on reflection. The problem with getting stuck in the endless cycle of attack and defence that blame invites is that it distracts us all from the equally important job of working out what happened and how it might be avoided in the future. We have sought to draw out diverse views to tell a persuasive version of the sociopolitical and cultural history of the expenses scandal; we hope it might contribute to reflections on what can be learned. We have done this by listening to a range of perspectives and drawing out their significance, but also by challenging ourselves to develop a new interpretation, under the influence of Hannah Arendt's approach to understanding and participating in the public realm. For Arendt, politics is about debating diverse opinions created by the plurality of humans in public spaces. Forming opinions is never a solitary activity. She writes:

> The more people's standpoints I have present in my mind while I am pondering a given issue, and the better I can imagine how I would feel and think if I were in their place, the stronger will be the capacity for representative thinking and the more valid my final conclusions, my opinion.[48]

So this involves more than holding up a mirror to the world: an author (or two) has to form an opinion through an act of imagination rather than merely listing many views. Anthropological method always relies on this way of thinking about how to develop knowledge. Tim Ingold wrote that to do anthropology means 'to ask questions of others, and of the world, and to wait upon their answers. It is what happens in any conversation. And like all conversations, it changes the lives of everyone involved.'[49]

In making visible the invisible, we have to give prominence to what we view as the key moments – a process of careful selection. In two years of research, interviews and writing in preparation for this book, both of us have developed our thinking. We started with a sense that past commentary on the 2009 scandal had oversimplified the issues – that the public discourse ten years ago had vilified Members of Parliament with too much zeal and not enough discernment, and that in turn may have damaged democracy. But that initial view of ours was itself, as we have tried to show, unduly simplistic. Through interviews with people who played parts on all sides of the scandal we have discovered new heroes: MPs whose honour was traduced, even when they did the right thing; *Telegraph* journalists who went to great lengths to get the facts right (most of the time) and even thought about the human impact on some of the MPs they were criticising; loyal Fees Office staff who endured brickbats from all sides; and – perhaps most of all – relentless campaigner Heather Brooke, who would not take 'no' for an answer.

But we went beyond seeking villains and heroes. We learned about privacy, secrecy and entitlement – the dangers of both concealment and exposure. Obscuring the truth for private gain is wicked, of that we have no doubt. MPs were beyond foolish to try and keep information about their expenses private once they passed the Freedom of Information Act. And the uniqueness of their job does not mean that blanket privilege is justified. Elected representatives would be wise to moderate the sense of entitlement many of them feel as a result of being voted into office. As we have shown, they had collectively – though with some exceptions – got into a way of thinking that the expenses system was theirs to do with as they wished, and had overlooked their accountability not just upwardly to auditors, but outwardly to citizens.

But it does not automatically follow that exposure always trumps secrecy as an aspiration. When navigating competing ethics, sometimes the more moral course of action means being discreet and keeping secrets. All human beings, including MPs, need personal lives, privacy for their families and space for themselves. MPs are not the property of their voters. Exposing MPs' private lives to the public gaze not only has a negative psychological effect on them, but increases the risks to their personal safety. Since the expenses scandal, the murder of Jo Cox MP and abuse directed towards MPs, and in particular at women and black and minority ethnic politicians, remind us that the threat of violence is acute and growing. MPs share in common with all of us the psychological and social need for privacy and have an unusual job that exposes them to more danger than most of us.

There is a wider lesson to learn here about transparency too. In 1997 Haridimos Tsoukas predicted that the obsessive production and collection of information could reduce people to bald facts, numbers and images, and it could be used to monitor and control them. The more information is mediated, the more its context and meaning has become distorted and the less we understand its complexity. The more information is put into the public domain without context or interpretation, or with malicious and disingenuous spin, the more distrust it generates. Twenty years ago he wrote, 'The light that the information society promises to direct upon itself may well constitute a new tyranny: the tyranny of radical doubt, of disorientation, and of heightened uncertainty.'[50] Since then, the information explosion has intensified and his cautionary words, if anything, ring more strongly. Tsoukas points out that more transparency in the public domain could lead to more confusion and weakening of the public interest, which he describes as a 'subtle and potentially more pernicious problem'. This, we believe, may have been the case with the expenses scandal. But the message for society in the information age goes broader: greater transparency is not automatically an unmixed blessing.

The expenses scandal was extraordinary but not for the obvious reasons. It wasn't corruption on a large scale; it was politicians being both secretive and out of touch with wider societal changes, partly brought about by them and partly by forces beyond their control. Of course if the Westminster Parliament was being invented from scratch in the 2000s, its founders might have created a more open expenses system, as they did in the Scottish Parliament 20 years ago.[51] But the accretion of years of habit was difficult to change. The philosopher John Dewey points out that this kind of moral failure is common: 'habits persist while the world which they have incorporated alters. Back of this failure lies the failure to recognize that in a changing world, old habits must perforce need modification, no matter how good they have been.'[52] People are accustomed to thinking of morality as a matter of individual reason and conscience, rather than the social habits of groups of people who fail to notice how society around them has shifted and to imagine how their routines could and should be modified if they wish to act more intelligently and ethically. Responsibility is both an individual and social matter. He argues that if we wish to change then we need to 'foster impulses and habits which experience has shown to make us sensitive, generous, imaginative, impartial in perceiving the tendency of our inchoate dawning activities.'[53] We need to understand what just happened, and what continues to happen, if we want satisfying reform. MPs' expenses are now transparent, displayed for all to see on the internet, but if representative democracy is to work better in the twenty-first century, a better understanding of the politics of knowledge needs to be developed. Working towards more intelligent and collaborative ways of interpreting, learning and debating might help society to cope better with the uncertainty of our times.

Glossary of acronyms

ACA	Additional Costs Allowance
APMA	Advisory Panel on Members' Allowances
CSPL	Committee on Standards in Public Life
DPA	Data Protection Act
F&S	Finance and Services Select Committee
FOI	Freedom of Information
FOIA	Freedom of Information Act 2000
GCW	Government Chief Whip
HoC	House of Commons
HOCC	House of Commons Commission
ICO	Information Commissioner's Office
IEP	Incidental Expenses Provision
IPSA	Independent Parliamentary Standards Authority
JCOS	Joint Committee on Security
MAC	Committee on Members' Allowances
MEAC	Members Estimate Audit Committee
MEC	Members Estimate Committee
MP	Member of Parliament
PASC	Public Administration Select Committee (since changed to the Public Administration and Constitutional Affairs Select Committee)
PCS	Parliamentary Commissioner for Standards
SSRB	Senior Salaries Review Body
TSO	The Stationery Office
UKIP	UK Independence Party

Image credits

p. 2: Cartoon licensed from www.CartoonCollections.com

p. 10: Cartoon by Joseph Lee © The Mail on Sunday, Evening News & Daily Mail, supplied by British Cartoon Archive, University of Kent

p. 20: © Theo Walker 2019

p. 41: © Theo Walker 2019

p. 46: Cartoon licensed from www.CartoonCollections.com

p. 77: Cartoon licensed from www.CartoonCollections.com

p. 80: © Theo Walker 2019

p. 137: Cartoon by Mac © The Mail on Sunday, Evening News & Daily Mail

p. 138: Front page of the *Mail on Sunday*, 10 May 2009 © The Mail on Sunday, Evening News & Daily Mail

p. 139: Headline in *The Guardian*, 15 May 2009 © Guardian News and Media Ltd. 2019

p. 142: Front page of *The Times*, 19 June 2009 © The Times/News Licensing

p. 146: © Theo Walker 2019

p. 167: Cartoon licensed from www.CartoonCollections.com

p. 185: © Theo Walker 2019

Notes

Preface and acknowledgements

1 Emma Crewe, *The House of Commons: An Anthropology of MPs at Work*, London: Bloomsbury, 2015.
2 Tim Ingold, *Anthropology: Why it Matters*, Cambridge: Polity Press, 2018, p. 118.
3 Although some Members of the House of Lords were caught up in the scandal, and two Peers (Lord Hanningfield and Lord Taylor of Warwick) served prison sentences, we have not sought to cover these aspects in this book. Some elements, such as the public anger with Parliament, were common, but there were big differences, too. For example, the House of Lords system of expenses was and still is much simpler, and operates on a very different basis; and members of the Lords are not elected, so the relationship with the public is not comparable with MPs.

1: A prelude

1 Gordon Brown has described it as the biggest political scandal for two centuries. See Katharine Viner, 'Gordon Brown interview: "It's a strange life, really"', *The Guardian*, 20 June 2009, www.theguardian.com/politics/2009/jun/20/gordon-brown-interview, accessed 19 March 2019.
2 Ben Worthy, 'Gone But Not Forgotten? The MPs' Expenses Scandal Four Years On', Political Studies Association website,

4 June 2013, www.psa.ac.uk/political-insight/blog/gone-not-forgotten-mps'-expenses-scandal-four-years, accessed 18 March 2019.

3 Jennifer van Heerde-Hudson, *The Political Costs of the 2009 British MPs' Expenses Scandal*, Basingstoke: Palgrave Macmillan, 2014.

4 Valentino Larcinese and Indraneel Sircar, 'Crime and Punishment the British Way: Accountability Channels Following the MPs' Expenses Scandal', *European Journal of Political Economy* 47, December 2016, pp. 75–99.

5 As pointed out by Ernest Gellner, cited in Dieter Haller and Cris Shore, Introduction, in *Corruption: Anthropological Perspectives*, London: Pluto Press, 2005, p. 8.

6 We use the short versions – MPs or Members – interchangeably. The former tends to be used by outsiders, whereas parliamentary staff nearly always use the latter.

7 Christopher Silvester, *The Pimlico Companion to Parliament: A Literary Anthology*, London: Pimlico, 1997, pp. 549 and 551, plus pp. 544, 558, 567.

8 For example, Gareth Jenkins, 'Rotten Barrel', *Socialist Review* 181, December 1994, www.pubs.socialistreviewindex.org.uk/sr181/jenkins.htm, accessed 27 June 2019.

9 Anonymous MP, interviewed by Emma Crewe, May 1998.

10 See 'Lobby Journalism' entry, Parliament UK website, www.parliament.uk/about/living-heritage/evolutionofparliament/parliamentwork/communicating/overview/lobbyjournalism, accessed 18 April 2019.

11 John Biffen, *Inside Westminster: Behind the Scenes at the House of Commons*, London: André Deutsch, 1996, p. 232.

12 Philip Norton, 'The Growth of the Constituency Role of the MP', *Parliamentary Affairs* 47, October 1994, pp. 710–11.

13 Edmund Burke, *The Works of the Right Honourable Edmund Burke* (1774), 6 vols. London: Henry G. Bohn, 1854–56, pp. 446–8.

14 Crewe, *House of Commons*, 2015, p. 88.

15 Michael Saward, 'The Representative Claim', *Contemporary Political Theory* 5, August 2006, pp. 297–318.

16 Biffen, *Inside Westminster*, 1996, p. 212.

17 See table below. Source: 'Members' pay, pensions and allowances', Parliament UK website, www.parliament.uk/documents/commons-information-office/fymp/m05.pdf, accessed 27 May 2019.

18 Simon Hattenstone, 'MPs' Expenses Scandal: What Happened Next?', *The Guardian*, 11 May 2012, www.theguardian.com/politics/2012/may/11/mps-expenses-scandal-what-next, accessed 19 March 2019. See also Andrew Eggers and Alexander Fisher, 'Electoral Accountability and the UK Parliamentary Expenses Scandal: Did Voters Punish Corrupt MPs?', Working Paper No. 8, London: London School of Economics, London, September 2011, pp. 29–30.

19 A brief outline is here: Richard Kelly, 'Members' pay and allowances – a brief history', Parliament and Constitution Centre, House of Commons Library, SN/PC/05075, 21 May 2009, https://researchbriefings.files.parliament.uk/documents/SN05075/SN05075.pdf, accessed 27 May 2019.

20 Recorded transcript. Former Government Chief Whip, interviewed by Emma Crewe, May 2000.

21 J. E. Neale, *The Elizabethan House of Commons*, Harmondsworth: Penguin, 1963, p. 322.

22 Private bills are those that had a specific purpose affecting a discrete group of people.

23 Cited in Neale, *The Elizabethan House of Commons*, 1963, p. 328.

24 Noted by various commentators, for example Gabrielle Bourke and Benjamin Worthy, 'The Sword and the Shield: The Use of FOI by Parliamentarians and the Impact of FOI on Parliament', London: The Constitution Unit at UCL, 2011, http://eprints.bbk.ac.uk/8713, accessed 3 May 2019.

25 See 'The Ibbs Report (1990)', Parliament UK website, https://publications.parliament.uk/pa/cm200607/cmselect/cmcomm/685/68518.htm, accessed 28 July 2019.

26 In the 1990s there had in fact been three budgets (called 'votes'): the Administration Vote, the Works Vote and the Members' Salaries etc Vote. When accruals accounting was introduced in 2001, the Administration and Works votes were merged

into a single budget (the House of Commons Administration Estimate).

27 Dick Allen, 'Cloud No Bigger Than a Man's Hand', available on the Poetry Foundation website, July/August 2009, www.poetryfoundation.org/poetrymagazine/poems/52681/cloud-no-bigger-than-a-mans-hand, accessed 28 July 2019. The idea is drawn from the Old Testament story of the prophet Elijah: 1 Kings 18:44.

28 Black Dog reporter, 'Amber Rudd's No Deal to a Brexit tipple', *Daily Mail*, 20 April 2019, www.dailymail.co.uk/news/article-6943377/BLACK-DOG-Amber-Rudds-No-Deal-Brexit-tipple.html, accessed 28 June 2019.

29 Department of Finance and Administration, *Parliamentary Salaries, Allowances and Pensions,* House of Commons, May 1997. The 1997 Green Book remains unpublished. Green Books from 2003 to 2009 are available at https://www.parliament.uk/mps-lords-and-offices/members-allowances/house-of-commons/house-of-commons-scheme-guides/, accessed 16 August 2019.

30 Richard Kelly, House of Commons Library Standard Note SN/PC/04641, *Additional Costs Allowance,* 3 March 2008, https://researchbriefings.files.parliament.uk/documents/SN04641/SN04641.pdf, accessed 16 August 2019.

31 HC Debates, Hansard 1803–2005, 5 July 2001, vol. 371, col. 424.

32 See 'Members' Allowances', Parliament UK website, www.parliament.uk/mps-lords-and-offices/members-allowances/house-of-commons, accessed 18 April 2019.

33 Review Body on Senior Salaries, *Review of Parliamentary Pay and Allowances 2001*, report no. 48, col. 4997. London: The Stationery Office, 2001.

34 HC Debates, Hansard 1803–2005, 19 July 2001, vol. 372, col. 317W.

35 Anonymous panel member, interviewed by Emma Crewe and Andrew Walker, October 2018.

36 Commission and Members Estimate Committee meetings took place together.

37 Sir Roger Sands, interviewed by Emma Crewe and Andrew Walker, January 2018.

38 Review Body on Senior Salaries, *Review of Parliamentary Pay and Allowances 2004*, report no. 57, col. 6354, London: The Stationery Office, 2004.

39 A transcript of the debate is available on the Parliament UK website: https://publications.parliament.uk/pa/cm200304/ cmhansrd/vo041103/debtext/41103-18.htm, accessed 18 April 2019.

40 Sir Roger Sands, interviewed by Emma Crewe and Andrew Walker, January 2018.

41 Biffen, *Inside Westminster*, 1996, p. 212.

42 From 2003, receipts were required for items costing £250 or more. At the same time, the Fees Office was tightening up by requiring MPs to give more detail on their claims to justify the expenditure, even for small items. Some MPs therefore started to submit receipts for items costing pence or a few pounds, but without the expectation that they would later be disclosed. Receipts for *all* expenses were not actually required until 2009.

43 Lord Kirkwood, interviewed by Emma Crewe and Andrew Walker, April 2018.

44 Robert Winnett, interviewed by Emma Crewe and Andrew Walker, December 2018.

2: Secrecy cracks open

1 See the Hansard archive via the Parliament UK website: www. data.parliament.uk/dataset/hansard-archive, accessed 17 April 2019.

2 Bourke and Worthy, 'The Sword and the Shield', 2011, p. 7. They add that Parliament has been taking steps towards greater transparency over several centuries, more so than many other public organisations. Transparency of decisions made by legislators on behalf of the people are a cornerstone of its functioning. The daily publication of Hansard, committee reports, submissions and library papers bears this out.

3 See Caroline Shenton, *The Day Parliament Burned Down*, Oxford: Oxford University Press, 2012.

4 Anonymous senior clerk, interviewed by Emma Crewe and Andrew Walker, date withheld for anonymity.

5 Wikipedia, s.v. 'Cash-for-questions affair', https://en.wikipedia. org/wiki/Cash-for-questions_affair, accessed 17 April 2019.

6 An online version of Erskine May is available here: https:// erskinemay.parliament.uk, accessed 4 July 2019.

7 Tony Blair, *A Journey: A Political Life*, London: Hutchinson, 2010, p. 516.

8 For example, Peter Hennessy, *Whitehall*, London: Pimlico, 1989.

9 Tony Blair, speech to the Campaign for Freedom of Information on 25 March 1996, transcript available at www.cfoi.org. uk/1996/05/speech-by-the-rt-hon-tony-blair-mp-leader-of-the-labour-party-at-the-campaign-for-freedom-of-informations-annual-awards-ceremony-25-march-1996, accessed 20 April 2019.

10 The OSA does not apply to 'proceedings in Parliament', but if parliamentary staff were given access to secret government information – as in the case of MP Mike Hancock's relationship with Ekaterina Zatuliveter – then disclosure of information other than in the course of proceedings *would* be covered by the Act.

11 Cabinet Office, 'Your Right to Know: The Government's Proposals for a Freedom of Information Act', London: The Stationery Office, 1997, col. 3818, para 2.3.

12 Select Committee on Public Administration, Third Report, May 1998, Parliament UK website, https://publications.parliament. uk/pa/cm199798/cmselect/cmpubadm/398-vol1/39807.htm#a5, accessed 17 April 2019.

13 Members of the committee at the time were Mr Peter Bradley, Helen Jones, Mr Ronnie Campbell, Mr Rhodri Morgan, Dr Lynda Clark, Mr David Ruffley, Mr Mike Hancock, Mr Richard Shepherd, Miss Melanie Johnson, Mr Andrew Tyrie, Mr Fraser Kemp.

14 Michael Carpenter, 'The Accountability of Members for their Expenses: Legal and Jurisdictional Issues', *Journal of Parliamentary and Political Law* 5, 2011, pp. 323–36.

15 'Public Administration – Third Report', Parliament UK website, 28 July 1999, https://publications.parliament.uk/pa/cm199899/ cmselect/cmpubadm/570/57002.htm, accessed 17 April 2019.

16 The Commission is a statutory body set up under the House of Commons Administration Act 1978. The Corporate Officer was created by the Parliamentary Corporate Bodies Act 1992.

17 Carpenter, 'The Accountability of Members', 2011. Following dissolution, the House of Commons ceases to exist until the day appointed for proclamation for the first meeting of the new Parliament. Following the 2010 general election, this was some time after Polling Day, because the negotiations to form the new coalition government took several days.

18 In common with some other legislation, such as the Health and Safety at Work Act 1974, and various aspects of employment law. Applicability of legislation to Parliament has from time to time been overlooked by government departments that sponsor legislation, and by drafters of parliamentary legislation. In the case of expenses, the arguments in Tribunal and the High Court turned to a large extent on the tension in the FOI and Data Protection legislation between MPs' right to privacy and the wider public interest in their expenses.

19 'Although Jack Straw and Derry Irvine (who later took over responsibility for FOI) both wanted to bring the Act into force for central government after 12–18 months, Tony Blair's personal intervention ensured it was delayed for over four years. The right of access did not take effect until January 2005.' 'The Blair Memories and FOI', Campaign for Freedom of Information website, 6 October 2010, www.cfoi.org.uk/2010/10/the-blair-memoirs-and-foi-2, accessed 17 April 2019.

20 Gabrielle Bourke and Benjamin Worthy, 'Open House? The Impact of the Freedom of Information Act on Westminster', Paper for the PSA Annual Conference, April 2011, www.ucl.ac.uk/constitution-unit/sites/constitution-unit/files/Open_House._The_Impact_of_FOI_on_Westminster.pdf, accessed 17 April 2019.

21 The latest version of the advice is at 'Privilege, Confidentiality and FOI for Select Committees', Parliament UK website, https://beta.parliament.uk/articles/Mk9xrfWe, accessed 17 April 2019.

22 Sir Nick Harvey, interviewed by Emma Crewe and Andrew Walker, January 2018.

23   Norman Baker, *Against the Grain*, London: Biteback, 2015, p. 191.

24   Anonymous staff member, interviewed by Andrew Walker and Emma Crewe, April 2018.

25   The House of Commons is not in any event subject to Corporation Tax, by agreement with HMRC.

26   Information Tribunal decision, 26 February 2008, paras 41–3, http://informationrights.decisions.tribunals.gov.uk/DBFiles/Decision/i85/HoC3.pdf, accessed 17 April 2019.

27   *On Expenses,* directed by Simon Cellan Jones and written by Tony Saint, 2010, BBC TV film.

28   Anonymous senior MP, interviewed by Andrew Walker and Emma Crewe, October 2018.

29   Quentin Letts, *Letts Rip!*, London: Constable, 2010, p. 24, from a sketch originally published 24 October 2000, just after Michael Martin had been elected Speaker.

30   Dalyell went on to say, 'Martin was born in the Anderston district of Glasgow, one of the five children of a merchant navy stoker and a cleaning lady. He always told me that the "Gorbals" tag irritated him because, he said with a twinkle, that Anderston made the Gorbals look like Weybridge and "most of my friends would have considered living there in the Gorbals a step up"'. Obituary, *The Independent*, 1 May 2018, www.independent.co.uk/news/obituaries/michael-martin-mp-death-commons-speaker-expenses-scandal-labour-trade-union-a8329981.html, accessed 17 April 2019.

31   Anonymous MP, interviewed by Emma Crewe and Andrew Walker, month withheld for anonymity 2018.

32   Baker, *Against the Grain*, 2015, p. 191.

33   Anonymous senior official, interviewed by Emma Crewe and Andrew Walker, month withheld for anonymity 2018.

34   Anonymous senior politician, interviewed by Emma Crewe and Andrew Walker, month withheld for anonymity 2018.

35   Sir Roger Sands, interviewed by Emma Crewe and Andrew Walker, January 2018.

36   Anonymous member of the Commission, interviewed by Emma Crewe and Andrew Walker, month withheld for anonymity 2018.

37 Sir Nick Harvey, interviewed by Emma Crewe and Andrew Walker, January 2018.

38 Anonymous official, interviewed by Emma Crewe, June 2018.

39 Ibid., January 2018.

40 Anonymous official, interviewed by Emma Crewe, June 2018.

41 Information Tribunal decision, 26 February 2008, para 44, http://informationrights.decisions.tribunals.gov.uk/DBFiles/Decision/i85/HoC3.pdf, accessed 17 April 2019.

42 The case is summarised in the House of Commons Standards and Privileges Committee report, 'Complaints against Mr Michael Trend', 13 February 2003, HC 435, Parliament UK website, https://publications.parliament.uk/pa/cm200203/cmselect/cmstnprv/435/435.pdf, accessed 17 April 2019

43 Brendan Carlin and George Jones, 'Blunkett fights for his political life', *The Telegraph*, 29 November 2004, https://www.telegraph.co.uk/news/uknews/1477734/Blunkett-fights-for-his-political-life.html, accessed 28 August 2019.

44 As explained by a former MP, interviewed by Emma Crewe and Andrew Walker, October 2018.

45 The Green Book: Parliamentary Salaries, Allowances and Pensions, 2003 edition, Parliament UK website, www.parliament.uk/documents/commons-finance-office/greenbook2003.pdf, accessed 17 April 2019.

46 The concordance of resolutions (the ones that were extant in the run-up to the crisis) can be found here: https://publications.parliament.uk/pa/cm200506/cmselect/cmmemest/950/950ii.pdf, accessed 17 April 2019.

47 Ibid., para 3.1.

48 'The Operation of the Parliamentary Standards Act 2009 – Committee on Members' Expenses', Parliament UK website, https://publications.parliament.uk/pa/cm201012/cmselect/cmmemex/1484/148404.htm, accessed 17 April 2019.

49 The Green Book: Parliamentary Salaries, Allowances and Pensions, 2006 edition, Parliament UK website, www.parliament.uk/documents/upload/hofcpsap.pdf, accessed 17 April 2019. 'It is your responsibility to satisfy yourself when you submit a claim, or authorise payments from your staffing allowance, that

any expenditure claimed from the allowances has been wholly, exclusively and necessarily incurred for the purpose of performing your Parliamentary duties.'

50 House of Commons Standards and Privileges Committee report, 'Conduct of Mr David Blunkett', 20 December 2004, HC 189, Parliament UK website, https://publications.parliament.uk/pa/cm200405/cmselect/cmstnprv/189/189.pdf, accessed 17 April 2019.

51 Curiously no such misused travel warrant was ever discovered. (In those days, convicts, squaddies and MPs were given warrants to travel by train. In the case of MPs, they filled them in and presented them at the station or on the train in return for a rail ticket. The warrants were collected by the rail companies, scanned, and sent to the Fees Office electronically for bulk payment. In this case, an extensive search for the warrant given to Mrs Quinn drew a complete blank – no warrant for the amount in question found its way back to the Fees Office for payment.)

52 David Hind and Gillian Peele, 'Integrity Issues in the United Kingdom: An Emerging Debate', in Dirk Tänzler, Konstadinos Maras and Angelos Giannakopoulos (eds.), *The Social Construction of Corruption in Europe*, Farnham: Ashgate, 2012, pp. 59–86.

53 For example, Alan Doig, 'Politics and Sleaze: Conservative Ghosts and Labour's Own Brand', *Parliamentary Affairs* 56, April 2003, pp. 322–33 discusses a number of cases of sleaze in the two main parties between 1980 and 2003, but the only reference to expenses is about election expenses, not parliamentary expenses.

54 'MPs' allowances and FoI requests' report, 22 June 2009, Parliament UK website, https://researchbriefings.parliament.uk/ResearchBriefing/Summary/SN04732#fullreport, accessed 17 April 2019.

55 Anonymous MP, interviewed by Emma Crewe and Andrew Walker, June 2018.

56 Anonymous MP, interviewed by Emma Crewe and Andrew Walker, June 2018.

57 Marc Johnson, 'John Stonborough: From Investigative Journalism to PR', Journalism.co.uk website, 2 November 2009,

https://blogs.journalism.co.uk/2009/11/02/john-stonborough-from-investigative-journalism-to-pr, accessed 18 April 2019.

58 Heather Brooke, 'Unsung Hero', *The Guardian*, 15 May 2009, www.theguardian.com/politics/2009/may/15/mps-expenses-heather-brooke-foi, accessed 18 April 2019.

3: Closing ranks on privacy

1 Heather Brooke, *The Silent State*, London: William Heinemann, 2010, p. 228.

2 Robert Winnett and Gordon Rayner, *No Expenses Spared*, London: Bantam Press, 2009, p. 19.

3 Brooke, *The Silent State*, 2010, p. 233.

4 Anonymous MP, interviewed by Emma Crewe, June 2012.

5 Baker, *Against the Grain*, 2015, p. 179.

6 'House of Commons: 2005 Freedom of Information Request Log', Parliament UK website, www.parliament.uk/documents/upload/05requestlog.pdf, accessed 29 April 2019.

7 Information Tribunal decision, 26 February 2008, para 5 (1–4), http://informationrights.decisions.tribunals.gov.uk/DBFiles/Decision/i85/HoC3.pdf, accessed 17 April 2019.

8 Ibid., para 5(4).

9 A recurring example concerned website hits from computers on the Parliamentary Estate. When asked what websites were accessed in a given period, it quickly became clear that pornographic websites had been visited on a number of occasions. In the early days, journalists simply attributed this to MPs, without apparently knowing that MPs as a group were only a small proportion of IT users on the Parliamentary Estate. Thus, after prompting negative press coverage, the House began to provide context when releasing such information in order to demonstrate that the data provided no direct evidence that MPs as a group, let alone any individual MP, had accessed pornography from their parliamentary computers.

10 The National Audit Office issued a critical report in 2002: www.nao.org.uk/wp-content/uploads/2002/04/0102750.pdf, accessed

18 April 2019, but media attention concentrated on the cost of the reception desk and the fig trees planted in the atrium. See HC Debates, Hansard 1803–2005, 31 October 2000, vol. 355, cols 352–3W, https://api.parliament.uk/historic-hansard/written-answers/2000/oct/31/portcullis-house, accessed 18 April 2019.

11 Members Estimate Committee, 'Concordance of Resolutions', HC 240-II, Parliament UK website, 6 May 2005, https://publications.parliament.uk/pa/cm200405/cmselect/cmmemest/240/240ii.pdf, accessed 18 April 2019.

12 Select Committee on Modernisation of the House of Commons, 'Connecting Parliament with the Public', HC 364, Parliament UK website, 26 May 2004, https://publications.parliament.uk/pa/cm200304/cmselect/cmmodern/368/368.pdf, accessed 18 April 2019.

13 Hansard Society and Gemma Rosenblatt (eds.), *Parliament in the Public Eye 2006: Coming into Focus? A Review of the Hansard Society Commission on the Communication of Parliamentary Democracy* (the 'Puttnam Commission'), London: Hansard Society, 2006.

14 John Pullinger (who became Director General of Information Services and in 2014 left the House of Commons to become the National Statistician), interviewed by Emma Crewe, February 2019.

15 This is not a direct quote but a summary of the typical view of MPs who were against parliament proactively doing outreach.

16 Andrew's press cuttings about expenses rose from 14 in four whole years (2003–06) to 51 in 2009, excluding the dozens of *Telegraph* entries.

17 For example, Jon Ungoed-Thomas and Robert Winnett, 'Two Jags and his mystery council tax bill', *Sunday Times*, 18 December 2005, www.thetimes.co.uk/article/two-jags-and-his-mystery-council-tax-bill-d2pvp28s273, accessed 29 July 2019; Norman Baker, 'Greedy, sly and unethical', *Mail on Sunday*, 26 March 2006, page 29; Gareth Walsh and Jon Ungoed-Thomas, 'Revealed: the 'black hole' in Blair's expenses', *Sunday Times*, 9 April 2006, www.thetimes.co.uk/article/revealed-the-black-hole-in-blairs-expenses-t55lxdh6cqn, accessed 29 July 2019.

18 Michael White, 'Red-faced MPs call for tougher line on expenses', *The Guardian*, 28 October 2004, https://www.theguardian.com/politics/2004/oct/28/uk.houseofcommons, accessed 20 August 2019.

19 Norman Baker, *Mail on Sunday*, 26 March 2006 page 29.

20 The books by Heather Brooke, by Robert Winnett and Gordon Rayner, and by Norman Baker tell a similar story. They each start with the FOI requests made in January 2005 and then fast-forward to the events of 2007. The figures are:

Year	Total FOI requests	Requests about MPs' expenses
2005	196	65
2006	141	37
2007	198	66
2008	358	180

Source: www.parliament.uk/site-information/foi/foi-and-eir/commons-request-disclosure-logs, accessed 20 April 2019.

21 Sir Nick Harvey, interviewed by Emma Crewe and Andrew Walker, January 2018.

22 See the House of Commons' internal note of a meeting between senior politicians and the Information Commissioner in late 2006: 'Jack Straw tried to conceal MPs' expenses: the minutes', *The Telegraph*, October 2009, www.telegraph.co.uk/news/newstopics/mps-expenses/6389793/Jack-Straw-tried-to-conceal-MPs-expenses-the-minutes.html, accessed 28 April 2019.

23 Cited in David Runciman, *Political Hypocrisy: The Mask of Power, from Hobbes to Orwell and Beyond*, Princeton, NJ: Princeton University Press, 2008, pp. 89–91. Viscount Bolingbroke is referring to the monarch, reflecting the conditions of political leadership in the eighteenth century.

24 Henry Bolingbroke, 'The Idea of a Patriot King', 1 December 1738, https://socialsciences.mcmaster.ca/econ/ugcm/3ll3/bolingbroke/king.html, accessed 17 April 2019. Runciman in *Political Hypocrisy* , 2008, p. 91, summarises this as 'those who are

serious about power should live as though their private lives were public'.

25 Jeremy Horder, *Criminal Misconduct in Office*, Oxford: Oxford University Press, 2018, p. 94.

26 Heather Brooke, 'There's Nothing Private about an MP's Expenses', *The Independent,* 10 April 2006, www.independent. co.uk/voices/commentators/heather-brooke-theres-nothing-private-about-an-mps-expenses-356821.html, accessed 27 July 2019.

27 David V. James et al., 'Aggressive/Intrusive Behaviours, Harassment and Stalking of Members of the United Kingdom Parliament: A Prevalence Study and Cross-National Comparison', *Journal of Forensic Psychiatry and Psychology* 27 (January 2016), www.tandfonline.com/doi/abs/10.1080/14789949.2015.1124908, accessed 19 April 2019.

28 Ibid.

29 Anonymous MP, interviewed by Emma Crewe and Andrew Walker, January 2018.

30 Sir Nicholas and Lady Winterton, both MPs, fell foul of this rule by renting a joint second home from a family trust, thereby benefiting themselves and their children (House of Commons Standards and Privileges Committee report, 'Conduct of Sir Nicholas and Lady Winterton', 17 June 2008, HC 744, Parliament UK website, https://publications.parliament.uk/pa/cm200708/cmselect/cmstnprv/744/744.pdf, accessed 28 July 2019).

31 Margaret Moran MP was later found to have claimed expenses on a home that did not qualify. Her case was more serious than Sayeed's: 'Fraud MP Margaret Moran given supervision order', BBC News, 14 December 2012, www.bbc.co.uk/news/uk-england-beds-bucks-herts-20725315, accessed 19 April 2019.

32 Philipp Nicolai, 'Wachet auf, ruft uns die Stimme', 1599 hymn based on Jesus's parable of the ten virgins – five of them were foolish, and were found not to have used the time while the bridegroom was away to fill their lamps with oil. So, when the bridegroom arrived, their lamps went out and they were not admitted to the feast (Matthew 25:1–13).

33 HC Debates, Hansard, 1 November 2006, vol. 451, col. 312. There
    is an excellent summary of the Communications Allowance and
    its history by Richard Kelly at http://researchbriefings.files.
    parliament.uk/documents/SN04615/SN04615.pdf, accessed 19
    April 2019.
34 HC Debates, Hansard, 1 November 2006, vol. 451, col. 385.
35 HC Debates, Hansard, 28 March 2007, vol. 458, col. 1524.
36 http://www.conservativehome.com/thetorydiary/2008/01/
    david-camerons-6.html, accessed 19 April 2019.
37 David Cameron, 'Cutting the Cost of Politics', Conservative
    Party speech, 8 September 2009. Cited in Kelly,
    'Communications Expenditure', House of Commons Research
    paper SN/PC/4615, 25 February 2010, https://researchbriefings.
    files.parliament.uk/documents/SN04615/SN04615.pdf, accessed
    19 April 2019.
38 This was another genuinely tricky issue, as public authorities did
    not necessarily set the same store by MPs or their constituents'
    confidentiality as MPs did. The issue took many months before a
    workable *modus operandi* was developed.
39 The story only came to light publicly in January 2009, following
    another FOI request by the *Telegraph*. Ben Leapman and
    Alastair Jamieson, 'Jack Straw "tried to conceal MPs' expenses"',
    The Telegraph, 17 October 2009, www.telegraph.co.uk/news/
    newstopics/mps-expenses/6360729/Jack-Straw-tried-to-conceal-
    MPs-expenses.html, accessed 19 April 2019.
40 https://www.telegraph.co.uk/news/newstopics/mps-
    expenses/6389793/Jack-Straw-tried-to-conceal-MPs-expenses-
    the-minutes.html; https://www.telegraph.co.uk/news/
    newstopics/mps-expenses/6389793/Jack-Straw-tried-to-conceal-
    MPs-expenses-the-minutes.html?image=1; and https://www.
    telegraph.co.uk/news/newstopics/mps-expenses/6389793/
    Jack-Straw-tried-to-conceal-MPs-expenses-the-minutes.
    html?image=2, accessed 16 August 2019.
41 Sir Nick Harvey, interviewed by Emma Crewe and Andrew
    Walker, January 2018.
42 For the bill see 'Freedom of Information (Amendment) Bill',
    Parliament UK website, https://publications.parliament.uk/pa/

cm200607/cmbills/039/07039.i-i.html, accessed 19 April 2019. For the comment see Baker, *Against the Grain*, 2015, p. 184.

43 The Leader of the House, shadow leaders and whips from the main government and opposition parties, who make agreements on the basis that they can usually (until recently) get their backbenchers to support the party line.

44 Brendan Carlin, 'Freedom of Information vote 'places MPs above law'', *The Telegraph* 19 May 2007, https://www.telegraph.co.uk/news/uknews/1552018/Freedom-of-Information-vote-places-MPs-above-law.html, accessed 16 August 2019.

45 David Hencke and Helene Mulholland, 'Lack of Lords sponsor wrecks plan to exempt MPs from FoI Act', *The Guardian,* 14 June 2007, https://www.theguardian.com/politics/2007/jun/14/uk.pressandpublishing, accessed 16 August 2009.

46 'The attempt to exclude Parliament from FOI through David Maclean's Private Member's Bill... [was] strongly opposed by the media, who portrayed them as self-interested attempts to limit FOI and keep embarrassing information secret.' Robert Hazell, Ben Worthy and Mark Glover, *The Impact of the Freedom of Information Act on Central Government in the UK*, Basingstoke: Palgrave Macmillan, 2010, p. 221.

47 The Slave Trade Act received Royal Assent on 25 March 1807.

48 'MP's Expenses Revealed After Two-Year Battle', *The Herald*, 3 November 2007, www.heraldscotland.com/news/12767165. MP_apos_s_expenses_revealed_after_two-year_battle/, accessed 19 April 2019.

49 Information Tribunal decision, appeal no. EA/2006/0074/0075/0076, 9 August 2007, para 17, http://informationrights.decisions.tribunals.gov.uk/DBFiles/Decision/i84/HoC2.pdf, accessed 19 April 2019.

50 Sir Christopher Kelly, interviewed by Emma Crewe and Andrew Walker, December 2018.

51 Committee on Standards in Public Life, Annual Report, March 2007 (the CSPL timeline erroneously says March 2006. There was no adverse comment about MPs' expenses in the March 2006 report), https://webarchive.nationalarchives.gov.uk/20131003071854/http://www.public-standards.gov.uk/

wp-content/uploads/2012/11/AnnualReport2006.pdf, accessed 19 April 2019.

52 His forensic and detailed report – when it finally appeared in 2008 – had two devastating effects: first, it exposed Conway as having committed a serious breach of the rules. It led to more media comment than the original *Sunday Times* exposé had. Secondly, the timing of the report's publication on 28 January 2008 was just over a week before the Information Tribunal heard the House's appeal in the main FOI case about disclosure of ACA details, raising the temperature of public opinion still further.

53 House of Commons Members Estimate, Audit Committee Annual Report, 2008–09, paras 16–17, Parliament UK website, www.parliament.uk/documents/commons-committees/ members-estimate-audit/Annual-Reports/Members-Estimate-Audit-Committee-2008-09-Annual-Report.pdf, accessed 19 April 2019.

54 Ibid.

55 Sir Thomas Legg, interviewed by Emma Crewe and Andrew Walker, 12 December 2018.

56 House of Commons Members Estimate, Audit Committee Annual Report, 2007–08, Parliament UK website, www. parliament.uk/documents/commons-committees/members-estimate-audit/Annual-Reports/Members-Estimate-Audit-Committee-2007-08-Annual-report.pdf, accessed 19 April 2019.

57 Richard Kelly, 'Review of parliamentary pay and allowances 2008', 17 January 2008, report SN/PC/04585, Parliament UK website, http://researchbriefings.files.parliament.uk/documents/ SN04585/SN04585.pdf, accessed 19 April 2019.

58 Thus it was not simply that successive governments persuaded MPs not to vote for pay rises, but that the formula used for automatic uprating was defective, ensuring that their pay inevitably slipped behind the pay of comparator groups.

4: Ebbing privilege

1 Martin Salter and Rob Wilson (report HC 1071, 17 October
  2007); Elfin Llwyd, Adam Price and Hywell Williams (HC 94,
  19 November 1997); Norman Baker, Malcolm Bruce and Sadiq
  Khan (HC 182, 13 December 2007).

2 Sir Nick Harvey, interviewed by Emma Crewe and Andrew
  Walker, January 2018.

3 David Amess MP, as reported in the *Basildon, Canvey and
  Southend Echo*: Michelle Archard, 'Expenses are a Trivial
  Matter, Claims MP Amess', *Basildon, Canvey and Southend
  Echo*, 3 July 2009, www.echo-news.co.uk/news/local_news/
  southend/4472744.Expenses_are_a_trivial_matter__claims_
  MP_Amess, accessed 28 April 2019.

4 The changes are summarised in a House of Commons Library
  briefing note: 'The Tebbit Review of Management and Services
  of the House of Commons', 26 February 2008, report SN/
  PC/04391, http://researchbriefings.files.parliament.uk/
  documents/SN04391/SN04391.pdf, accessed 28 April 2019.

5 Information Tribunal decision, 26 February 2008, para 80,
  http://informationrights.decisions.tribunals.gov.uk/DBFiles/
  Decision/i85/HoC3.pdf, accessed 17 April 2019.

6 Sir Nick Harvey, interviewed by Emma Crewe and Andrew
  Walker, 18 January 2018.

7 'Review of Parliamentary Pay, Pensions and Allowances 2007',
  January 2008, report no. 64, https://assets.publishing.service.
  gov.uk/government/uploads/system/uploads/attachment_data/
  file/243117/7270.pdf, accessed 19 April 2019.

8 HC Debates, Hansard, 16 January 2008, cols 32–36WS.

9 Robert Winnett and Holly Watt, 'MP hires son on expenses',
  Sunday Times, 27 May 2007, www.thetimes.co.uk/article/
  mp-hires-son-on-expenses-qn06jmdztjw, accessed 6 August 2019.

10 House of Commons Standards and Privileges Committee report,
  'Conduct of Mr Derek Conway', 25 January 2008, HC 280,
  Parliament UK website, https://publications.parliament.uk/pa/
  cm200708/cmselect/cmstnprv/280/280.pdf, accessed 19 April
  2019.

11 Interview with Derek Conway, *Mail on Sunday*, 3 February 2008,
    p. 8.

12 Letts, *Letts Rip!*, 2010, p. 195.

13 There was an FOI request for the information in January 2008.
    The requester was told that the information was not held by
    the House of Commons: 'House of Commons: 2008 Freedom
    of Information Request Log', Parliament UK website, www.
    parliament.uk/documents/foi/FOI-requestlog-2008-HOC.pdf,
    accessed 19 April 2019.

14 House of Commons Standards and Privileges Committee report,
    'Conduct of Mr Iain Duncan Smith', 26 March 2004, HC 476–I,
    Parliament UK website, https://publications.parliament.uk/pa/
    cm200304/cmselect/cmstnprv/476/476.pdf, accessed 19 April
    2019.

15 Simon Walters, 'After a week of vilification, defiant Derek
    Conway speaks out and says: "I did nothing wrong"', *Daily Mail*,
    2 February 2008, www.dailymail.co.uk/news/article-511948/
    After-week-vilification-defiant-Derek-Conway-speaks-says-I-did-
    wrong.html, accessed 27 July 2019.

16 The House of Commons Standards and Privileges Committee
    rapidly conducted an inquiry into MPs' employment of family
    members. It recommended that the practice should be allowed
    to continue, but MPs would have to disclose employment of
    family members on a public register. The Chair of the Committee
    on Standards in Public Life had written to the committee in
    a similar vein: House of Commons Standards and Privileges
    Committee report, 'Employment of family members through
    the Staffing Allowance', 18 March 2008, HC 436, Parliament
    UK website, https://publications.parliament.uk/pa/cm200708/
    cmselect/cmstnprv/436/436.pdf, accessed 6 August 2019. IPSA
    announced in March 2017 that the practice would be banned
    from the next General Election: Emilio Casalicchio and Tom
    Barnes, 'MPs to be Banned from Employing Family Members
    in Major Expenses Crackdown', PoliticsHome website, 15 March
    2017, www.politicshome.com/news/uk/politics/public-affairs/
    news/84270/mps-be-banned-employing-family-members-major-
    expenses, accessed 19 April 2019.

17 Nick Cohen, 'When Will It Dawn on MPs How Bad They Look to Us?', *Evening Standard*, 6 February 2008, p. 12.

18 Richard Kelly, 'Members' Allowances – Reporting Requirements', 2 April 2008, report SN/PC/04624, Parliament UK website, http://researchbriefings.files.parliament.uk/documents/ SN04624/SN04624.pdf, accessed 19 April 2019.

19 There is a good summary of both the tribunal judgement and the later High Court judgement in Carpenter, 'The Accountability of Members', 2011, pp. 323–36.

20 Brooke, 'Unsung Hero', 15 May 2009. Heather Brooke, interviewed by Emma Crewe, April 2019.

21 Anonymous House of Commons official, interviewed by Emma Crewe, April 2018.

22 A phrase made famous by Sir Robert Armstrong in the *Spycatcher* trial of 1986, though the idea is said to go back to Edmund Burke.

23 Carpenter, 'The Accountability of Members', 2011, p. 327.

24 There was no transcript of the proceedings, but Sam Coates of the *Times* reported some of the evidence in his Red Box blog on 9 February 2008, referred to by Richard Kelly (see n. 18).

25 Information Tribunal decision, 26 February 2008, paras 24–5, http://informationrights.decisions.tribunals.gov.uk/DBFiles/ Decision/i85/HoC3.pdf, accessed 17 April 2019.

26 Ibid., paras 52–62.

27 Ibid., paras 70–73.

28 It is not clear how the tribunal established this as a finding of fact rather than opinion (see Carpenter, 'The Accountability of Members', 2011).

29 Information Tribunal decision, 26 February 2008, paras 74, 81(a), 82, 79(g), http://informationrights.decisions.tribunals. gov.uk/DBFiles/Decision/i85/HoC3.pdf, accessed 17 April 2019. Interestingly, it was the MPs who had submitted most receipts and details that attracted the most attention during the crisis the following year.

30 The Green Book: Parliamentary Salaries, Allowances and Pensions, 2003 edition, para 3.8.1, Parliament UK website, www.parliament.uk/documents/commons-finance-office/ greenbook2003.pdf, accessed 19 April 2019.

31 'Additional Cost Allowance Claims Guide (the "John Lewis
    list")', Parliament UK website, 13 March 2008, www.parliament.
    uk/documents/upload/HofCClaimsGuide.pdf (the list as at 13
    March 2008), accessed 19 April 2019.

32 Jake Morris, 'Every Little Helps: MPs can put weekly shop on
    expenses', *Daily Mirror*, 9 February 2008, www.mirror.co.uk/
    news/uk-news/every-little-helps-mps-can-292779, accessed 29
    July 2019.

33 Lord Touhig, interviewed by Emma Crewe and Andrew Walker,
    September 2018.

34 Sam Coates, the Red Box blog, 9 February 2008. See n. 18.

35 Jason Lewis, 'Speaker used his business air miles to get free trips
    for his family', *Mail on Sunday*, 17 February 2008.

36 Jonathan Oliver, 'Top aide Mike Granatt quits over Michael
    Martin's expenses', *Sunday Times*, 24 February 2008, www.
    thetimes.co.uk/article/top-aide-mike-granatt-quits-over-speaker-
    michael-martins-expenses-mphjzx0kml9, accessed 6 August 2019.

37 'Show some dignity... and go swiftly', *Mail on Sunday*, 24
    February 2008, www.dailymail.co.uk/news/article-517846/
    COMMENT-Show-dignity-swiftly.html, accessed 6 August
    2019.

38 In a written answer in March 2008, the House disclosed to David
    Winnick MP that the defence costs of the tribunal cases so far
    had been nearly £52,000, before taking account of the cost that
    would later have to be paid to the other parties. HC Debates,
    Hansard, 5 Mar 2008, vol. 472, col. 2487W.

39 Sir Nick Harvey, interviewed by Emma Crewe and Andrew
    Walker, January 2018.

40 The full court judgement can be found here: [2008] EWHC
    1084 (Admin), www.right2info.org/resources/publications/
    case-pdfs/uk_corporate-officer-of-the-house-of-commons-v.-
    information-commissioner-et-al, accessed 19 April 2019.

41 'Blair was chased over unpaid bill', BBC News, 23 May 2008,
    news.bbc.co.uk/1/hi/uk_politics/7417017.stm, accessed 27 May
    2019.

42 'Decisions 19 May 2008', Parliament UK website, www.
    parliament.uk/mps-lords-and-offices/offices/commons/

house-of-commons-commission/minutes/minutes-2008/
hccfm190508, accessed 19 April 2019.

43 The Freedom of Information (Parliament and National Assembly
for Wales) Order 2008, No. 1967, www.legislation.gov.uk/
uksi/2008/1967/contents/made, accessed 6 August 2019.

44 Information Tribunal decision, 26 February 2008, para 76,
http://informationrights.decisions.tribunals.gov.uk/DBFiles/
Decision/i85/HoC3.pdf, accessed 17 April 2019.

45 Sir Stuart Bell, David Maclean and Nick Harvey.

46 The dates were 4, 20, 25 February 2008; 5, 10, 19, 26 March 2008;
3, 23, 30 April 2008; 7, 14 May 2008; and 4 June 2008.

47 Members Estimate Committee, 'Review of Allowances: Third
Report of Session 2007–08', vol. 1, HC 578-I, Parliament UK
website, 23 June 2008, www.publications.parliament.uk/pa/
cm200708/cmselect/cmmemest/578/578i.pdf, accessed 6 August
2019. Vol. 2, HC 578-II, can be found here: www.publications.
parliament.uk/pa/cm200708/cmselect/cmmemest/578/578ii.
pdf, accessed 19 April 2019.

48 David Hencke, 'MPs' expenses: these reforms are long
overdue', *The Guardian*, 25 June 2008 www.theguardian.com/
politics/2008/jun/25/houseofcommons3, accessed 27 July 2019.

49 Joe Murphy, 'London MPs pay bonanza', *Evening Standard*,
25 June 2008, www.standard.co.uk/news/london-mps-pay-
bonanza-6885190.html, accessed 6 August 2019.

50 Lord Touhig, interviewed by Emma Crewe and Andrew Walker,
September 2018.

51 Ibid.

52 HC Debates, Hansard, 3 July 2008, vol. 451, cols 1101, 1114.

53 Andrew Porter, 'MPs Vote to Keep "John Lewis" list', *The
Telegraph*, 4 July 2008 and Ben Russell and Nigel Morris, 'Nice
work if you can get it: MPs keep their perks', *The Independent*,
4 July 2008. Both extracts cited in Richard Kelly, 'Members'
Allowances: decision of 16 July 2008 and the revised Green
Book', House of Commons Library, Standard Note SN/
PC/04813, 20 January 2009.

54 Christopher Hood, 'A Public Management for All Seasons',
Public Management 69, Spring 1991.

55 See for example Thomas Yarrow et al., 'Introduction: reconsidering detachment', in *Detachment: Essays on the Limits of Relational Thinking*, Manchester: Manchester University Press, 2015, p. 17.

56 Reported in Kelly, 'Members' Allowances...', 2008, report SN/PC/04624.

57 For example, John Spellar MP, 'Is it not slightly odd, however, that – as has already been said a number of times – what is essentially a matter of House business should be raised in Opposition time and thus become a matter of party business?' HC Debates, Hansard, 16 July 2008, vol. 479, col. 288. This foreshadowed the attempts of backbenchers to take control of the business of the House in relation to Brexit.

58 Ibid., col. 304.

59 The government's consultation paper 'Audit and Assurance of MPs' Allowances', August 2008, report CM7460, made it clear that MPs would continue to be able to claim for household goods.

60 Sir Christopher Kelly, interviewed by Emma Crewe and Andrew Walker, December 2018.

61 The same committee that ten years previously had recommended that Parliament should be subject to the FOI Act.

62 'Review of MPs' Expenses and Allowances', https://webarchive.nationalarchives.gov.uk/20131003071446/http://www.public-standards.gov.uk/wp-content/uploads/2012/11/Background_Paper_No_2.__Timeline_of_Events.pdf, accessed 19 April 2019.

63 CSPL press notice, 28 July 2008, quoted in Richard Kelly, 'Members' Allowances – Decision of 16 July 2008 and the Revised Green Book', 20 January 2009, report SN/PC/04813, Parliament UK website, http://researchbriefings.files.parliament.uk/documents/SN04813/SN04813.pdf, accessed 19 April 2019.

64 Unlike previous Speakers, Michael Martin had been in the habit of continuing to meet his old party friends in the Members' Tea Room. 'Tea Room talk' was the phrase used in the House of Commons for the chatter between MPs over a cup of tea or a snack, where MPs gathered with party colleagues.

65 Lord Touhig, interviewed by Emma Crewe and Andrew Walker, September 2018.

66 Stephen Robinson, 'Michael Martin: The Speaker Cornered', *Sunday Times Magazine*, 27 July 2008, www.thetimes.co.uk/article/michael-martin-the-speaker-cornered-0z9cpmshlh8, accessed 6 August 2019.

67 Leader of the House of Commons, 'Audit and Assurance of MPs' Allowances', August 2008, report CM7460, London: The Stationery Office, 2008.

68 HC Debates, Hansard, 10 September 2008, vol. 479, col. 127WS.

69 HC Debates, Hansard, 9 October 2008, vol. 480, col. 20WS.

70 The Green Book: A Guide to Members' Allowances, 2009 edition, Parliament UK website, www.parliament.uk/documents/commons-finance-office/greenbook.pdf, accessed 19 April 2019.

5: The leak

1 At the meeting of the MEC on 19 May 2008, they decided not to appeal again, and to publish receipt-level information about all MPs' expenses: 'Decisions 19 May 2008', Parliament UK website, www.parliament.uk/mps-lords-and-offices/offices/commons/house-of-commons-commission/minutes/minutes-2008/hccfm190508, accessed 19 April 2019.

2 HC Debates, Hansard, 1 July 2008, vol. 478, col. 742W.

3 Formerly Her Majesty's Stationery Office, but now a private company.

4 Anonymous Fees Office official, interviewed by Emma Crewe, April 2018.

5 HC Debates, Hansard, 3 April 2008, vol. 474, col. 1142W.

6 HC Debates, Hansard, 20 May 2008, vol. 476, col. 174W.

7 Winnett and Rayner, *No Expenses Spared*, 2011.

8 HC Debates, Hansard, 31 March 2009, vol. 490, col. 789.

9 The review was initially about the early disclosures (in particular regarding the Home Secretary, Jacqui Smith), but after the *Telegraph* started publishing extensive leaked information, the review was extended to cover those disclosures too.

10 On 23 July 2008: The Freedom of Information (Parliament and National Assembly for Wales) Order 2008, No. 1967. See Chapter 4.

11 HC Debates, Hansard 1803–2005, 21 November 1989, vol. 162, col. 7.

12 Paul Flynn, *How to be an MP*, London: Biteback, 2012, p. 142.

13 Professor Tony Wright, interviewed by Emma Crewe, December 2013.

14 Oliver Wright, '"Some of the emails I've had are simply appalling": MPs complain of vitriolic lobbying ahead of historic vote', *The Independent*, 5 February 2013, www.independent. co.uk/news/uk/politics/some-of-the-emails-ive-had-are-simply-appalling-mps-complain-of-vitriolic-lobbying-ahead-of-historic-vote-8481240.html, accessed 27 July 2019.

15 Anonymous MP, interviewed by Emma Crewe, March 2012.

16 HC Debates, Hansard, 28 January 2009, vol. 487, col. 542W.

17 HC Debates, Hansard, 4 June 2009, vol. 493, col. 611W. The Advisory Panel on Members' Allowances had been replaced by the Committee on Members' Allowances in January 2009 (see 'At sixes and sevens in Byzantine bureaucracy', below).

18 BBC Radio 4, *The Reunion: Parliamentary Expenses Scandal*, 14 April 2019, www.bbc.co.uk/programmes/m0004629, accessed 6 August 2019.

19 Lord Touhig, interviewed by Andrew Walker and Emma Crewe, September 2018.

20 In a resolution adopted by the House on 16 July 2008 that stated: 'There should be a re-writing of the Green Book by the Advisory Panel on Members' Allowances, augmented by two independent external appointees.'

21 House of Commons Commission, 'Decisions 21 July 2008', Parliament UK website, www.parliament.uk/mps-lords-and-offices/offices/commons/house-of-commons-commission/minutes/minutes-2008/hccfm210708, accessed 23 April 2019.

22 House of Commons Members Estimate, Audit Committee Annual Report, 2008–09, Parliament UK website, www.parliament.uk/documents/commons-committees/

members-estimate-audit/Annual-Reports/Members-Estimate-Audit-Committee-2008-09-Annual-Report.pdf, accessed 30 April 2019.

23 'Michael Fabricant (Con Lichfield) will ask the Commons Administration Committee... to investigate claims that officials lost crucial documents, and failed to check expenses claims properly.' Jonathan Walker, 'Midland MP wants inquiry into Commons staff's handling of expenses claims', *Birmingham Post*, 16 October 2009, www.business-live.co.uk/news/local-news/midland-mp-wants-inquiry-commons-3938403, accessed 6 August 2019.

24 Practice notes were the detailed guidance and instructions needed to underpin the general principles set out in the new version of the Green Book, published in 2009. Few practice notes were written before the system was abolished.

25 Anonymous official, comment made to Emma Crewe and Andrew Walker, June 2019.

26 The MEAC made a Delphic comment in its 2008/09 Annual Report, stating that 'It was disappointed that various complexities in governance which remained to be resolved, together with logistical issues, meant the new system [of audit and assurance] would not be in place from 1 April 2009.' House of Commons Members Estimate, Audit Committee Annual Report, 2008–09, para 21, Parliament UK website, www.parliament.uk/documents/commons-committees/members-estimate-audit/Annual-Reports/Members-Estimate-Audit-Committee-2008-09-Annual-Report.pdf, accessed 23 April 2019.

27 Now Sir Paul Silk, previously Clerk of the National Assembly of Wales, and subsequently author of the 'Silk Commission Report' into government financing in Wales: https://webarchive.nationalarchives.gov.uk/20140605075122/http://commissionondevolutioninwales.independent.gov.uk, accessed 23 April 2019.

28 In the House of Commons Service, clerks are the most senior staff, not the most junior. Bob Castle, interviewed by Emma Crewe, April 2018.

29 The Green Book: Parliamentary Salaries, Allowances and Pensions, July 2006 edition, Parliament UK website, www.parliament.uk/documents/upload/hofcpsap.pdf and The Green Book: A Guide to Members' Allowances, July 2009 edition, Parliament UK website, www.parliament.uk/documents/commons-finance-office/greenbook.pdf, accessed 23 April 2019.

30 House of Commons Members Estimate Committee, 'Revised Green Book and audit of Members' allowances', First Report of Session 2008–09, HC 142, Parliament UK website, https://publications.parliament.uk/pa/cm200809/cmselect/cmmemest/142/142.pdf, accessed 30 April 2019.

31 HC Debates, Hansard, 22 January 2009, vol. 486, col. 945.

32 Brendan Carlin, 'How Gorbals Mick used our money to pulp guide to MPs' expenses', *Mail on Sunday*, 25 January 2009, www.dailymail.co.uk/news/article-1127248/How-Gorbals-Mick-used-money-pulp-guide-MPs-expenses.html, accessed 6 August 2019.

33 'Neighbours make a new complaint against Jacqui Smith: "She only stays here for four months a year"', *Mail on Sunday*, 15 February 2009, www.dailymail.co.uk/news/article-1145571/Neighbours-make-new-complaint-Jacqui-Smith-She-stays-months-year.html, accessed 6 August 2019.

34 Simon Walters and Martin Delgado, 'Lodger deal earns Jacqui Smith £100,000', *Mail on Sunday*, 8 February 2009, www.pressreader.com/uk/the-mail-on-sunday/20090208/281487862243199, accessed 6 August 2019.

35 Jason Groves and Marco Giannangeli, 'WORLD EXCLUSIVE: Jacqui Smith put adult films on expenses', *Sunday Express*, 29 March 2009, https://www.express.co.uk/news/uk/91920/WORLD-EXCLUSIVE-Jacqui-Smith-put-adult-films-on-expenses, accessed 19 August 2019.

36 Gordon Brown: 'Let Jacqui Smith get on with her job as Home Secretary', *The Telegraph*, 30 March 2009, https://www.telegraph.co.uk/news/politics/labour/5076151/Gordon-Brown-Let-Jacqui-Smith-get-on-with-her-job-as-Home-Secretary.html, accessed 15 August 2019.

37 House of Commons Standards and Privileges Committee report, 'Mr Tony McNulty', 27 October 2009, HC 1070, Parliament

UK website, https://publications.parliament.uk/pa/cm200809/cmselect/cmstnprv/1070/1070.pdf, accessed 30 April 2019.

38   Winnett and Rayner, *No Expenses Spared*, 2011, p. 54.

39   The letter is printed in full at the end of Chapter 6.

40   See Chapter 4, 'A watchdog watches'.

41   'Review of MPs' Expenses and Allowances', https://webarchive. nationalarchives.gov.uk/20131003071446/http://www.public-standards.gov.uk/wp-content/uploads/2012/11/Background_ Paper_No_2.__Timeline_of_Events.pdf, accessed 23 April 2019. The dates given on the CSPL website are inconsistent.

42   Sir Christopher Kelly, interviewed by Emma Crewe and Andrew Walker, December 2018.

43   Letters, *The Guardian*, 1 April 2009.

44   HC Debates, Hansard, 1 April 2009, vol. 490, col. 911.

45   Winnett and Rayner, *No Expenses Spared*, 2011, pp. 59–83.

46   Sam Coates, 'MPs' expenses receipts were hawked by City businessman', *The Times*, 1 April 2009, www.thetimes.co.uk/ article/mps-expenses-receipts-were-hawked-by-city-businessman-rv9cp8v385s, accessed 6 August 2019.

47   Peter Oborne, 'Sorry, but a Tory victory is far from certain', *Daily Mail*, 11 April 2009, www.dailymail.co.uk/debate/article-1169141/PETER-OBORNE-Sorry-Tory-election-victory-far-certain.html, accessed 6 August 2019.

48   Government ministers with grace-and-favour homes would not get the subsistence allowance.

49   It appeared on the Cabinet Office website, and is still available on YouTube: 'MPs expenses', YouTube video, uploaded 23 April 2009, www.youtube.com/watch?v=sBXj5l6ShpA, accessed 23 April 2019.

50   'Rory Bremner does Gordon Brown's expenses video', YouTube video, uploaded 11 June 2009, www.youtube.com/watch?v=lfcNZmRkKLo, accessed 23 April 2019.

51   Gordon Brown, *My Life, Our Times*, London: Bodley Head, 2017. On pp. 12–14 he deals with the expenses crisis, but does not mention this episode. See also Harriet Harman, *A Woman's Work*, London: Penguin Random House, 2017. Although her memoir

covers the period when she was Leader of the House, it does not deal with the expenses crisis.

52 Andrew Sparrow, 'Party leaders clash as Gordon Brown urges MPs' expenses overhaul', *The Guardian*, 21 April 2009, www. theguardian.com/politics/2009/apr/21/gordon-brown-mps-expenses-reform, accessed 29 July 2019.

53 HC Debates, Hansard, 23 April 2009, vol. 491, col. 376.

54 Sam Coates et al., 'Gordon Brown's YouTube plan for MPs' £150 a day expenses collapses', *The Times*, 27 April 2009, www.thetimes. co.uk/article/gordon-browns-youtube-plan-for-mps-pound150-a-day-expenses-collapses-s2vbmntnchd, accessed 23 April 2019.

55 Andrew Grice, 'Brown backs down on plan for MPs to "clock in"', *The Independent*, 28 April 2009. Cited in Richard Kelly, 'Members' Allowances – the Government's proposals for reform', House of Commons Library Standard Note SN/PC/05046, 5 May 2009, p. 17.

56 The motion agreed by the House was 'That this House welcomes the Prime Minister's decision of 23 March 2009 to invite the Committee on Standards in Public Life to inquire into Members' allowances; believes that in order to command maximum public support for change the House should defer its conclusions until after the Committee has reported; and further believes it would be desirable for the House to have an opportunity to consider any recommendations from the Committee as early as possible.' HC Debates, Hansard, 30 April 2009, vol. 491, col. 126.

6: 'A tempest dropping fire'

1 William Shakespeare, *Julius Caesar*, 1599, Act I, scene 3, line 5.

2 Robert Winnett, interviewed by Emma Crewe and Andrew Walker, December 2018. The story is engagingly told in detail in Winnett and Rayner, *No Expenses Spared*, 2011. By the end of the investigation, the *Telegraph* had sold an extra 1.26 million newspapers.

3 Brown, *My Life, Our Times*, 2017, pp. 12–14.

4   Technically, the 'Comptroller General of the Receipt and Issue
    of Her Majesty's Exchequer and Auditor General of Public
    Accounts'.

5   A term borrowed by the *Telegraph*'s Christopher Hope from the
    USA, where it is used to describe purchasing a revenue-generating
    asset and quickly reselling it for profit. In the UK context, it was
    used by the media to apply to MPs who had switched between
    main and second homes in order to maximise their expenses and/
    or to profit from the ultimate sale of the property.

6   Robert Winnett, interviewed by Emma Crewe and Andrew
    Walker, December 2018.

7   Rosa Prince, 'Clearing the moat at viscount's manor', *The
    Telegraph*, 2 May 2009, p. 7.

8   'The Complete Expenses Files', supplement included with *The
    Telegraph*, 20 June 2009.

9   'MPs' expenses editor "more resolute" after Queen talk', BBC
    News, 25 March 2019, www.bbc.com/news/uk-47669586,
    accessed 16 April 2019.

10 'The Complete Expenses Files', *The Telegraph*, 23 June 2009, p. 2.

11 Anonymous MP, interviewed by Emma Crewe and Andrew
    Walker, June 2018.

12 In fact, the police did not launch an investigation. The internal
    investigation of the leak resumed once the police had responded.

13 HC Debates, Hansard, 11 May 2009, vol. 492, col. 548.

14 MPs interviewed by Emma Crewe and Andrew Walker, January
    and October 2018. Also see Baker, *Against the Grain*, 2015,
    pp. 191–2. Baker described his attitude as 'sneering'. One retired
    official told us that he could simply have left it, that it was a
    matter for the Clerk, and moved on, rather than commenting on
    Ms Hoey's media appearances.

15 Lord Touhig, interviewed by Emma Crewe and Andrew Walker,
    September 2018.

16 Anonymous MP, interviewed by Emma Crewe, June 2013.

17 Anonymous official, interviewed by Emma Crewe, June 2018.

18 Anonymous senior Conservative MP, interviewed by Emma
    Crewe and Andrew Walker, October 2018.

19 Michael Savage, 'Climate-change envoy Morley sacked over
    £16,000 mortgage', *The Independent*, 15 May 2009, https://www.
    independent.co.uk/news/uk/politics/climate-change-envoy-
    morley-sacked-over-pound16000-mortgage-1685196.html,
    accessed 20 August 2019.

20 Martin Beckford and Nick Allen, '£50,000 to rent a cottage from
    his sister-in-law', *The Telegraph*, 23 May 2009, p. 3.

21 For example, according to Patrick Wintour, 'Speaker Martin's
    stay of execution', *The Guardian*, 18 May 2009, www.theguardian.
    com/politics/2009/may/18/gordon-brown-michael-martin-
    speaker, accessed 6 August 2019.

22 HC Debates, Hansard, 18 May 2009, vol. 492, col. 1205.

23 David Heath MP, ibid., col. 1206.

24 Benedict Brogan, 'Now critics accuse Brown of dithering', *The
    Telegraph*, 20 May 2009, p. 5.

25 HC Debates, Hansard, 19 May 2009, vol. 492, col. 1323.

26 Shirley Williams, 'Much to be done, but a shotgun election won't
    help', *The Independent*, 21 May 2009, p. 9.

27 The Speaker called the MEC 'the Commission' in his statement
    to the House: HC Debates, Hansard, 19 May 2009, vol. 492, col.
    1421.

28 This would later become the Legg review. See below.

29 For example the rule about capital gains tax (CGT) was based on
    a misunderstanding of how the tax worked, and the differences
    in 'main home' definition as between the tax authorities and the
    ACA. Walker recalls that the MEC was in no mood to grapple
    with these details.

30 HC Debates, Hansard, 20 May 2009, vol. 492, cols 1505–19.

31 What was ultimately enacted in the Parliamentary Standards Act
    a couple of months later differed from the announcement, in that
    IPSA was not required to implement the Kelly recommendations
    – they carried out their own consultation and went their own
    way. Nor were the proposals to bring the House of Lords within
    the scope of IPSA pursued.

32 HC Debates, Hansard, 20 May 2009, vol. 492, col. 1508.

33 As the authors find when they travel to overseas parliaments, the
    three things that are usually known about the political world in

Britain are the Queen, Mrs Thatcher, and the expenses scandal. Brexit can now, of course, be added to the list.

34 HC Debates, Hansard, 20 May 2009, vol. 492 cols 1513–14.

35 Bob Castle, interviewed by Emma Crewe, April 2018.

36 In the end, all staff other than senior managers who wanted to transfer to IPSA were offered the opportunity to do so.

37 Simon Walters, 'Speaker's Scapegoat: Official who signed off MPs' expenses didn't even have a qualification in accountancy', *Mail on Sunday*, 10 May 2009, www.pressreader.com/uk/the-mail-on-sunday/20090510/281483567333895, accessed 6 August 2019.

38 Walker had a 20-year history at the Inland Revenue, and had qualified as an accountant in 2008.

39 He was accused of breaching the Ministerial Code, but was later exonerated by Sir Philip Mawer, the Prime Minister's independent adviser on the Code (Press Association report in *The Independent*, 9 June 2009).

40 Brooke, 'Unsung Hero', 15 May 2009.

41 Lord Touhig, interviewed by Andrew Walker and Emma Crewe, September 2018.

42 Ex-Liberal Democrat MP, interviewed by Emma Crewe and Andrew Walker, June 2018. The newspaper story can be found here: Jon Swaine, 'MPs' expenses: Lord Kirkwood did up flat on expenses then sold it cheaply to daughter', *The Telegraph*, 3 June 2009, www.telegraph.co.uk/news/newstopics/mps-expenses/5431827/MPs-expenses-Lord-Kirkwood-did-up-flat-on-expenses-then-sold-it-cheaply-to-daughter.html, accessed 6 August 2019.

43 Larcinese and Sircar, 'Crime and punishment the British way', 2016, pp. 75–99, and 'Singing from the same broadsheet?' in van Heerde-Hudson (ed.), *The Political Cost*, 2014, pp. 153–74.

44 Georgina Waylen and Ros Southern, 'Gender, Informal Institutions and Corruption: The UK Parliamentary Expenses Scandal', paper prepared for the Gender and Corruption Conference, University of Gothenburg, 23–24 May 2016.

45 Anonymous lobby correspondent, interviewed by Emma Crewe, month withheld for anonymity 2019.

46 Anonymous lobby correspondent, interviewed by Emma Crewe and Andrew Walker, month withheld for anonymity 2018.

47 Anonymous lobby correspondent, interviewed by Andrew Walker, month withheld for anonymity 2018.

48 This was the first time new rules for the election of a new Speaker by secret ballot had been used. See House of Commons Library briefing paper SN05074, Richard Kelly, 'The Election of a Speaker', 9 June 2017, Parliament UK website, https:// researchbriefings.parliament.uk/ResearchBriefing/Summary/ SN05074#fullreport, accessed 6 August 2019.

49 John Bercow, interviewed by Andrew Walker and Emma Crewe, June 2018.

50 There is a good summary of the background to the bill in House of Commons Research Paper 09/61: Oonagh Gay, 'Parliamentary Standards Bill', House of Commons Library Research Paper 09/61, 25 June 2009.

51 For example *The Times* headline on 24 June 2009: 'MPs will regret rushing into tough looking legislation on expenses'.

52 House of Commons Justice Committee report, 'Constitutional Reform and Renewal: Parliamentary Standards Bill', 1 July 2009, https://publications.parliament.uk/pa/cm200809/ cmselect/cmjust/791/791.pdf, Parliament UK website, accessed 23 April 2019. The Committee's report also includes the Clerk's memorandum.

53 Sir Christopher Kelly, interviewed by Emma Crewe and Andrew Walker, December 2018.

54 House of Commons Committee on Standards in Public Life report, 'MPs' Expenses and Allowances: Supporting Parliament, safeguarding the taxpayer', 1 November 2009, 12th report, Cm 7724, Parliament UK website, www.gov.uk/government/ publications/twelfth-report-of-the-committee-on-standards-in- public-life-november-2009, accessed 29 April 2019.

55 Some Scandinavian parliaments provide living accommodation for their MPs in their parliamentary buildings or nearby.

56 See Chapter 3.

57 The legal immunities for witnesses and Members of both Houses of Parliament to allow them to perform their duties without

interference from outside Parliament. This includes freedom of speech within parliamentary proceedings and the right of each House of Parliament to regulate its own affairs.

58 Supreme Court press summary, 1 December 2010, Supreme Court website, www.supremecourt.uk/cases/docs/uksc-2010-0195-press-summary.pdf, accessed 1 May 2019.

59 David Chaytor, Jim Devine, Eric Ilsley, Denis MacShane, Margaret Moran and Elliot Morley. All were found guilty. Margaret Moran was found not fit to plead through mental illness, but she was sentenced to a two-year supervision and treatment order.

60 That is, the additional costs of having to live in two places – both Westminster and constituency – as required by their roles as MP.

61 HC Debates, Hansard, 23 June 2009, vol. 494, col. 678. His terms of reference were agreed by the MEC on 1 July: www.parliament.uk/mps-lords-and-offices/offices/commons/house-of-commons-commission/minutes/minutes-2009/hccfm010709, accessed 23 April 2019.

62 Sir Thomas Legg, interviewed by Emma Crewe and Andrew Walker, December 2018.

63 Nicholas Watt and Allegra Stratton, 'Anger and anarchy among MPs at extent of Legg's demands', *The Guardian*, 14 October 2009, www.theguardian.com/politics/2009/oct/14/mps-expenses-legg-labour-brown, accessed 24 May 2019.

64 The review covered all MPs who had claimed ACA during the previous 5-year period. When there was no money to be repaid, the entry read 'x has no issues'.

65 Office insider, communication with Emma and Andrew, June 2019.

66 Ann Widdecombe, *Strictly Ann*, London: Phoenix, 2014, p. 411.

67 Anonymous MP, interviewed by Emma Crewe and Andrew Walker, October 2018. The issue was taken up by Deborah Orr, 'The MPs' expenses row exposes the attitude to pay in this country', *The Guardian*, 15 October 2009, www.theguardian.com/commentisfree/2009/oct/15/mps-expenses-cleaners-low-pay, accessed 27 June 2019.

68 House of Commons Members Estimate Committee, 'Review of Past ACA Payments', HC 348, London: The Stationery Office, 2010.

69 Jonathan Rose, *The Public Understanding of Political Integrity: The Case for Probity Perceptions*, Basingstoke: Palgrave Macmillan, 2014, pp. 120–21. 'In this analysis, the specific (per MP) effect of 'MPs' expenses' remains conspicuous by its absence ... The effect of wrongfully claiming more than £1000 is statistically indistinguishable from the effect of claiming entirely appropriately.'

70 Hansard Society, 'Audit of Political Engagement: The 2019 Report', Hansard Society website, www.hansardsociety.org.uk/projects/research/audit-of-political-engagement, accessed 23 April 2019. The 2019 report shows a sustained dip in political engagement and trust since the expenses scandal. The ratings worsened further in 2019 as a result of the Brexit crisis.

71 House of Commons Reform Committee report, 'Rebuilding the House', 12 November 2009, HC 1117, Parliament UK website, https://publications.parliament.uk/pa/cm200809/cmselect/cmrefhoc/1117/1117.pdf, accessed 23 April 2019.

72 See 'Rise of the backbenchers' in Chapter 7 for how this worked out.

7: Aftershocks

1 Larcinese and Sircar, 'Crime and punishment the British way', 2016, pp. 75–99.

2 Anonymous MP, interviewed by Emma Crewe, June 2013.

3 J. L. Newell, 2010, 'Understanding and Preventing Corruption: Lessons from the UK Expenses Scandal', 2010 conference paper, University of Salford, Manchester, http://usir.salford.ac.uk/id/eprint/10373/6/Paper-2.pdf:public, accessed 20 April 2019, p. 2.

4 Anonymous Labour MP, interviewed by Emma Crewe and Andrew Walker, December 2018.

5 Anonymous MP, interviewed by Emma Crewe, May 2012.

6 Anonymous MP, interviewed by Emma Crewe, March 2013.

7 Anonymous MP, interviewed by Emma Crewe, September 2012.

8 Anonymous colleague of Hogg, interviewed by Emma Crewe, May 2012.

9 Anonymous MP, interviewed by Emma Crewe, March 2019.

10 Ashley Weinburg, 'A Longitudinal Study of the Impact of Changes in the Job and the Expenses Scandal on UK National Politicians' Experiences of Work, Stress and the Home–Work Interface', *Parliamentary Affairs* 68, 2015, pp. 248–71.

11 Ibid.

12 BBC Radio 4, *The Reunion: Parliamentary Expenses Scandal*, 14 April 2019, www.bbc.co.uk/programmes/m0004629, accessed 6 August 2019. On the programme the presenter, Sue MacGregor, said that the BBC had approached more than 60 MPs and peers who had been accused of or found guilty of fiddling their expenses. All of them apart from Ann Cryer had turned down the invitation to appear.

13 Proverbs 22:1.

14 'Blears to face confidence motion', BBC News, 13 June 2009, http://news.bbc.co.uk/1/hi/uk_politics/8097955.stm, accessed 20 April 2019.

15 Crewe, *House of Commons*, 2015, pp. 99–100.

16 Stephen Pound, interviewed by Emma Crewe, 7 August 2012.

17 Richard Fenno, *Home Style: House Members in their Districts*, New York: Harper Collins, 1978, p. 56.

18 Ibid., pp. 64, 85.

19 Crewe, *House of Commons*, 2015, p. 100.

20 Nick Vivyan, Markus Wagner and Jessica Tarlov, 'Representative Misconduct, Voter Perceptions and Accountability: Evidence from the 2009 House of Commons Expenses Scandal', *Electoral Studies* 31, 2012, p. 761.

21 The case was only taken to the regulator in 2016 after the *Telegraph* republished an image of the front page of their original story featuring Gordon Brown and his brother in 2009: 'IPSO Upholds Gordon Brown Expenses Complaint', *The Telegraph*, 15 May 2017, www.telegraph.co.uk/news/2017/05/15/ipso-upholds-gordon-brown-expenses-complaint, accessed 24 April 2019.

22 Ed Miliband, 'Full Transcript: Speech on the Riots', delivered at Haverstock School and published by the *New Statesman*, 15 August 2011, www.newstatesman.com/politics/2011/08/society-young-heard-riots, accessed 28 April 2019.

23 Anonymous Labour MP, interviewed by Emma Crewe, November 2011.

24 Christopher Hope, Chief Political Correspondent for the *Telegraph*, on BBC Radio 4, *The Reunion: Parliamentary Expenses Scandal*, 14 April 2019, www.bbc.co.uk/programmes/m0004629, accessed 6 August 2019.

25 https://www.parliament.uk/business/commons/the-speaker/speeches/speeches/designing-a-parliament-for-the-21st-century/, accessed 28 August 2019.

26 https://www.conservativehome.com/thetorydiary/2009/06/john-bercow-sets-out-his-3000-word-manifesto-for-a-21st-century-speakership.html, accessed 28 August 2019.

27 Speaker Bercow, interviewed by Emma Crewe and Andrew Walker, June 2018.

28 *The Argus*, 8 September 2012 as cited by Crewe, *House of Commons*, 2015, p. 169.

29 Tony Wright, interviewed by Emma Crewe, 15 December 2011.

30 Commons Select Committee, 'How the Backbench Business Committee Works', Parliament UK website, www.parliament.uk/business/committees/committees-a-z/commons-select/backbench-business-committee/how-the-backbench-business-committee-works, accessed 27 June 2019.

31 Meg Russell, '"Never Allow a Crisis to Go to Waste": The Wright Committee Reforms to Strengthen the House of Commons', *Parliamentary Affairs* 64, 2011, pp. 612–33.

32 Ibid.

33 House of Commons Library, 'General Election 2010' research paper, 2 February 2011, http://researchbriefings.files.parliament.uk/documents/RP10-36/RP10-36.pdf, accessed 30 April 2019.

34 Letter to Members on the Wright Committee recommendations, 1 March 2010, http://wrightreforms.files.wordpress.com/2010/05/support-wright-reforms-letter-2-march-2010.pdf, accessed 4 December 2013.

35 David Foster, 'Going "Where Angels Fear to Tread": How
    Effective was the Backbench Business Committee in the 2010–
    2012 Parliamentary Session?', *Parliamentary Affairs* 68, 2015,
    pp. 116–34. One reason for the increase in viewing (perhaps the
    main one) is that the Petitions Committee contacts people who
    signed the petition that led to the debate, letting them know
    when the debate is going to take place and how they can view it.

36 Now Baron Young of Cookham, cited in ibid.

37 The Hansard Society conducts annual audits of political
    engagement: www.hansardsociety.org.uk.

38 *Expenses: The Scandal That Changed Britain*, BBC Two, 25
    March 2019, www.bbc.co.uk/iplayer/episode/m0003mtg/
    expenses-the-scandal-that-changed-britain, accessed 27 March
    2019.

39 Emma Crewe, 'Magi or Mandarins? Contemporary Clerkly
    Culture', in Paul Evans (ed.), *Essays on the History of
    Parliamentary Procedure*, Oxford: Hart Publishing, 2018,
    pp. 45–68.

40 In October 2018, Dame Laura Cox reported that bullying both by
    MPs and by senior staff had not been addressed adequately, and
    that a major culture change was required. Dame Laura Cox, 'The
    Bullying and Harassment of House of Commons Staff' report,
    15 October 2018, Parliament UK website, www.parliament.uk/
    documents/dame-laura-cox-independent-inquiry-report.pdf,
    accessed 27 April 2019. This was what she was asked to look at, so
    she followed her remit, but the consequences of failing to inquire
    into why these patterns emerge has led to considerable confusion.

41 Chloe Chaplain, 'Westminster Bullying: Full List of 83 House of
    Commons Employees Who Have "Experienced or Seen Bullying
    Firsthand" in Parliament', *iNews*, 22 October 2018, https://inews.
    co.uk/news/politics/westminster-bullying-house-of-commons-
    employees-letter-full-list-parliament, accessed 29 June 2019.

42 Anonymous official interviewed by Emma Crewe, October 2013.

43 One senior clerk did, however, stand in for the Fees Office's
    Director of Operations for a few months in 2008.

44 See Emma Crewe 'Magi or Mandarins? Contemporary
    Clerkly Culture', in Paul Evans, (ed.), *Essays on the History of*

Parliamentary Procedure. Oxford; Portland: Hart, pp. 45–68 and Marilyn Strathern (ed.), Audit Cultures: Anthropological Studies in Accountability, Ethics and the Academy, London: Routledge, 2000. For more about management of the House, see Richard Kelly and Ed Potton, 'The Administration of the House of Commons', House of Commons Library Standard Note SN/PC/6976, 21 January 2015, researchbriefings.files.parliament.uk/documents/SN06976/SN06976.pdf, accessed 15 August 2019.

45 The Clerk's Department had taken over Hansard and the Serjeant-at-Arms Department in 2008.

46 Anonymous ex-staff member, interviewed by Andrew Walker, April 2019.

47 Made Lord Lisvane in December 2014.

48 Andrew gave evidence to the Committee that a 'two-pillar model of equals is likely to be quite disastrous'. House of Commons Governance Committee report, HC 692, 6 November 2014, https://www.parliament.uk/business/committees/committees-a-z/commons-select/house-of-commons-governance-committee/publications/?type=Oral#pnlPublicationFilter, accessed 27 April 2019.

49 Ibid, HC 692. Emma advised the committee that the role of the top Clerk should clearly be above the role of Director General/Chief Executive. Andrew advised the opposite.

50 House of Commons Governance Committee report, HC 692, 6 November 2014, para 9, https://www.parliament.uk/business/committees/committees-a-z/commons-select/house-of-commons-governance-committee/publications/?type=1#pnlPublicationFilter, accessed 15 August 2019.

51 See the quote by David Heathcoat-Amory in 'Rise of the backbenchers' in Chapter 7.

52 Heather Brooke on BBC Radio 4, *The Reunion: Parliamentary Expenses Scandal*, 14 April 2019, www.bbc.co.uk/programmes/m0004629, accessed 6 August 2019.

53 Crewe, *House of Commons*, 2015, p. 111.

54 Chairs are elected by the whole House; other Members are elected by their party colleagues (with no results published).

55 Daniel Boffey, 'Cameron did not think EU referendum would happen, says Tusk', *The Guardian*, 21 January 2019, www.theguardian.com/world/2019/jan/21/donald-tusk-warned-david-cameron-about-stupid-eu-referendum-bbc, accessed 20 April 2019.

56 House of Commons Select Committee on Public Administration and Constitutional Affairs, 'Lessons Learned from the EU Referendum' report, HC 496, 11 April 2017, Parliament UK website, https://publications.parliament.uk/pa/cm201617/cmselect/cmpubadm/496/49602.htm, accessed 20 April 2019, pp. 12–13.

57 Alexis de Tocqueville, *Democracy in America* (1889), Washington, DC: Regnery, 2002, p. 200.

8: Ordinary MPs in an extraordinary scandal

1 Lucinda Maer and Richard Kelly, 'Members' pay and allowances: arrangements in other parliaments', 23 April 2009, House of Commons Research Briefing report SN/PC/05050, Parliament UK website, https://researchbriefings.files.parliament.uk/documents/SN05050/SN05050.pdf, accessed 29 April 2019.

2 John Dunn, *Democracy: The Unfinished Journey, 508 BC to AD 1993*, Oxford: Oxford University Press, 1992.

3 Stephen Coleman, 'Direct Representation: Towards a Conversational Democracy', Institute for Public Policy Research exchange, 11 November 2005, www.ippr.org/files/ecomm/files/Stephen_Coleman_Pamphlet.pdf, accessed 23 May 2019.

4 Haller and Shore, *Corruption*, 2005, p. 6.

5 In 2019 MPs earn £79,468, so more than double the annual mean basic full-time pay of less than £30,000 in 2018, according to the Office of National Statistics.

6 Virginia Woolf, 'This is the House of Commons' (1932), *Virginia Woolf Miscellany* 87, Spring/Summer 2015, p. 30.

7 See J. Dunn, *Setting the People Free, The Story of Democracy*, London: Atlantic Books, 2005, p. 174.

8   Aneurin Bevan, *In Place of Fear*, London: William Heinemann, 1952, p. 7.

9   Florence Sutcliffe-Braithwaite, *Class, Politics and the Decline of Deference in England 1968–2000*, Oxford: Oxford University Press, 2018.

10   Ibid., pp. 8–9.

11   Ibid., p. 11.

12   Jack Ashley, interviewed by Emma Crewe, May 1998.

13   Crewe, *House of Commons*, 2015, p. 106.

14   Philip Cowley, 'Why not ask the audience? Understanding the public's representational priorities', *British Politics* 8, 2013, pp. 138–63.

15   Decca Aitkenhead, 'Sarah Wollaston interview: "If it ain't broke, don't fix it… but it is a bit broke"', *The Guardian*, 20 September 2013, www.theguardian.com/politics/2013/sep/20/sarah-wollaston-interview, accessed 23 April 2019.

16   Four months later she quit that party (Change UK) and sat as an independent.

17   Len McCluskey, 'Peter Mandelson's selection argument is about politics not procedure', *The Guardian*, 21 May 2013, www.guardian.co.uk/commentisfree/2013/may/21/peter-mandlesons-selection-argument-politics-procedure, accessed 7 July 2013.

18   *Today Programme*, BBC Radio 4, 20 October 2012, www.bbc.co.uk/programmes/b01ng03q, accessed 6 August 2019.

19   Georgia Gaden and Delia Dumitrica, 'The "real deal": Strategic authenticity, politics and social media', *First Monday* 20, January 2015, www.ojphi.org/ojs/index.php/fm/article/view/4985/4197, accessed 23 April 2019.

20   Frankfurt, as quoted by Gaden and Dumitrica, ibid.

21   For example Daniel Kawczynski MP said in March 2019 that he would now support the Prime Minister's deal because in his constituency 'the mood has changed': Darren Hunt, 'Brexiteer MP reveals constituency's "UNPRECEDENTED" Brexit shift', *Daily Express*, 18 March 2019, www.express.co.uk/news/uk/1101814/Brexit-news-UK-EU-BBC-Theresa-May-Conservative-Party-European-Union, accessed 29 April 2019. But compliance with constituents' wishes has not been universal:

David Wooding, 'The Brexit Wreckers: MPs who are betraying their constituents by trying to thwart Brexit – from Anna Soubry to Amber Rudd', *The Sun*, 2 March 2019, www.thesun. co.uk/news/brexit/8548383/brexit-mps-ignoring-leave-voting-constituents, accessed 29 April 2019.

22 'Secret Diary of an MP: I want to help but it's humiliating – a dead cat would be as useful', *The Times*, 25 March 2019, www. thetimes.co.uk/article/secret-diary-of-an-mp-i-want-to-help-but-its-humiliating-a-dead-cat-would-be-as-useful-06sq2wll5, accessed 6 August 2019.

23 Bronwen Weatherby, 'North East Somerset MP Jacob Rees-Mogg calls Remainers "cave-dwellers"', *Bristol Post*, 2 April 2018, www. bristolpost.co.uk/news/bristol-news/north-east-somerse-mp-jacob-1409498, accessed 29 April 2019.

24 Runciman, *Political Hyprocrisy*, 2008, p. 71.

25 Ibid., p. 210.

26 Matt Korris, 'A Year in the Life: From Member of Public to Member of Parliament', June 2011, Hansard Society, London, interim briefing paper, https://assets.ctfassets.net/rdwvqctnt75 b/4ZgkQrromIO4I6y6QooWCE/5a186b1ba880d4b5780aee6 7f03f6564/Publication__A-Year-In-the-Life-From-Member-of-Public-to-Member-of-Parliament.pdf, accessed 25 May 2019.

27 Anonymous staff member, interviewed by Andrew Walker, April 2019.

28 *World at One*, BBC Radio 4, 21 May 2009, www.bbc.co.uk/ programmes/bookcrmx, accessed 6 August 2019. See also Wikipedia, s.v. 'Anthony Steen', https://en.wikipedia.org/wiki/ Anthony_Steen, accessed 23 April 2019.

29 'Cameron warns "jealousy" MP Steen', BBC News, 22 May 2009, http://news.bbc.co.uk/1/hi/uk_politics/8062786.stm, accessed 29 April 2019.

30 S. Fielding, introduction to 'Fiction and British Politics: Towards an Imagined Political Capital?', *Parliamentary Affairs* 64, 2011, p. 227.

31 Blair, *A Journey*, 2010, p. 516.

32 As told by Sir Malcolm Rifkind, interviewed by Emma Crewe, September 2012.

33 Robin Butler, interviewed by Anthony Seldon, www.
cabinetsecretaries.com/#butler, accessed 27 July 2019.

34 Leveson Inquiry, 14 May 2012, afternoon session, National
Archives website, http://webarchive.nationalarchives.gov.
uk/20140122145147/http://www.levesoninquiry.org.uk/
hearing/2012-05-14pm, accessed 15 May 2014.

35 I. Gaber, 'The Lobby in Transition', *Media History* 19, 2013,
pp. 45–58.

36 As quoted by Gaber, ibid.

37 Anonymous Labour MP, interviewed by Emma Crewe, January
2019.

38 As quoted by Gaber, 'The Lobby in Transition', 2013, p. 54.

39 Peter Bull, Ralph Negrine and Katie Hawn, 'Telling it like it is or
just telling a good story?: Editing techniques in news coverage
of the British parliamentary expenses scandal', *Language and
Dialogue* 4, January 2014, pp. 213–33.

40 Interviewed by Emma Crewe and Andrew Walker, December
2018.

41 See Chapter 7 *MPs and staff accuse one another.*

42 Information Tribunal decision, 26 February 2008, para 33, http://
informationrights.decisions.tribunals.gov.uk/DBFiles/Decision/
i85/HoC3.pdf, accessed 17 April 2019.

43 John Bercow, interviewed by Emma Crewe and Andrew Walker,
June 2018.

44 'Stop MP humiliation – archbishop', BBC News, 23 May 2009,
http://news.bbc.co.uk/1/hi/uk/8064828.stm, accessed 4
December 2013.

45 Runciman, *Political Hyprocrisy*, 2008, p. 199.

46 Information Tribunal decision, 26 February 2008, para 81(a) and
para 82, http://informationrights.decisions.tribunals.gov.uk/
DBFiles/Decision/i85/HoC3.pdf, accessed 17 April 2019.

47 Michael Lambek (ed.), *Ordinary Ethics. Anthropology, Language
and Action*, New York: Fordham University Press, 2010, p. 4.

48 Hannah Arendt, *Between Past and Future*, New York: Penguin
Books, 1977, p. 241.

49 Ingold, *Anthropology: Why it Matters*, 2018, pp. 129–130.

50 Haridimos Tsoukas, 'The Tyranny of Light, the temptations and paradoxes of the information society', *Futures* 9, November 1997, pp. 827–43. Thanks to Thomas Yarrow for bringing this article to our attention.

51 See the 'Scotland Act 1998', Section 83 ('Remuneration: supplementary'), Legislation.gov.uk website, www.legislation.gov.uk/ukpga/1998/46/section/83 for details, accessed 30 June 2019.

52 John Dewey, *Human Nature and Conduct: An Introduction to Social Psychology*, New York: Henry Holt and Co., 1922, p. 56. We would like to thank Emma's colleague Karina Solsø for drawing our attention to this brilliant part of Dewey's work.

53 Ibid, p. 207.

Index

Runciman, Professor David, 186, 187, 196

S
salary, MPs' *see* pay, MPs'
Sands, Sir Roger, 26, 27, 42, 118
Saward, Michael, 8
Sayeed, Jonathan MP, 62–63
Second Homes Allowance *see* Additional Costs Allowance (ACA)
Security Co-ordinator, Parliamentary, 100–01
Senior Salaries Review Body (SSRB), 23, 24, 27, 71–72, 75–76, 84, 88, 91, 118
Serjeant-at-Arms, 14–15, 61, 63, 100–01
Shadow Cabinet, 126, 131
Shadow Leader of the House of Commons, 109, 113
signature, MP's, 11, 21, 119, 124–25, 128
Silk, Sir Paul, 114–115
Sinn Fein, 126
Sircar, Indraneel, 140
Smith, Jacqui MP, 116–17, 118–19
Smith, Tim, 31
Southern, Ros, 140
Speaker's Advisory Panel, 24–25, 27, 112
Speaker's Counsel, 34, 114
SSRB *see* Senior Salaries Review Body
Staffing Allowance, 22, 24, 44, 91

Standards and Privileges Select Committee, 63, 76, 78, 110, 117, 121
Standards Commissioner, Parliamentary, 43, 48, 62, 71, 77–78
Standing Orders, 26
Stationery Office, The (TSO), 101, 102–03
Steen, Anthony MP, 189–90
Stonborough, John, 44, 50, 54
strangers, 5
Straw, Jack MP, 66, 165, 173–74
Stuart, Gisela MP, 49
Sunday Times, The, 53, 69, 71, 76, 96
Supreme Court, 146–47
Sutcliffe-Braithwaite, Florence, 182
Swinson, Jo MP, 63–64, 107

T
Taylor, David FCA, 71
Taylor, David MP, 158
Telegraph, Daily, 61, 137–38, 190
Telegraph, Sunday, 192
Thatcher, Margaret MP, 70, 191, 193
Times, The, 49, 82, 119, 121, 139, 184–85
Timms, Stephen MP, 60
Tocqueville, Alexis de, 176
Tomlinson, Hugh, QC, 79, 82
Touhig, Don MP, 89, 91, 96, 98, 109, 130, 134, 135, 139
Travel Warrant, 25–26, 48